DAVID

COOKING *for* FRIENDS

WOOD

DAVID
COOKING *for* FRIENDS
WOOD

PHOTOGRAPHS BY **Gillean Proctor**

whitecap

Whitecap Books is known for its expertise in the cookbook market, and has produced some of the most innovative and familiar titles found in kitchens across North America. Visit our website at www.whitecap.ca.

EDITORS Penny Hozy and Patrick Geraghty
DESIGN Andrew Bagatella
FOOD PHOTOGRAPHY Gillean Proctor
FOOD STYLING Gillean Proctor
PROOFREADER Penny Hozy

Library and Archives Canada Cataloguing in Publication

Wood, David, 1944 May 7-, author
Cooking for friends / David Wood.

ISBN 978-1-77050-300-7 (softcover)

1. Cooking. 2. Entertaining. 3. Cookbooks. I. Title.

TX731.W66 2018   641.5'68   C2017-908081-4

We acknowledge the financial support of the Government of Canada through the Canada Book Fund (CBF) for our publishing activities and the Province of British Columbia through the Book Publishing Tax Credit.

Nous reconnaissons l'appui financier du gouvernement du Canada et la province de la Colombie-Britannique par le Book Publishing Tax Credit.

17 18 19 20 21 22   6 5 4 3 2 1

Printed in China by Regent Publishing Services

···

To my Family, my Friends, and our loyal Customers near and far, whose encouragement and enthusiasm over many years have enabled me to expand and deepen my understanding and enjoyment of food. Your open hearts and curious minds have taught me the many ways in which both food and friendship are enriched by the presence of the other.

···

....

CONTENTS

....

Foreword

••

Toronto to Salt Spring Island

When *David Wood Food Book* was published in the fall of 1987, the Food Shop in downtown Toronto had been open for three and a half years and we were enjoying a certain popular success. But financially the business was not doing well, and I was at a loss as to what to do about it.

Our food costs were high, but so too were our prices, despite my egalitarian desire to have the shop be accessible to anyone interested in food. The unfortunate fact was that I did not value my own efforts enough to be comfortable raising our prices, and was not hard-headed enough to manage the business with a firmer hand. I had not yet learned Einstein's definition of insanity: continuing to do everything the same way while hoping for a different result.

Around this time, I was introduced to a businessman with a background in supermarkets who felt ready to move into the world of specialty food. Backing him was a small group of investors prepared to build a newer, larger version of the two shops we already had. We came to an agreement that instead of starting from scratch, they would invest in our company, expand the business, and build a new shop with us. It was an attractive idea that at the very last minute fell victim to the stock market crash of October 1987, and I was back to solving our problems on my own.

The following January, Nancy and I went to the Fancy Food Show in California. We rented a car and drove up the coast to Mendocino, only to find the restaurant that we had wanted to visit closed. We turned back and stopped late in the afternoon at the Station House Café in Point Reyes. While we waited for the food, away from the intensity of daily life with our minds free to wander, we jotted down on a placemat the things that we wanted in our lives. Our wish list contained things most people would include—time for family and friends, a compatible community, safe surroundings, a benign climate—as well as things more specific to us, like living in the country. Opposite this we wrote down the things we actually had: we lived downtown in a big city with little time for anything except work and holding things together at home; from my perspective, there was not enough time with the kids, from her perspective, there was perhaps too much. The gap between what we had and what we said we wanted was enormous, but by the time we were on the plane home, I was determined to bring the two lists together.

It was clear that freeing myself from the business would be an essential part of this, and I wondered whether the agreement that had almost happened in October might provide the answer, and whether it could be revived. It turned out that it could, and we closed the deal in June 1988: the investors put in the money to build a large new store, while I agreed to stay on for two years and remain as a minority shareholder. At the end of two years I would be free to leave.

The store we built opened in June 1989. In many ways it was an immediate success: the store was beautiful, overflowing with food from around the world (local was not on our radar), and people loved it. But parking was very difficult, and we did not get the customers we needed. In a stronger cash position, we could have weathered a year or two of slow sales, but cash was a luxury we did not have. I found out later that our Vietnamese cooks were not impressed with my explanations about parking or needing more time and, after the store closed, they told me they were not surprised the store did not make money. Opposite the front door of the shop, on the other side of Yonge Street, a side street ran away to the west. According to feng shui, a road running away from your front door will carry away all your money. It would have been nice to know this before we signed the lease—but I doubt that it would have made any difference: even today it's hard to imagine myself turning down a location because of feng shui.

At Christmas we had good but not great sales, and in the New Year the investors brought in a consultant to replace the man they had backed. Over the following months, as consultants came and went, I discovered that almost everyone who looked at our business from the outside was convinced that they could do a better job of running it than we did. They thought buying, cooking, and selling food should be as simple as it sounds, although I could not for the life of me understand why—all I saw were the many parts we tried to make work together that stubbornly refused to cooperate. There was a certain satisfaction when one of the consultants—himself on the way out, walking papers in hand—acknowledged that running a food shop was more complicated than it looked.

Nine months after opening the doors to the new store, the company was out of money and the board decided to look for a buyer. They were not able to find one. We were saved by two things: the first was that everyone thought running our business was not as difficult as we made it; the second was our catering manager's talent for friendship. Krystyna Schmidt was brilliant at her job and, in the course of it, she had got to know one of our very good customers, whose husband turned out to be in the business of buying and selling companies. Krystyna suggested she and I talk to him. I remembered a piece of wisdom once offered to a fundraiser friend: If you go to a potential donor and ask for money, what you are most likely to get is free advice. But if what you want is money, ask for advice. Krystyna and I went to see our customer's husband and we asked for advice. Within six weeks he had bought the company—for $100, it's true—but he had also assumed all of the liabilities, including those to the Canada Revenue Agency, for which the directors (including me) were personally liable.

The sale came with new management, some new money, and it bought some time. But the light of this sale, which we had briefly hoped might be shining at the end of the tunnel, turned out to be an oncoming train, and by the end of June we had little choice but to close down the new store, hoping to slow the cash drain and give the other two stores and catering business another lease on life. Barely a year after opening, we walked away from the new store and spent the night moving out as much of the inventory as we could. As the sun came up, I locked the front door of the shop, posted a note of thanks to our customers, and turned out the lights. Two weeks later, Nancy and I, the three children, and the dog climbed into our minivan, turned north out of the city, and headed for the West Coast. The two other stores and the catering business, which we had hoped to save, did not survive much longer. They were sold to two different buyers who ran them for a while and eventually closed them. They, no more than we, were able to find the magic formula to make them successful.

Shortly after arriving on Salt Spring, I got in touch with the dairy inspector for Vancouver Island and explained my newly formed plan to get a small flock of sheep, milk them, make cheese, and sell it locally. My inspiration came from Olivia Mills, an English woman who almost single-handedly revived sheep dairying in Britain in the 80's and literally wrote the book on it (*Practical Sheep Dairying*, for anyone with the same ambition). If the inspector thought milking sheep on Salt Spring Island was a poor career choice, he was gracious enough not to say so.

Olivia had talked about how big you had to be to make a go of making sheep cheese. I thought I could survive if I had just enough sheep for me to handle the milking, cheese making, and selling all by myself—like they do in France and Spain, I said. She gave me a pitying look: "It depends on how much like a peasant you want to live."

I learned from the inspector that a goat dairy had recently closed its doors on Gabriola Island, just up the coast from Salt Spring. A few years earlier, a young woman had enrolled in agricultural college in Quebec, where she had met and fallen in love with a young French-Canadian. They shared a desire to milk goats and make cheese, which eventually led them to a honeymoon spent driving a school bus full of goats from Montreal to the West Coast. Over the next three years they built a goat farm, a milking parlour, and a dairy on her father's property, with the father as engineer and their own hands doing the work. It was not made any easier by a very challenging health inspector, but eventually they began production late in 1987. Less than a year later they closed it down, worn out by the hard labour and a hesitant market for goat cheese, which was new to the West Coast at the time. They mothballed their cheese plant, closed the doors, and handed the keys to her father.

I had heard this story in 1990, but it was not until 1995 that I was ready to do something about it. By then I had nearly five years' experience looking after sheep and some limited experience in sheep milking (not limited enough, from the sheep's point of view). I had travelled, studied, experimented, and got to know sheep in a way that I had never imagined, but in truth, I had very little to show for it but a succession of doubtful looks and bad jokes. I realized it was time to get down to business or stop talking about it.

I called Jim Brown, the owner of the mothballed goat farm, and asked if he was interested in selling his dairy equipment. He suggested I come take a look, and I asked a friend to come along to temper my enthusiasm. Jim met us at the milking parlour, showed us around, and left us to our own devices. It was much larger than

XII
•••••
DAVID WOOD

I had expected, and the way it was put together was clearly the work of an engineer. Everything I would need to get started was here; for an aspiring cheese maker, it was perfect.

We were invited back to the house for lunch and Jim asked for my thoughts. I told him the truth, that my intention was to start on a smaller scale, and he smiled politely. When lunch was over, he slipped away for a few moments, reappearing as we were leaving, his hand in his pocket. In front of everybody, he asked me how much I planned to pay for the milking and cheese-making equipment I would need. I had no idea—I hadn't thought that far ahead yet (foreshadowing financial bumps on the road ahead …). I grasped for a plausible number and finally came up with twenty-five thousand dollars. Jim took his hand out of his pocket and handed me a piece of paper. On it, he had written $20,000. I shook his hand and thanked him.

Two days later, Nancy came out of the house looking for me. She said the bank was on the phone; they wanted to know whether I had written a large cheque to someone called Jim. I had to confess to her and to the bank that that was exactly what I had done. We had passed the point of no return.

For most of the last five years in Toronto, I had been squeezed out of the kitchen and into a suit, and I knew what I wanted when we arrived on Salt Spring was to get my hands back in the dirt. Learning how to look after a sheep and milk it is a fool-proof and quite pleasant way to do that.

Sheep have small teats with just enough room for a finger and thumb, and milking one by hand is not easy. I did master the technique in the end and used the milk for cheese-making practice. After we received our dairy license we switched to machine milking, which was more productive but decidedly less pleasant for both sheep and milker. Because most sheep produce milk only between spring and fall, I looked forward to having the winter off. But seasonality has its drawbacks, as I learned at the end of the first summer, when the sheep dried up and cheese sales came to an end. I could not build a business on a seasonal product, and searched out a year-round source of goat milk on Vancouver Island. It was the first step away from my plan for a simple life.

One of the things Salt Spring offered was the opportunity for a fresh start in business, to avoid the mistakes I had made in Toronto. A major one was growing too big and too fast. Soon after we started to sell cheese in 1996, a journalist asked me about my plans; I said I hoped I would have the brains to know when to stop growing. Of course I did not. "Big enough" is a point that is gone before you know you are at it. Over the twenty two years we have been in business, we have relied on growing sales to cover escalating costs like a dog chasing its tail, on the road to profitability. I don't think there was any time during those years when we were at a perfect size, no point that I would choose to go back to, even if it were possible. Perfect is relative to the life that you want and what you like to do—a constantly moving target.

My vision of a small farm operation where everything could be done by a few people has long since gone out the window. The turning point came after we had been making cheese for six years, as a result of a conversation I had had many times before that started with someone asking how things were going in the cheese busi-ness. I would launch into a long explanation about how it was not really a business, more a way of life, and that things were pretty good, but if truth be told, it was a lot of work for not much return. Eventually I could no longer believe my own answer. Getting up at five in the morning to milk sheep did not have the appeal it once had, and I was tired of making excuses. If I was not happy with what I was getting from my work, it was time for a change.

The past 10 years have been devoted to changing a way of life into a business. We are getting there. We have an excellent and committed staff, a dedicated man-agement team, and very loyal customers. I cannot imagine living and working in a better place. I am particularly fortunate having my three children work in the business. They bring very different skills than mine, and I know that many of those skills are what the business needs in order to grow. I don't want to disparage what I have done in creating it, but I feel that we have been stuck for a few years now at a size and in a way of doing things that are no longer appropriate to our stage of growth. I am optimistic that my children and our other managers have the balance of talents to imagine the future and bring it about.

Introduction

Food is about much more than nourishment. There are many wonderful things about food, but the greatest is that it opens a Pandora's box full of doors, to variety and excitement, memory, comfort, texture, and flavour, and most of all to the company and conversation of good friends.

We all want our friends to know how much we appreciate and value their friendship, and there are many ways in which we can do that, but they all, in one way or another, involve an act of generosity on our part. Cooking is my way of giving, and I suspect there is a good chance that it is yours, too, given that you are reading this rather than leafing through a coffee table door-stopper entitled "Drywalling for Friends."

Like you, many things draw me to food, but near the top of the list is the way that food works its magic in our lives two or three times a day, seven days a week. Not every meal has to be a star-studded gala (I am told it would get dull after a while, like staying in hotels); but twice a day we have an opportunity for personal pleasure and expressing gratitude. Cooking for our friends provides us with the opportunity for both.

Gratitude is something we think about a lot these days, and properly so: we routinely take too much in life for granted, and forget to say thank you to both people and to the food we eat. If this sounds a bit New Age for a sensible cookbook (which this one is, obviously), I apologize, but there is no question that the more I understand what it takes to get food onto a plate, the more I appreciate the contributions made by all the different parts. At the very least, gratitude is in order. And enjoyment; I would not want to be killing and eating things and not appreciating their gift (even if it was not exactly their choice to end up on the plate . . .).

But overall and hands down, the best thing about food is that it brings us together with friends and family (who are also friends)—it eases conversations and opens our hearts and minds, even to those who on first acquaintance we did not imagine could be our friends. As Dr. Johnson observed more than 250 years ago: "A man, Sir, should keep his friendship in constant repair." While today we would wish he had used a more inclusive pronoun, his sentiment cannot be faulted. There is no better way to keep our friendships in good repair than to invite our friends into our homes and cook for them.

WHAT MAKES GOOD FOOD?

I owe my taste in food to a Scottish upbringing and Elizabeth David.

I grew up in post-war Scotland, a world of grey days and soot-blackened buildings. Food was for sustenance, not pleasure, and anyone who was interested in what they were eating was probably foreign, maybe even English. Scottish machismo prided itself on being able to subsist, as Dr. Johnson noted, on what in England they feed to horses. I have no idea where the idea came from that well brought-up people did not discuss food at the table; it was, like so much else in British life, one of those rules you were just meant to know. So we did not talk about food—at the table or anywhere else.

There were, even in Scotland, houses where people cared about their food, and I was fortunate enough to live in one of them. The quality of our food was always good at home, although the preparation tended toward the basic end of the spectrum. My stepfather was a Scot of the old school variety and his favourite meal was "mince and breakups"—ground beef in a thin gravy and potatoes boiled until they fell apart. My mother had been at school in France before the war but it did her no good when it came to cooking for him. She talked to us, the children, about real food, but not at the table.

In those grey days before the Beatles, Carnaby Street, and avocado pears came into our lives, good cooking still followed the rules set by Escoffier and others during the Golden Age, even though post-war shortages made it impossible to actually make any of the recipes. This was the time when Britain earned its reputation for stodgy puddings and overcooked vegetables, and menus featured Brown Windsor soup and the memorably named Spotted Dick. The food may have been monotonous and lacking in imagination, but in our house there was always plenty of it, and for that I will always be grateful.

The seeds of my interest in food and cooking sowed by my mother eventually sprouted and then grew through trial, error, and books. My first attempts to cook were not for friends, but for myself. In my early twenties, I worked briefly for a company that had once been the family business, and where I still had enough connections to get a job. I was very fortunate to be sent for training to Mexico City.

I lived alone and quickly grew tired of eating on my own in restaurants. The alternative was to try cooking for myself (there being no other volunteers) and I fell into reading the recipe column in the *London Times*. I am embarrassed to admit that I received this every day by airmail, a lapse from life in the real world I can only explain by having had a very sheltered upbringing. But I did learn to cook, and to this day I retain a soft spot in my heart for Katie Stewart, the author of the column at the time.

My early heroes were the stars of "Nouvelle Cuisine," many of whom, like Paul Bocuse, had trained under Fernand Point at La Pyramide in Vienne. But most of all I admired the English food writer Elizabeth David. For pure food reading pleasure, there is for me nothing that can touch the Introduction to *French Provincial Cooking*. Largely because of her, the food I am most drawn to is what used to be called *la cuisine bourgeoise*, the thoughtful and economical cooking of the French middle classes—the doctors, lawyers, priests, and modest landowners. Long before the 100-mile diet, this cooking style depended almost entirely on the careful use of local and seasonal ingredients, although in season they were able to supplement their larders with wonderful things from all across France—melons from Cavaillon, asparagus and butter from Normandy, fish from Brittany, and oysters from Les Landes, all as fresh as if they had picked them themselves. To us, FedEx is a marvel (on most days), but it is nothing compared to the railways of the late nineteenth century (which I am just about old enough to remember).

The result of these bourgeois tastes (as well as age, I suspect) is that I would much rather eat in a bistro than a modern fusion restaurant. I think the chefs who are in the forefront of modern cooking are wonderfully creative and brilliant, but my preference is for two or three sensibly sized courses rather than a dozen different plates so small that I need to stop for a hamburger on the way home. I prefer that the chef be more of an artisan, less of an artist. I like to be the one who decides if what I am eating needs more salt, and not be told by the server that Chef likes it the way it is. Much as I am in favour of keeping food and cooking alive and relevant, and admire creative cooks who push boundaries with foams and essences, for my own pleasure I like to be able to recognize what is on my plate for what it was before it entered the kitchen. If I sound like a curmudgeon, it is because I am (a bit).

WHAT MAKES A GOOD COOK?

A good cook must love to cook. Without that, you can forget it, for a cook who cannot find pleasure in the processes of cooking will easily become bored. It is a good sign if you enjoy cooking for yourself alone, and are quite happy to take the time to make something interesting even when no one is coming to dinner.

Nothing else is essential. Qualities like great technique, the ability to come up with interesting new recipes, or a powerful belief in your own talent are certainly nice to have, but are only necessary if you are planning on opening a three-star restaurant. But most of us, wisely, are not, for there is no shorter route to a life of fatal stress and financial ruin.

There are other qualities I admire in cooks who do food well, and one thing they will almost certainly agree on is that it takes more than good food to make a meal memorable. Meals that leave a lasting impression do not always necessitate amazing food—in fact, the food can sometimes be quite ordinary. My definition of good food is not that it stands out, but just the opposite: that it fits in. Without harmony between all the different elements of an evening—food, atmosphere, setting, conversation, mood—there is no balance, and the chances of creating an experience that people will remember are shot in the foot.

As people who love to cook, we can be tempted into making amazing food for our friends, simply because we can. The time for that is when your friends are as passionate about food as you are, and are happy to spend the evening talking about it; go for it and let your passion show. But when, as sometimes happens, your friends are not as food-obsessed as you, serving amazing food runs the risk of upsetting the applecart of the evening. Food that does not demand to be the centre of attention will be a much better background for a broad-ranging conversation, and allow for some other element, such as the pleasure of the first outdoor dinner of the summer, to be the memory that people take away.

Bear in mind, too, that the consequence of serving amazing food to non-foodies is that you will never be invited anywhere again. Friends will be convinced their food can never come up to your standards (which may be true), and they may also be convinced that you only eat things that are very exotic, very expensive, or very difficult to make, and this is almost certainly not true. We who love food must take care not to intimidate our friends by dazzling them with our own brilliance. It can easily be mistaken for smugness.

I am not particularly good at technique (though I get better with practice), nor especially creative when it comes to inventing new dishes. But there is one thing I am good at, and that is making food that works for the occasion at hand, whatever it may be. I can come up with a menu that reflects the setting, enhances the atmosphere, and supports the conversation, and when that is done, that is within my skill set. (It is not a good idea to plan a menu around recipes you cannot make!)

There is another talent I have observed in cooks I admire, and which I have tried to cultivate within myself—the ability to produce something interesting out of not very much. A good cook can look in a sparsely populated fridge and find the makings of a meal; non-cooks look in the same fridge and complain there is nothing to eat. I like the challenge of the sparse fridge, supplemented by supplies from the larder (usually pasta, I admit).

At the end of the day, what a good cook wants is to be able to cook for themselves and their family and friends, to make satisfying and delicious things to eat, to welcome guests to the table with warmth and generosity, and, in the process, to give pleasure to themselves and to others. Learning to trust your instincts is an important part of the process. It is easier said than done, of course, but remember that inside each of us is a feeling for food that is ours and ours alone. No one else can cook like you. If food is one of the ways you show your talents to the world, trust that you know what you're doing and do not hold back. Take risks but don't be stupid. Some people say that you shouldn't try out a new dish on guests; I would say it depends on the guests. With that in mind I would also say: just the one course.

One last piece of advice that over the years has made me appear a better cook than I am, which I have always attributed to Julia Child (perhaps wrongly, but if anyone deserves the credit, it is she): a cook should never apologize (for their food, at least). You may think you have made the most unholy mess of a recipe, and perhaps you have, but the chances are good that your friends will have no idea unless you make the mistake of telling them. Julia's advice, and mine to you, is to let them enjoy your food in blissful ignorance.

AN APPRECIATION OF TASTE

What is it that makes some foods go so well together? Think of all the taste combinations we come across every day that are so commonplace we don't even question them: lemon with fish; salt and vinegar on French fries; horseradish or mustard with roast beef; duck and orange; eggs and bacon; tart apples and sharp cheese; coffee and chocolate. Why do these combinations work so well and others not at all?

I have wondered about this for a long time, but did not understand the reasons until Helen, my wife, gave me a copy of *Taste* by Sybil Kapoor, an English cookery writer who has made it her mission to understand the workings of our taste buds. To summarize her work and that of many others, there are just five tastes, each experienced by a different part of the mouth. The familiar four are: sweet, sour, bitter, and salt. The fifth, which has been identified only quite recently, is "umami," a combination of the Japanese words meaning "delicious" and "taste." In English it is normally referred to as "savoury," and the classic examples are soy sauce and chicken stock; meat and cheese are both umami.

Sybil Kapoor has done a wonderfully thorough job of exploring how the five tastes work together, and I have no intention of plagiarizing her work here. I have however tried to introduce some of her ideas into these recipes. I completely recommend her book to anyone interested in food. (*Taste*, by Sybil Kapoor. Mitchell Beazley, London, 2003.)

Have you ever tried putting a twist of lemon zest into a sweet espresso? The coffee is bitter, the sugar is sweet, and the combination can be delicious and satisfying at the end of a meal. But adding a zing of lemon transforms it, and here's why: almost no food has just one taste—most are a combination of two or even more. In this case, the sugar is only sweet, but the coffee, while mainly bitter, has a little sweetness of its own. The lemon is mostly sour, but it, too, has some sweetness and also some bitterness. The bitter element of the lemon tempers the much more pronounced bitterness of the coffee, and the lemon's sourness reveals the coffee's hidden sweetness. And, more obviously, the sugar sweetens the lemon.

You might say: If you want your coffee to be sweeter, just add more sugar. But that would be to ignore the subtleties of taste. The lemon does not just make the coffee taste sweeter—it transforms it into a different drink. It introduces sourness, a taste element that was not there before, and allows interactions between the different tastes to produce a much more sophisticated drink than sugar alone can do. Another example is adding an anchovy or Parmesan cheese to a pasta sauce instead of salt; both anchovy and Parmesan are umami, and anchovies introduce sweetness as well. The result is a complexity of taste that you cannot easily put your finger on, but which is the opposite of flat, bland, and boring. It stimulates the appetite and leaves us wanting more.

To the best of my understanding, there is no simple set of rules to tell us how to combine tastes and produce wonderful food—at this point, at least, there are only the experiences of our taste buds and the tastes of others to educate us. When you come across something that works, particularly if it is an unfamiliar combination, try to identify what is going on. If you understand why it works, you can begin to play with taste in your own cooking and open the door to a whole new way of thinking about and experiencing food. You do not need to add a lot; in most cases I have found that it only takes a small amount of a new taste element to add a sophisticated complexity to a recipe.

RAW MATERIALS
··························

After a couple of months of living on Salt Spring, we acquired a small number of sheep, who, in the natural way of things, gave birth to lambs, and eventually it came time to turn these into lamb chops. Mike Byron, a local farmer with a heart of gold, took me under his wing and showed me how to do it. It was a practical decision on my part (it's good to know how to do the things that need to be done on a farm), and a philosophical one, too (as a meat eater, I wanted to understand how meat arrives on my plate). The reality was not as unpleasant as I had expected, and I particularly liked the fact that the deed was done right where the animals were raised, with the lambs subjected to as little stress as we could manage. There was no getting away from the fact that death was part of the process, but knowing that I had had a hand in giving the lambs a comfortable life made it less difficult to accept. They were not the most tender lamb chops I have ever eaten, but it was the meat I felt the least conflicted about eating. When we buy meat from the store, we don't know about the conditions by which the animal was slaughtered—in fact, no one wants us to know what goes on in there. However, we can ask these question where we buy meat, and, sooner or later, the butchers and stores will get the message that this is something they need to care about.

Animal welfare is just one of many food issues we deal with every time we pick up a carton of milk in the supermarket or a bunch of carrots at a farmers' market. These issues are not quite as confusing as we might think, because the fact is that we already have an opinion on many of them. Do you only buy wild fish? Are you a vegetarian or vegan? What about free range eggs? What do you think about GMO products? Would you like some foie gras? Or veal? Unpasteurized cheese? Organic, or local, or both? There is no wrong answer here—whatever our answer, it is the correct one, because although the list goes on and on, most of the time we know where we stand.

As cooks, we are people who like to eat, and our choices put a strong emphasis on taste. Of course, there is more to food than flavour; if that was all we cared about, veal, foie gras, and raw milk cheese would be flying off the shelf. We would only eat strawberries in June and July, never in winter, and only choose foods that are locally grown and raised, not transported halfway around the world to get to us.

All of us—carnivores, vegetarians, and vegans alike—have to consider whether we buy local or global, where we stand on organic and genetically modified production, what we think about the scale on which food is produced, and monoculture crops.

For meat eaters, the issues are climate change, animal welfare and the use of hormones. We have all heard stories about the cattle rancher who keeps a few animals for his own consumption, not willing to eat those he raises commercially because he knows what he pumps into them—scary stuff if the stories are true. For all the regulations that exist around food, there are none for happy meat. We are taking steps along the road, however: labelling chickens as free range, for a start (assuming they are). Free range may not guarantee happiness (if happiness for animals is as complicated as it is for people, we may be doomed before we start), but it is a huge improvement over the caged, constrained, and air-conditioned lives lived by most of the chickens we buy. And it would be great to see farmers get together and develop standards for raising and slaughtering animals.

What about salmon? This is a big issue here on the West Coast. The best salmon from several perspectives is wild Atlantic, but it is expensive and not local, which is only fine for special occasions. The available alternative is farmed salmon, but this is not a popular choice here when most farms raise their fish in open nets that can pass sea lice on to the wild stock and make a desert of the seabed underneath; so far only a few fish are raised in land-based closed containment systems. One day we will get fish farming right (we had better if we want to keep eating it), and when that day comes, we can eat farmed salmon with no more environmental guilt than the chicken we eat—some guilt to be sure, but we eat it nonetheless, particularly when it's raised in the open air and happy as the day is long.

What level of risk are we prepared to accept on food safety? Do we let our kids eat dirt? Or does everything we put in our mouths have to be squeaky clean and scrubbed within an inch of its life before it is safe? That is certainly what our government appears to believe, and maybe it is what we want as a country. The price we pay is that everything starts to taste the same, distinguished only by different amounts of salt and sugar.

What does all this mean for our own food shopping? Buying free range and farm raised is a good place to start. As the Eat Local movement has grown and spread over the last 20 years, it has become clear, even if it was not before, that the best food we can buy is local and seasonal—and organic, too, although I don't put it on quite the same level.

At the end of the day, after thinking our way through all the issues around food, knowing where we stand is one thing, sticking to it is another. My personal food choices are more about taste and being able to buy from friends and neighbours, but even as this idea of local and seasonal becomes more widely accepted there still remain massive, even insurmountable, practical difficulties, not least the Canadian winter. We all fall off the wagon and buy food that goes against our ethical grain, from places we don't approve of, simply because we are human. But that does not absolve us from making up our own mind about the issues that food raises.

Here are a few things that I think it is worth spending more on, to get the best:

Vinegar for salad dressing

Parmesan cheese

Bread

Tomato paste in a tube

Olive oil for drizzling

Farm eggs

Cultured butter

Saffron

Meat, chicken, and fish with a known source

Dried pasta

Black peppercorns

Tomatoes in winter

....

BREAKFAST

....

APPLE PANCAKES 13

APRICOT *and* BLUEBERRY PANCAKES (VARIATION) 14

BANANA PANCAKES 14

FRENCH TOAST 15

WAFFLES *with* STRAWBERRIES *and* WHIPPED CREAM 17

PERFECT SCRAMBLED EGGS 20

SOFT BOILED EGGS *with* SOLDIERS 21

BREAKFAST WRAP *with* EGGS, TOMATOES, *and* GOAT CHEESE 23

POACHED EGGS *on* TOAST 23

HUEVOS RANCHEROS 24

LENTILS *with* TORTILLAS, EGGS, *and* FETA 24

A FULL HOUSE (BREAKFAST *in*
the AFTERNOON) 27

....

Breakfast is in danger of losing its soul. Take for example (and because I am most familiar with it) the English breakfast as served today. The parts are present—sausage, baked beans, fried bread, tomato, fried egg, bacon, black pudding for the brave-hearted—but the soul is missing. It is poetry read by the marine weather forecaster. When was the last time you came across a tomato cooked properly, deep reds and yellows, burned at the edges, soft enough to squish into the toast? In most places, they do not understand toast. They probably just made it that morning. Breakfast toast should not be just made; it needs to sit and cool and become slightly leathery, for how else can you spread the butter thick enough? At university, the landlady of one of my friends stored toast in the toast rack overnight so that by the morning it had just the right amount of bend, and we would fight for invitations to breakfast. When eating it with marmalade at breakfast, buttered toast is two things: toast and butter, and they should remain so until you, and not someone in the kitchen, bring them together, preferably one bite at a time. That other thing—where the butter has melted into the hot toast and is dripping onto your hand and the toast is soggily soft—is for teatime, and soft-boiled eggs.

Most of us are adventurous and broadminded when it comes to lunch and dinner (even elevenses) but less so at breakfast. You don't need a wide repertoire, but you do need to care about it. Let's give breakfast back its soul.

Apple Pancakes

There is one key to making perfect waffles and pancakes, and it is this: separate the eggs. Add the yolks to the batter; beat the whites to stiff peaks and fold them in very gently at the last minute. This introduces air and lightness into the batter and makes a much fluffier pancake or waffle. The difference is chalk and cheese.

These are the best pancakes I know. The modern hybrid apples—Jazz, Braeburn, Gala, etc.—are good as they don't go mushy when cooked.

Warm the oven to 175°F (80°C).

Peel, quarter, and core the apples. Cut each quarter cut into 3 or 4 slices.

Heat a large frying pan or griddle over medium heat, add the butter, and arrange the apple slices in the pan. Cook a few minutes on one side until lightly browned and softened; turn and cook the other side until tender but not mushy. Remove from the pan and set aside.

Whisk the yolks, yogurt, and milk in a large bowl until smooth. In a separate bowl, whisk together the flour, baking soda, and baking powder.

Sprinkle most of the flour mixture on top of the liquids, and fold together gently with a spatula. Add more of the flour as necessary to make a soft and slightly soupy mixture, erring on the side of softness as the batter will firm up as it sits—remember that it is easier to add flour to a batter that is too wet than liquid to one that is too dry.

In a stand mixer or by hand, beat the egg whites to stiff peaks, adding the sugar halfway through. (The sugar is optional, but it gives the whites a firmer texture and makes folding easier.) With a rubber spatula, gently fold half the whites into the batter, then add the rest of the whites and fold again until just a few pockets of unincorporated egg white remain.

Heat the frying pan or griddle over medium-low heat. Spoon mounds of batter (about ½ cup [125 mL] each) onto the frying pan or griddle, leaving a little space between. Arrange 3 or 4 slices of the cooked apple on top of each pancake.

When a few small air bubbles begin to appear on top, turn them over and cook the other side. The outside should be a lovely golden brown, so adjust the temperature of the cooking surface as you go—up if they are too pale, and down if too dark. Take care not to overcook the pancakes—the inside should be just cooked.

They are best eaten as soon as they are ready. Serve with Greek yogurt, butter, or maple syrup. Breakfast does not get much better.

. . . recipe continued

SERVES 4
....

3 apples

1 Tbsp (15 mL) butter + extra
for serving

3 eggs, separated, whites set aside
in a large clean bowl

½ cup (125 mL) plain yogurt
(the higher the fat the better, but low
fat is okay)

2 cups (480 mL) milk

2 cups (480 mL) all-purpose flour

1 Tbsp (15 mL) baking powder

1 tsp (5 mL) baking soda

2 tsp (10 mL) granulated sugar
(optional)

Greek yogurt, for serving

Maple syrup, for
serving

. . . Apple Pancakes (cont.)

APRICOT AND BLUEBERRY PANCAKES (VARIATION) This is the second best pancake, perhaps the best of all on a summer morning. The tartness of the apricots is lovely with maple syrup.

Cut 3 or 4 apricots in half, remove the pits, and cut the halves into ⅛-inch (3 mm) slices; cut these slices in half if they are large. Have ready 1 cup (250 mL) of fresh blueberries.

Following the same method as the Apple Pancake recipe, fold the beaten egg whites into the batter and scoop it into the pan. Arrange a few blueberries and some slices of apricot on top of the pancakes, and cook on a low to medium heat until the bottom is golden; turn carefully and cook until the other side is just done—the batter should be cooked through, but overcooking will detract from the delicate puffiness of the pancakes.

Serve with the fruit side up, along with maple syrup and butter.

Banana Pancakes

A good way to use ripe bananas. These pancakes are delicate little things, and quite sweet—but delicious nonetheless. As always with pancakes, don't forget to separate the eggs.

SERVES 2
••••••••••••

2 ripe bananas

2 egg yolks

½ cup (125 mL) yogurt

½ cup (125 mL) whole wheat flour

½ tsp (2 mL) baking powder

2 egg whites

1 tsp (5 mL) sugar

Butter

Greek yogurt, for serving

Maple syrup, for serving

Place a large frying pan or griddle over medium-low heat.

Mash together the bananas, egg yolks, and yogurt until smooth.

Whisk together the flour and baking powder; sprinkle it on top of the bananas and mix gently. Add enough flour to make a medium batter.

Whisk the egg whites to stiff peaks, adding 1 tsp (5 mL) sugar halfway through, and gently fold them into the batter in two additions.

Drop 1 tsp (5 mL) butter into the heated pan. Scoop ⅓ to ½ cup (80 to 125 mL) of batter per pancake into the pan and cook them slowly over quite low heat until little bubbles appear on the surface and the pancakes are firm enough to flip—which, being so delicate, can be a bit tricky.

These are best served straight from the pan, with Greek yogurt and maple syrup.

French Toast

The bread for French Toast has to be able to absorb the batter without falling apart. Very heavy breads don't have this sponge-like quality; white or whole wheat breads will work, but the crèmes de la crème of French toast are challah, egg bread, raisin bread, or perhaps best of all, croissants.

The eggs are not separated here, the opposite of what we would do for waffles and pancakes.

Warm a serving platter in a 175° F (80°C) oven.

Whisk the milk, eggs, spices, and salt together until well combined. Soak the bread in this batter for up to 15 minutes.

Set a large frying pan or griddle over medium-low heat.

Melt a knob of butter in the pan or griddle until foaming, then add as many slices as will fit comfortably. Cook 2 to 3 minutes until golden brown; turn and cook the second side. Transfer to the serving dish in the warm oven, and keep going until all the slices are done.

Serve with maple syrup and butter.

SERVES 4
••••••••••

2 cups (480 mL) milk

3 eggs

Large pinch mixed spices (cinnamon, nutmeg, allspice, a hint of clove)

Pinch salt

8 slices bread or 4 croissants, split

Butter

Maple syrup, for serving

Waffles *with* Strawberries *and* Whipped cream

....

You can serve these any way you like—with maple syrup and butter is pretty good—but the combination of strawberries and cream is hard to beat. The bags of frozen berries are excellent and have more flavour than fresh ones for about 330 days of the year.

A non-stick waffle iron with deep indentations is essential, and a silicone pastry brush is very useful for spreading the butter on the waffle iron.

....

Thaw the strawberries overnight, then warm them in a 300°F (150°C) oven, sprinkled with sugar. Bake for 40 minutes, until softened and warm and the juices have started to run. Remove and set aside; reduce the oven to 175°F (80°C).

Whisk together the egg yolks, yogurt, and milk in a large bowl until smooth. In a separate bowl, whisk together the flour, baking powder, and soda (whisking is easier than sifting, and just as effective).

Sprinkle most of the flour mixture on top of the liquids, and mix gently with a spatula. Vigorous mixing makes for tough waffles, so be gentle. You want a soft and quite loose mixture, but only experience will show the consistency that works best. Add more of the flour as necessary, but err on the side of softness as the batter will firm up as the baking soda kicks in—it is easier to add flour to a batter that is too wet, than liquid to one that is too dry.

Whip the cream to soft peaks and set aside; serve it with the waffles when they are ready.

In a stand mixer or by hand, beat the egg whites to stiff peaks, adding 1 Tbsp (15 mL) sugar halfway through. (The sugar is optional, but it gives the whites a more robust texture and makes them less likely to collapse when folding.)

With a rubber spatula, gently fold half the whites into the batter, then add the rest of the whites and fold again. Small pockets of unincorporated egg white are fine, and preferable to over-folding.

Make sure the waffle iron is up to temperature. Brush it top and bottom with butter. Gently spoon about a cup of batter onto the surface. Close the lid and cook for 2 to 3 minutes until golden brown. Serve immediately, or transfer to the warm oven while you make the rest.

Serve with the prepared strawberries and whipped cream.

SERVES 4
....

1⅓ lbs (600 g) fresh or frozen strawberries

½ cup (125 mL) sugar

4 eggs, separated, whites set aside in a large clean bowl

1 cup (250 mL) plain yogurt (the higher the fat the better, but low fat is okay)

2 cups (480 mL) milk

2 cups (480 mL) all-purpose flour (could be half white, half whole wheat)

1 Tbsp (15 mL) baking powder

1 tsp (5 mL) baking soda

1 cup (250 mL) whipping cream

1 Tbsp (15 mL) sugar

Butter

BAKING POWDER *and* BAKING SODA

....

These are leavening agents that produce bubbles of carbon dioxide when activated. Baking soda is activated by acid, and baking powder by heat. In most recipes a combination of the two is a good idea as it extends the leavening period—the soda kicks in as soon as it comes in contact with the acid (from the yogurt or sour cream), the powder when it comes in contact with the heat in the oven or on the griddle.

If you are out of baking powder, you can make it by mixing baking soda with cream of tartar, one to one (unless you are out of that, too . . .).

Perfect Scrambled Eggs

••

It is hard to say which is the best way to cook an egg, but a good scrambled one is right up there—actually, 2 eggs or more; it is hard to scramble just one (if you are faced with having to do that, use the microwave, although they will not be the perfect scrambled eggs this recipe makes). You can cook at least 18 eggs at a time for a large group.

••

Whisk together the eggs, salt, and milk or cream.

Set a saucepan, in which the egg mixture will fit comfortably, over a medium-low heat.

Add the butter; let it foam but not brown. Turn down the heat to low and pour in the egg mixture. Success here is about heat and stirring. Too much heat and the egg proteins will become rubbery; too little and the curds will not form. If you don't stir enough then the curd will form a solid mass; stir just right and, with practice, you can create smooth and silky curds of egg suspended against a background of gently cooked custard.

Stir briefly, stop, and let the eggs set for a few seconds. Scrape the spoon or spatula across the bottom of the pan—if a small lump of curd has formed on the spoon, gently scrape the rest of the curd from the bottom of the pan. Stir briefly, and let the eggs set for 15 seconds; it may take more or less time for the curd to form. If it is shorter, turn down the heat; if it is longer, leave the heat where it is (unless it is a lot longer, in which case, turn up the heat a little).

Continue scraping the curd from the bottom and letting it rest. Let it take its time. Just before the eggs are cooked, pull the pan off the heat and keep stirring gently until the curd is no longer forming on the bottom. If you have left the eggs on too long, add cold butter, cream, or milk to cool them down and stop the cooking.

Voila! The eggs are ready.

EGG READINESS If there is one thing that drives me to distraction, it is people who are not. Why, just at the moment when the eggs have been so carefully nurtured to perfection, do they find something that apparently cannot wait? Do they not know that Louis XVI considered punctuality the courtesy of kings? Do not waste perfect scrambled eggs on peasants.

The flip side is that you have to be ready, too. Whatever you are serving with these perfect eggs, be it bacon or smoked salmon, warm croissants, grainy toast or bagels, even toasted brioche, these things must all be ready before you start on the eggs. They will stay warm longer than your eggs will stay perfect, so get them done ahead of time.

SERVES 1
(MULTIPLY RECIPE AS NEEDED)
••••••••••••••••••••••••••

2 eggs

¼ tsp (1 mL) salt

1 Tbsp (15 mL) milk or cream

1 Tbsp (15 mL) butter

Soft Boiled Eggs *with* Soldiers

••

A boiled egg is the ultimate test of egg quality. Apart from the toast soldiers, salt, and pepper, there is nothing to detract from the egg itself, and it is well worth seeking one fresh from a farm chicken.

••

If you like your egg with the white fully cooked and the yolk still completely soft, the first step is to take the eggs out of the fridge and place them in a bowl of warm water, even if only for a few minutes.

Bring a small pan of water to a boil and gently lower the warmed eggs into the water with a slotted spoon. Set the timer for 4 minutes and adjust the heat to a simmer. When the time is up, lift out the eggs and set them in the egg cups, with the big end up. (Or not; there are arguments for both sides—just more convincing ones for the big end pointing up.)

Make the soldiers while the eggs are cooking, or before: toast the bread and butter it while still warm. Len Deighton, writer of thrillers *(The Ipcress Files)* and cookbooks *(The Action Cookbook; Où est le Garlic?)*, recommends sprinkling salt and pepper on the toast, not on the egg, so that each mouthful is pre-salted and peppered, and you do not interrupt the natural flow of breakfast in seasoning each spoonful. Either way, cut the toast into soldiers and serve with the eggs.

**SERVES 1
(MULTIPLY RECIPE AS NEEDED)**

••••••••••••••••••••••••••••••

1 or 2 eggs

1 or 2 slices of bread

Butter

Salt

Fresh ground black pepper

FRYING EGGS

••

Every cuisine has its own way of frying an egg, but none can match the United States in the number of ways it can be done. Here we'll stick with "sunny side up" and "over easy" (or medium).

A small non-stick pan used only for frying eggs and saved from all other abuses is a very handy piece of equipment, and not as extravagant as it might seem. After all, what else does a toaster do apart from toast bread, and yet we don't think twice about giving it counter space, and at considerably greater cost.

Break 1 or 2 eggs into a small cup—it makes things a little easier. Heat the pan over medium heat and, when hot, add ½ tsp (2 mL) of fat; it can be anything you like—butter, vegetable oil, lard. Let it melt, then pour the eggs gently into the pan. Sprinkle with salt.

For "sunny side up," let them cook until the white is firm and the yolk still yellow; a sunny egg will always have a thin film of uncooked white over it. If you don't like it, you can cover the pan with a lid while the egg cooks, but I am not sure that it then qualifies as a fried egg—half-fried for sure, but also half-steamed.

The better solution to the uncooked film of white is to cook the egg "over easy." Heat the pan and add the fat and the eggs in the same way. When the white starts to firm up, gently separate the eggs from one another—it makes flipping easier. As soon as the whites are firm enough that you can lift the eggs one at a time with a spatula, turn them over and cook for another 30 seconds on the other side. I think over-easy eggs look better turned once more, with the top side facing up.

When the eggs are done, the non-stick pan makes it easy to slide them out onto a plate.

Breakfast Wrap *with* Eggs, Tomatoes, *and* Goat Cheese

··

Gently frying the tortillas before filling them greatly improves their texture.

··

Fry the tomato slices in 1 Tbsp (15 mL) olive oil over medium-high heat until soft and a little burnt at the edges. Set aside.

Warm a large frying pan over medium heat, add 1 Tbsp (15 mL) olive oil, swirl it around, and put in the tortilla; heat briefly until warm but not crispy, then turn and warm the other side. Set aside in a towel or foil.

Whisk the egg with salt and fresh pepper, add a little oil to the frying pan, turn down the heat and pour in the eggs. Stir constantly until cooked to your liking.

Unroll a tortilla on a plate, spread goat cheese down the centre, top with a line of tomato, and finish with the eggs. Roll up the tortilla and serve.

SERVES 1
(MULTIPLY RECIPE AS NEEDED)
······························

1 medium tomato, in ¼-inch (6 mm) slices

Olive oil

1 large flour tortilla

1 egg

Salt

Pepper

1 oz (30 g) goat cheese (chèvre or feta)

Poached Eggs *on* Toast

··

After my father died, one of his best friends quietly and gently insinuated himself into our family and took on the role of adoptive grandfather to our children. That they learned their table manners is entirely thanks to Ian. He would come and visit us on Salt Spring for a couple of weeks every year, and each morning he would ask for two poached eggs for breakfast. Over the years we learned how to do it properly: break two eggs into a tea cup first, then pour them together into the swirling water and you will get eggs that emerge surprisingly separate from the pan.

··

Bring a small saucepan of water to a boil.

Toast the bread, butter it while still warm, and set aside. (This is different from English breakfast toast, which is meant to be eaten with marmalade and therefore needs to be dry and "leathery.")

Add the salt and vinegar to boiling water; turn the heat down to medium.

Break the eggs, no more than two at a time, into a teacup short enough to allow for easy tipping into the centre of the pan.

With a large spoon, stir the water to create a whirlpool. Stop stirring, allow the water to settle for a couple of seconds, and pour the eggs into the centre. Turn the heat down to a gentle simmer.

After 4 minutes, lift the eggs with a slotted spoon. They are ready (whites cooked and yolk soft) when they hold their shape but still flatten slightly under their own weight; cook a little longer for a firmer yolk. Lift out onto paper towels, pat them dry, and transfer to buttered toast.

Repeat with the rest of the eggs. Sprinkle with salt—it is essential.

SERVES 1
(MULTIPLY RECIPE AS NEEDED)
······························

1 slice bread

Butter

1 tsp (5 mL) salt + extra for serving

2 Tbsp (30 mL) white vinegar

2 eggs

Huevos Rancheros

14 oz (396 g) can refried beans

2 Tbsp (30 mL) oil

Small can salsa (red, green, or both)

½ bunch cilantro (fresh coriander), stemmed and coarsely chopped

4 green onions, finely sliced

1 avocado, peeled and sliced

Salt

4 corn tortillas

4 eggs

On the occasions when you need a change from bacon and eggs, Huevos Rancheros are a good alternative—a reminder of hot sun any time you want it.

There is a variation on this dish: instead of a red salsa on both eggs, the second egg is topped with a green tomato or tomatillo salsa. They are now called "Huevos Divorceados"—divorced eggs. The eggs now look quite different and are not speaking to each other except through their lawyers.

Heat the beans in a small pan over medium heat, or in the microwave, and keep warm.

To warm the tortillas, heat a frying pan over medium heat, add 1 Tbsp (15 mL) oil for 2 tortillas. Heat and flip until all 4 sides are warm. Set them on a plate and cover with a lid while you heat the remaining 2 tortillas.

Arrange 2 tortillas on each plate and spread the warm beans on top.

Fry the eggs (see page 22) and place 1 on top of each tortilla. Spoon the salsa on top—red, green, or both—and sprinkle with green onions and cilantro. Arrange the avocado slices around the eggs.

Lentils *with* Tortillas, Eggs, *and* Feta

One 19-oz (450 mL) can lentils OR 1 cup (250 mL) dried green lentils

½ tsp (2 mL) salt

½ medium red onion, finely chopped

1 tsp (5 mL) fresh herbs, finely chopped

Pinch ground cumin

3 Tbsp (45 mL) olive oil + extra for frying

8 corn tortillas

8 eggs

1 cup (250 mL) crumbled feta cheese

Lentils and eggs go well together, and feta provides just the right amount of salt.

Bring a small pan of water to a boil, add the dried lentils, cover, and allow to simmer for about 25 minutes, checking for doneness and adding more water as necessary—the lentils should be tender but not mushy. When lentils are cooked, drain them and transfer to a clean bowl. Mix in the diced onions, herbs, cumin, and olive oil. Set aside in the fridge if for more than an hour or two. When you are ready to serve, reheat the lentils.

Set a frying pan over medium heat; when it is warm, add 1 Tbsp (15 mL) vegetable oil (olive oil is fine).

Put in 2 tortillas, one on top of the other. Allow to cook on the bottom for a few seconds, then turn both tortillas over together so that what was the uppermost side is now heating against the bottom of the pan. Turn over the top tortilla only and flip the stack again. Again, turn only the new top tortilla and, after several seconds, flip the stack once more. Now both sides of each tortilla have been warmed in the oil. Set aside on a plate covered with a pot lid or a second plate while you repeat the process with another stack of 2 tortillas.

In the same pan, fry 2 eggs at a time (see page 22). While they are frying, set out 2 tortillas on each plate, spoon the lentils over them, and slide the eggs on top.

Serve with crumbled feta cheese.

ROASTING TOMATOES

....

Roasting a tomato evaporates some of its moisture and browns the edges; it is a useful technique when a recipe calls for a more intense tomato flavour. Fried tomatoes are more liable to fall apart, which makes roasting a good idea for breakfast, too—but it does take more time.

Preheat the oven to 400°F (200°C).

Line a baking sheet with parchment paper—it should not burn at this temperature.

Cut the tomatoes in half and arrange on the paper, cut side facing up. Drizzle them with olive oil and sprinkle with salt. Roast in the preheated oven for 20 to 40 minutes, depending on how dried and browned you want them—generally less for breakfast, more for other recipes.

A Full House
(Breakfast *in the* Afternoon)

···

Some of the best breakfasts I have eaten have not been at breakfast time, but later in the day, after I've been outside, getting cold and wet in the wind and the rain. We call it a "Full House," and nothing hits the spot quite like it. Despite all the rich and fatty components, there is a perfect balance to it: the starch of the baked beans offset by the fattiness of the fried bread; the acid edge of the tomatoes cutting the succulence of the sausage; and the soft egg yolk providing a foil for the firmness of the bacon as well as a sauce for everything else. To me, these are the essential ingredients, but add or subtract whatever you choose—it is what touches your soul that matters.

If you have the time, roast the tomatoes instead of frying them (see page 25).

···

Preheat the oven to 175°F (80°C), to keep everything warm.

Warm the baked beans in a small saucepan (or heat them later in the microwave).

Heat a frying pan over medium heat and add the oil or lard. Prick the sausages with a fork and add to the pan; cook until browned on the outside and done on the inside. Remove to a platter in the oven; put the serving plates in the oven, too.

Cook the bacon in the same frying pan until done as you like it. Add to the platter in the oven to keep warm.

Fry the bread in the same pan until golden, using the fat from the sausages and bacon, adding more oil or fat if necessary; put it in the oven, too.

If frying the tomatoes, slice them thickly and add them to the frying pan with more oil. Cook until soft and a bit browned on the edges: overcooking is better than not cooking them enough.

Check that the beans are heated through.

Fry the eggs (see page 22) two at a time in a non-stick frying pan. While they are cooking, take the platter and plates out of the oven. Assemble the Full House one plate at a time: put a slice of fried bread on the plate and spoon some beans on top, then arrange the sausages, bacon, and fried tomato alongside. When the eggs are done, slide them on top of the beans and, voila, there you have it.

Serve with strong tea or Newcastle Brown Ale.

SERVES 1
············

Half 14-oz (396 mL) can baked
beans

1 Tbsp (15 mL) cooking oil or lard
+ extra as needed

2 pork sausages

2 strips thick cut bacon

1 ripe tomato

1 slice bread

2 eggs

....

SOUPS

....

PASTA E FAGIOLI 30

WILD MUSHROOM *and* SHALLOT SOUP 31

LEEK *and* STILTON SOUP 33

CALDO VERDE 33

GAZPACHO 35

....

Nothing says friendship like soup.

When the very first restaurants opened in Paris in the heady days (excuse the expression) before the French Revolution, the very word "restaurant" was coined because owners promoted their fare as restoring. We should not be surprised to learn that the food was, in the beginning, entirely soup. With the possible exception of Kraft Dinner, there is no food that is more deeply embedded in our unconscious than soup. We eat it on cold nights, share large pots of it with friends, and when sad things happen we give it as an expression of our sympathy and care.

It used to be that soup was part of almost every dinner, from the elaborate multi-course affairs of the rich and famous, to the simple potage that began the evening meal in every French household, rich or poor. At home in Scotland, soup was the start of every dinner I ever ate. In these affluent days many people find that starting a meal with soup is more food than they can manage, to the point where it has lost its place as the first course of choice. To me, we are throwing the baby out with the bathwater. As with everything food, what is important is finding the right soup for the right occasion, and there are many sophisticated and elegant soups that can fit right in with even the most formal dinner.

That said, it is a fact that today we usually find soup standing alone, a meal in itself (although often with the addition of something to round it out). These stand-alone soups are more substantial, often originating from times and places where sustenance, not the equilibrium of a meal, was the primary concern. With their rustic earthiness, there is nothing like them for comfort and warmth.

Pasta E Fagioli

¾ cup (180 mL) dried Romano beans (or one 28-oz [794 g] can of Romano beans)

½ cup (125 mL) finely chopped celery

½ cup (125 mL) finely chopped carrot

1 cup (250 mL) finely chopped onion

1 tsp (5 mL) finely chopped garlic

2 Tbsp (30 mL) finely chopped parsley

2 Tbsp (30 mL) olive oil

One 28-oz (794 g) can Italian plum tomatoes

10 cups (2.4 L) chicken stock

1 thick slice prosciutto, cut in matchstick size pieces

Piece of Parmesan rind (or other hard cheese)

1 tsp (5 mL) salt

½ lb (227 g) short dried pasta

Romano or Parmesan cheese, for serving

Peppery olive oil, for serving

This wonderful dish from Italian country cooking is halfway between a pasta and a soup. It is earthy, rustic, and very substantial—perfect for supper on a winter evening with crusty bread, a green salad, and a big glass of red wine.

The beans can be fresh, dried, or canned—all of these work fine. The Parmesan rind adds body and complexity to the dish; it's a good idea to keep rinds from hard cheeses in the freezer and use them for occasions like this.

If you are using dried beans, soak the beans overnight in a large bowl of water. The next day, drain the beans and put in a large saucepan with fresh water to cover. Bring to a boil, turn down the heat, and simmer for 1½ to 3 hours, until barely tender (timing depends on the age of the beans). For canned beans, rinse them in a sieve or colander under cold water. Drain and set aside.

In a large saucepan, sauté the finely chopped celery, carrot, onion, garlic, and parsley in olive oil over medium heat until lightly browned.

Drain the tomatoes and mash them briefly with a potato masher, immersion hand blender, or food processor. Add them to the vegetables along with the chicken stock, sliced prosciutto, and cheese rind. Bring to a boil, reduce the heat to a simmer, and cook for 1 hour, stirring occasionally.

If using dried beans, add them now and cook the soup for another hour. Add the canned beans later, after the soup has simmered for 2 hours.

Cook the pasta al dente in a large pot of salted boiling water, drain, and add to the soup; taste and adjust for salt. Heat until piping hot.

Serve in large bowls. Pass around Romano or Parmesan cheese and a peppery olive oil.

Wild Mushroom *and* Shallot Soup

....

A soup earthy enough for an evening by the fire, and sophisticated enough for a formal dinner.

....

Soak the porcini mushrooms and morels in separate bowls of warm water for an hour. Squeeze the mushrooms and strain their liquids through a fine filter into a single bowl, removing sand particles; reserve liquid. Cut the morels in half and trim any hard parts from the porcini. Put all the mushrooms in a fresh bowl of water and rub them with your fingers to remove any remaining sand. Drain, squeeze dry, and chop them coarsely. Discard the water.

In a medium saucepan, heat the chicken stock until almost boiling. Remove from the heat and set aside.

Melt the butter in a large heavy saucepan over medium heat, add the chopped shallots, and sauté until translucent. Add the sliced brown or white mushrooms and cook until their juices run and evaporate. Add the flour and stir for 2 minutes. Pour in the chicken stock and the strained mushroom liquid. Bring to a boil, stirring steadily to make a smooth sauce. Add the chopped wild mushrooms, reduce the heat, and simmer for 1 hour. Taste for seasoning, adding salt and pepper if needed. (May be done up to 2 days ahead to this point.)

Reheat the soup over medium heat and whisk in the sherry and Crème Fraîche before serving.

SERVES 8
....

1 oz (28 g) dried porcini (ceps) mushrooms

1 oz (28 g) dried morels

6 cups (1.4 L) chicken stock

½ cup (125 mL) butter

1 cup (250 mL) finely chopped shallots

1 lb (454 g) sliced fresh white or brown mushrooms

3 Tbsp (45 mL) all-purpose flour

¼ cup (60 mL) sherry

1 cup (250 mL) Crème Fraîche (page 232)

CROUTONS

....

You can use good quality stale white bread cut into small cubes, which is traditional, or more modern croutons by baking bread cubes in the oven, with or
without olive oil. Spread the croutons on a large baking sheet and bake in a 350°F
(180°C) oven for about 8 minutes, turning a couple of times. If using olive oil, pour
a few tablespoons of oil onto the baking sheet and toss the croutons in it until
lightly coated, baking for the same amount of time.

Leek *and* Stilton Soup

An elegant soup with flavours that complement each other beautifully. Stilton's balance of sweet and sharp gives the best result; other blue cheeses just don't quite cut it here.

Bring the chicken stock to a boil in a large saucepan; remove from the heat and set aside.

Melt the butter in another large saucepan and add the chopped leeks and onions. Cook over medium heat until soft and translucent, then add the garlic, thyme, potatoes, and flour. Pour in the hot stock, bring it all to a boil, and reduce the heat to a simmer; cook for 1½ hours, until the potatoes are very soft.

Remove the soup from the heat and allow to cool a little before ladling into a food processor, or use an immersion blender to purée until smooth. (There is a risk of scalding when blending very hot liquids with a machine.)

Before serving, reheat the soup and add the cream and crumbled Stilton, stirring just enough to melt the cheese.

SERVES 10
•••••••••••

10 cups (2.4 L) chicken stock

5 Tbsp (75 mL) butter

3 leeks, white parts only, finely chopped

3 white onions, finely chopped

3 cloves garlic, crushed

1 Tbsp (15 mL) thyme leaves (fresh or dried)

5 medium white fleshed potatoes, peeled and diced

¼ cup (60 mL) all-purpose flour

1 cup (250 mL) whipping cream

1 cup (250 mL) crumbled Stilton

Caldo Verde

This substantial country soup from Spain makes a lovely informal dinner combined with a green salad and cheeses from the same part of the world; Manchego, Cabrales, Idiazábal, or a Portuguese cheese would all be great choices.

In a large saucepan over medium heat, sauté the onions in olive oil until very soft. Pour in the chicken stock, add the sliced potatoes, turn the heat down to a gentle bubble, and cook until the potatoes are very tender—about 45 minutes.

Remove from the heat and allow to cool a little before blending in a food processor or with an immersion blender until very smooth. (Beware of scalding when blending very hot liquids with a machine.) The recipe may be done ahead up to this point.

Bring the soup back to a simmer and add the chorizo, either fresh or dried. The dry sausage will need 20 minutes in the soup; if the sausage is fresh, put it in for 5 minutes to firm up, slice into ¼-inch (6 mm) rounds, and cook 5 minutes longer.

Wash the kale and slice it finely; add to the soup and cook until just wilted.

Ladle the soup into bowls and pass around some extra olive oil.

SERVES 8
•••••••••••

3 medium onions, thinly sliced

¼ cup (60 mL) olive oil + extra for serving

10 cups (2.4 L) chicken stock

2 lb (900 g) potatoes, peeled and sliced

½ lb (227 g) chorizo sausage (fresh or dried)

1 lb (454 g) kale

Gazpacho

••

Perfect in the summer when the tomatoes are full of flavour, and very simple to make if you let a food processor do the chopping.

••

Remove the skin from the tomatoes, using a vegetable peeler if the tomatoes are firm; otherwise, nick the skins of riper tomatoes with the point of a knife, drop them in boiling water for about 20 seconds, remove from the water, and slip off the skins.

Cut all the tomatoes in quarters and discard the seeds; cut out the cores and reserve. Slice the flesh of 3 tomatoes into thin strips, then across into a small dice; set aside. Chop the last tomato and the reserved cores coarsely, and drain them in a sieve for half an hour.

Peel the cucumber and chop coarsely. Remove the stem and core from the pepper and chop coarsely. Chop the onion. Put everything except the bread and the neatly diced tomatoes into the food processor. Pulse to chop, to the point where the texture is still grainy without any large lumps. Transfer to a large bowl, stir in the diced tomato, and set aside in the fridge for an hour or longer for the flavours to blend.

The recipe may be prepared up to a day ahead. Serve with croutons.

SERVES 6
•••••••••••

4 ripe tomatoes

⅓ English cucumber

1 green pepper

½ red onion

½ tsp (2 mL) garlic

½ tsp (2 mL) salt

¼ tsp (1 mL) fresh ground black pepper

½ tsp (2 mL) red pepper flakes

1 Tbsp (15 mL) red wine vinegar

2 cups (480 mL) cold water

1 Tbsp (15 mL) chopped parsley

1 Tbsp (15 mL) chopped fresh coriander

2 Tbsp (30 mL) olive oil

6 slices day old bread, in ½-inch (13 mm) cubes for croutons (see page 32)

PASTA *and* RISOTTO

SPAGHETTI CARBONARA 38

SPAGHETTI PUTANESCA 39

SPAGHETTI *with* MUSSELS *and* ROASTED TOMATOES 40

LINGUINE *with* CLAMS (LINGUINE ALLE VONGOLE) 42

FETTUCINE *with* ASPARAGUS, PROSCIUTTO,
AND GORGONZOLA 43

TAGLIATELLE *with* SPICY GINGER CRAB 44

TAGLIOLINI ALLA SICILIANA 45

TAGLIATELLE *with* FRESH SALMON, CRÈME FRAÎCHE,
and CHIVES 47

PENNE *with* BUTTERNUT SQUASH, SAGE, *and* PROSCIUTTO 48

TORTELLINI *with* SPICY SAUSAGE 50

LASAGNE 51

VEGETABLE LASAGNE 52

FUSILLI PASTA SALAD *with* TOMATO, BASIL,
and BUTTERMILK 53

RISOTTO MILANESE 54

RISOTTO *with* PORCINI MUSHROOMS
(VARIATION) 55

....

Wherever I go in the world of food, pasta is what I return to time after time. I love it in all its shapes and forms; it is so endlessly versatile and deeply satisfying that it is hard to conceive of a world without it. And for me, risotto is not far behind.

Cooking pasta (and risotto) "al dente" is standard practice—or so we think. But what we mean by al dente, and what those words mean to Italians, are two very different things. Over here, like the frog in the slowly heated pot of water, our senses have been lulled by gradual change to the point where now we would send a plate of genuinely al dente pasta right back to the kitchen. I am all for cooking our food the way we like it and not kowtowing to fashion or received opinion, but I will say that it is worth experimenting with cooking pasta and risotto for a shorter time. The result will be a greater contrast between the pasta and its sauce—a firmer pasta in a more liquid sauce—rather than the pasta and sauce sharing a single texture, like the canned spaghetti of our childhood. Try it and if you don't enjoy it you can always go back.

So how do you tell when pasta is cooked the way you want, however that may be? The time shown on the pasta package is a good guide, another is to watch as the yellow colour of the dry pasta takes on a whiter hue; but in the end, the only way is to taste it, looking for more or less of that firm centre, depending on your taste. All pastas will continue to soften after they are drained, so drain it while it still has that firmness at the centre. Good pasta will retain its al dente texture all the way to the plate, which is why it is worth spending extra money on quality.

When cooking pasta, remove about 1 cup (250 mL) of the cooking water and set it aside just before you drain it. The liquid is full of starch and very useful for extending a sauce without watering it down.

Spaghetti Carbonara

··

This is my favourite pasta. With a glass of wine and a green salad, Spaghetti Carbonara is the perfect supper when we come home late from work or a movie. Open a bottle of red wine and pour two glasses while you cook.

··

Bring a large pot of water to a boil, salt it, and add the spaghetti.

While the pasta is cooking, whisk the eggs together in a small bowl and set aside.

Grate the Parmesan and set aside.

Cook the pasta until al dente, 9 or 10 minutes. Before draining, scoop out 1 cup (250 mL) of the cooking water and reserve it.

Leave the pasta to drain, return the pan to the heat, add the olive oil and prosciutto strips, and stir together for 30 seconds. Add the pasta and stir to coat with the olive oil and prosciutto. Pour in the beaten eggs and mix thoroughly, adding enough of the reserved pasta water to keep it saucy. Stir in the grated Parmesan.

Serve in warmed pasta bowls. Grind black pepper on top—in one version of the origin of the name "Carbonara," the pepper represents the coal dust that the miners brought home on their clothes.

SPAGHETTI CARBONARA WITH BACON (VARIATION) If you don't have prosciutto, you can still make a very good Spaghetti Carbonara with bacon. The ingredients are the same except that instead of the prosciutto, use 4 oz (113 g) thick smoked bacon, cut into batons.

Set a small frying pan over medium heat and cook the bacon in olive oil until just starting to crisp, then set it aside. Reheat it when the pasta is almost ready; drain the pasta and return it to the pan, pour in the bacon and the oil, and stir to coat. Add the eggs and Parmesan as before.

SERVES 2

············

1 tsp (5 mL) salt

7 oz (200 g) dried spaghetti

2 eggs

1 cup (250 mL) freshly grated Parmesan cheese

2 Tbsp (30 mL) olive oil

3 oz (85 g) thinly sliced prosciutto, cut across into narrow strips

½ tsp (2 mL) coarsely ground black pepper

Spaghetti Putanesca

··

Putanesca is tomato sauce with attitude, supposedly spicy enough to rekindle the ardour of ladies of the night. Simple though it is, it remains a long-standing favourite and is easily made.

The sauce is versatile and works with most kinds of pasta, fresh or dried, although I prefer it with dried. It is robust enough to stand up to pastas made from whole wheat or ancient grains.

··

In a medium saucepan over medium-low heat, cook the onion in 1 Tbsp (15 mL) oil until soft and translucent. Add the tomatoes, breaking them up with a potato masher, and bring to a boil; turn the heat down and simmer uncovered for 20 minutes.

Add the anchovies, capers, olives, chili flakes, and remaining ¼ cup (60 mL) olive oil. Cook over low heat for 10 minutes to blend the flavours.

Bring a large pot of water to a boil over high heat; salt the water and cook the spaghetti, uncovered, until al dente. Scoop out 1 cup (250 mL) of the cooking water and drain the pasta.

Return the pasta to the pan, pour in half the sauce, and stir to coat. Add some of the reserved cooking water if needed.

Divide the pasta between bowls, top with the rest of the sauce, and serve with grated Parmesan.

SERVES 4
············

1 small onion, finely chopped

5 Tbsp (75 mL) olive oil, divided

One 28-oz (794 g) can Italian plum tomatoes (whole or diced)

4 anchovy fillets, chopped

2 Tbsp (30 mL) capers

½ cup (125 mL) pitted black olives, chopped

½ tsp (2 mL) chili flakes

1 tsp (5 mL) salt

1 lb (454 g) dried spaghetti

Parmesan cheese, grated, for serving

SERVES 2

············

½ lb (227 g) cherry or other
small tomatoes

5 Tbsp (75 mL) olive oil, divided

Salt

1 small onion, finely chopped

½ cup (125 mL) white wine

2 lb (900 g) mussels, washed and
drained

1 tsp (5 mL) garlic, finely chopped

¼ tsp (1 mL) chili flakes

8 oz (227 g) dried
spaghetti

Spaghetti *with* Mussels *and* Roasted Tomatoes

···

A satisfying combination of mussels and roasted tomatoes in a reduction of the mussel cooking liquid, with a bit of fire in the tail. A pound (454 g) of mussels per person may sound like a lot, but they seem to get eaten without any trouble.

···

Preheat the oven to 375°F (190°C).

Cut the tomatoes in half lengthwise (cut Roma in quarters or smaller) and toss with 2 Tbsp (30 mL) olive oil in a bowl to coat. Arrange the tomatoes, skin side down, on a large baking sheet lined with parchment (it makes cleaning much easier). Sprinkle with salt and bake in the preheated oven for 30 to 45 minutes, until starting to colour and still slightly soft, but not burned. Remove from the oven and set aside.

While the tomatoes are roasting, set a medium saucepan with a lid over medium-low heat and cook the onion in 2 Tbsp (30 mL) oil until translucent. Turn the heat up to medium, pour in the white wine, bring to a boil, add the mussels, and cover the pan. Steam for 5 minutes, or until all the shells open. Discard any that do not open. Remove from the heat and set aside to cool.

Reserve 6 or 8 mussels in their shells for decorating the plates, and remove the meat from the rest; discard the shells; strain and reserve the liquid.

In a small pan, sauté the garlic in the remaining 1 Tbsp (15 mL) oil until pale gold. Add the chili flakes and stir for 20 seconds; pour in the mussel liquid and reduce to about ⅓ cup (80 mL). Add the tomatoes and stir in the mussels; remove from the heat and set aside while you cook the pasta.

Bring a large pot of water to a boil, then add salt and the spaghetti. Cook until al dente, about 9 minutes; drain, reserving ½ cup (125 mL) of the cooking liquid.

Add the pasta to the pan and reheat the mussel sauce, stirring it into the pasta; add just enough of the cooking liquid to keep it from drying out.

Serve in warmed bowls and decorate with the mussels in their shells.

1 cup (250 mL) dry white wine

2 lb (900 g) washed and drained
Manilla clams

1 Tbsp (15 mL) finely chopped garlic

3 Tbsp (45 mL) olive oil

6 Tbsp (90 mL) flat leaf parsley,
finely chopped

1 tsp (5 mL) salt

14 oz (400 g) dried linguine

Linguine *with* Clams
(Linguine alle Vongole)

···

*A classic combination, simple and very delicious, of garlic and parsley, briny
clams, and the robust flavour of semolina. In Italy they would not let cheese anywhere near this dish, and I can see their point, but those who say they will have
their Parmesan where and when they want it have a point, too—food is about
pleasure, not rules.*

···

Pour the wine into a saucepan large enough to hold all the clams, bring it to a
boil, and add the clams. Cover the pan and cook for 5 minutes over medium
heat, until the shells are fully open. Drain them in a colander set over a large
bowl to catch the liquid.

When cool enough to handle, remove the clam meat from most of the
shells and reserve. Discard the empty shells and set aside a few full ones for
decoration. Strain the clam juice into a small bowl.

In a small frying pan, sauté the garlic in the olive oil until pale gold; add
the clam juice and reduce it to about half a cup (125 mL). Turn down the
heat, add the clam meat, and reheat.

Boil a large pot of water; salt the water and add the pasta. Cook until just
done, about 10 or 11 minutes (3 to 5 minutes for fresh).

Return the pasta to the pot; pour in the clams and clam juice, and stir to
coat thoroughly. Stir in the chopped parsley.

Serve in warmed pasta bowls, decorated with the reserved clams in shells.

Fettucine *with* Asparagus, Prosciutto, *and* Gorgonzola

••

This is a simple and substantial pasta dish with a great mix of flavours. Gorgonzola is a creamy blue cheese toward the middle of the sharpness spectrum; Stilton or Saint Agur make good substitutes. The sharper blues, like Roquefort or Danish Bleu, are a little too powerful, while the mild ones like Cambozola or Dolcelatte (a milder Gorgonzola) do not deliver enough of a punch.

••

Hold an asparagus spear with both hands—one on each end and a few inches apart—and bend it gently until it breaks; discard the hard stem piece. Cut the spears into 1-inch (2½ cm) lengths and set aside.

In a medium saucepan, sauté the prosciutto in butter until lightly browned. Pour in the cream and bring to a boil; reduce the heat to medium and add the Gorgonzola. Stir until the cheese has melted; set aside and keep warm.

Boil a large pot of water. Salt the water, add the asparagus, and boil for 1 minute. Leave asparagus in the pan and add the fettucine. Bring the water back to a boil and cook until the pasta is just done, 2 or 3 minutes; drain in a colander and reserve 1 cup (250 mL) of the cooking water.

Return the pasta and asparagus to the pot; pour in the cheese sauce and stir to mix, adding some of the cooking water if necessary.

Serve in heated pasta bowls. Pass around the Parmesan and pepper grinder.

SERVES 4
••••••••••••

8 oz (227 g) fresh asparagus

3 Tbsp (45 mL) finely diced prosciutto

1 Tbsp (15 mL) butter

1 cup (250 mL) whipping cream

8 oz (227 g) Gorgonzola, cut into small cubes

1 tsp (5 mL) salt

1 lb (454 g) fresh fettucine

Parmesan cheese, for serving

Fresh ground black pepper, for serving

Tagliatelle *with* Spicy Ginger Crab

SERVES 4 AS A FIRST COURSE,
2 AS A MAIN COURSE

2 Tbsp (30 mL) vegetable oil

¼ tsp (1 mL) chili flakes

1 inch (2½ cm) piece of fresh ginger,
grated or finely chopped

1 tsp (5 mL) finely chopped garlic

1 cup (250 mL) dry white wine

1 tsp (5 mL) salt

8 oz (227 g) dried egg taglliatelle
(or regular spaghetti)

7 oz (200 g) crab meat

1 Tbsp (15 mL) Vietnamese fish
sauce

½ cup (125 mL) cilantro leaves,
coarsely chopped

Considering it has a very delicate flavour, crab goes surprisingly well with ginger and chili. If you are fortunate enough to have access to fresh crab, there is a pleasurable half hour to be had with a pair of claw crackers and a glass of wine, extracting the meat from the shell before dinner. There may not be a lot of meat in them, but this pasta makes a little go a long way—definitely a point in its favour given the price of crab these days.

Pour the oil into a medium frying pan over medium-low heat. Stir in the chili flakes and cook for 30 seconds. Add the ginger and garlic and cook, stirring, for another 30 seconds. Pour in the white wine, reduce by half, and remove pan from the heat.

Bring a large pan of water to a boil. Salt the boiling water and add the pasta; cook according to package directions until barely done.

While the pasta is cooking, reheat the wine mixture, add the crab meat, and heat gently on medium-low. Stir in the fish sauce and keep warm.

Drain the pasta and reserve 1 cup (250 mL) of the cooking liquid. Add the pasta to the pan, and gently stir in the crab along with the cilantro leaves, adding enough of the cooking liquid to keep it moist (there has to be a better word, but you get the meaning: it should not be dry).

Serve in warmed pasta bowls. No cheese, please.

Tagliolini alla Siciliana

••

A quick and easy pasta made with the ingredients of Sicily; it's a combination that may be hard to find on a local menu, but which tastes very good nonetheless. Pantelleria, off the west coast of the island, is famous for its capers and tomatoes; Bronte, on the slopes of Mount Etna, produces the best pistachios, and, surprisingly, anchovies still seem to abound in the surrounding seas.

Tagliolini are narrow tagliatelle made with eggs that are, consequently, more tender than other pastas. If tagliolini is not available, substitute regular spaghetti, adjusting the cooking time as required.

••

Preheat the oven to 375°F (190°C).

Line a small baking sheet with parchment paper. Cut the tomatoes in half and arrange them on the paper, cut side facing up; drizzle with 1 Tbsp (15 mL) olive oil and sprinkle with salt. Bake in the preheated oven for 30 to 40 minutes, until lightly browned and partly dried; set aside.

Heat a small saucepan over medium-low heat, add the remaining 2 Tbsp (30 mL) olive oil and the drained capers. Cook them for about 5 minutes, stirring occasionally. Pour in the white wine; let it bubble and reduce briefly, then add the chopped anchovies and stir until dissolved.

Bring a pot of water to a boil; salt the boiling water and add the pasta. Cook until al dente, then drain when ready, reserving 1 cup (250 mL) of the cooking liquid.

Add the roasted tomatoes to the capers and heat through. Return the pasta to the cooking pot or a bowl, pour in the sauce, and toss to combine, adding reserved cooking liquid as needed.

Serve in pasta bowls, sprinkled with chopped pistachios.

SERVES 2
•••••••••••

½ lb (227 g) cherry or other small tomatoes

3 Tbsp (45 mL) olive oil, divided

Salt

¼ cup (60 mL) small capers, drained

½ cup (125 mL) white wine

6 salted anchovy fillets, chopped

6 oz (160 g) dried tagliolini or spaghetti

¼ cup (60 mL) pistachios, very finely chopped, for serving

Tagliatelle *with* Fresh Salmon, Crème Fraîche, *and* Chives

••

A spring dish with the fresh colours of salmon and chives in a sauce that is lightened by the pasta cooking water. The strips of salmon are cooked just right by the heat of the pasta.

••

In a small bowl, beat together the egg yolks and add ½ cup (125 mL) crème fraîche, Parmesan, chives, lemon zest, black pepper, and parsley. Set aside.

In a saucepan large enough to hold the cooked pasta, bring the remaining 1½ cups (360 mL) crème fraîche to a boil; turn down the heat, and allow to simmer.

Cut the salmon into ¼-inch (5 mm) slices, then cut the slices across into strips, each about the size of 4 matchsticks tied together. Set them aside while you cook the pasta.

Bring a large pot of water to a boil on high. Salt the boiling water and add the pasta. Cook until just done, 3 to 5 minutes for fresh and for tagliolini, longer for regular dried pasta. Drain in a colander, reserving 1 cup (250 mL) of the cooking water.

Transfer the drained pasta to the pan of simmering crème fraîche and stir to coat. Add the egg mixture and stir again; the pasta will absorb a generous amount of sauce—add some of the cooking liquid to prevent it from drying out. Finally, add the salmon strips, stirring very gently to prevent them from breaking up.

Transfer to heated serving bowls and sprinkle with chopped parsley.

SERVES 4
AS A MAIN COURSE,
6 AS A STARTER

••••••••••••••••••

2 egg yolks

2 cups (480 mL) crème fraîche, divided

½ cup (125 mL) grated Parmesan cheese

¼ cup (60 mL) chopped chives

1 tsp (5 mL) grated lemon zest

1 tsp (5 mL) coarsely ground black pepper

2 Tbsp (30 mL) chopped Italian parsley + extra for garnish

12 oz (340 g) boneless salmon fillet

1 tsp (5 mL) salt

1 lb (454 g) fresh tagliatelle (or dried tagliolini)

Penne *with* Butternut Squash, Sage, *and* Prosciutto

•••

A perfect combination of flavours for fall and winter.

•••

SERVES 4

•••••••••••

1 large butternut squash

2 Tbsp (30 mL) olive oil

1 medium onion

5 Tbsp (75 mL) butter, divided

8 thin slices prosciutto

16 to 24 sage leaves (fresh or dried)

1 tsp (5 mL) salt

10½ oz (300 g) dried penne

Parmesan cheese, grated, for serving

Preheat the oven to 350°F (180°C).

Peel the squash (with a vegetable peeler), cut in half lengthwise, scoop out the seeds (a melon baller works well), and cut the flesh into roughly ½-inch (13 mm) cubes. Toss the cubes in a large bowl with the olive oil and spread them on a large baking sheet. Bake in the preheated oven for 30 minutes, turning them at half-time and cooking until just tender; set aside.

Chop the onion and sauté in 2 Tbsp (30 mL) butter over medium-low heat until soft and translucent; add to the baked squash, but hang on to the pan.

Heat the onion pan over medium heat and add 1½ Tbsp (22 mL) butter and prosciutto, then cook until slightly crisped. Remove the prosciutto and set aside. Add the sage leaves and remaining 1½ Tbsp (22 mL) butter to the pan and cook until the sage is starting to crisp; set aside.

Bring a large pot of water to a boil, salt it, and add the penne. Cook until al dente, drain, and reserve 1 cup (250 mL) of the cooking water. Stir the drained pasta into the squash and onions. Add the prosciutto and sage leaves and stir gently to mix. Add the reserved cooking liquid as needed to keep it creamy.

Serve with freshly grated Parmesan.

SERVES 4
••••••••••

4 fresh hot Italian sausages

1 cup (250 mL) whipping cream

1 tsp (5 mL) salt + extra as needed

1 lb (454 g) tortellini (preferably
cheese filled)

½ cup (125 mL) grated Parmesan
cheese + extra for serving

Fresh ground black
pepper

Tortellini *with* Spicy Sausage

This makes a quick, simple, and delicious supper.

With a sharp knife, slit the skin down one side of the sausages and remove the meat from the casing.

Set a frying pan over medium heat, add the sausage meat, break it up with a potato masher, and cook until it is no longer pink. Pour in the cream, bring to a boil, reduce the heat, and cook briefly. Set aside and keep warm.

Boil a large pot of water; salt the boiling water and add the tortellini. Bring the water back to a boil, reduce the heat, and cook until tender (check the package for the proper timing). Reserve 1 cup (250 mL) of cooking water, drain the pasta, and return it to the pot.

Reheat the sausages and cream and stir in the pasta, adjusting the consistency of the sauce with the reserved cooking liquid if necessary.

Stir in the Parmesan and fresh black pepper, adding salt if necessary.

Serve in warm pasta bowls and pass around more Parmesan.

Lasagne

••

This is my sons' version of lasagne, and it's good. They like to pursue some-thing—often a discussion, but in this case a recipe—as far as it will go. In this situation, they have refined lasagne down to the bare essentials: it contains no cheese and definitely no spinach, and the lasagne noodles are the oven-ready kind, which saves time. Before it goes in the oven the lasagne is very sloppy, but any liquid gets absorbed during cooking.

••

Sauté the onion in olive oil in a large saucepan over medium heat until soft and translucent. Add the ground beef and pork, breaking them up with a potato masher, and cook until no longer pink.

Add the canned tomatoes, red wine, salt, and herbs. Bring to a boil, turn the heat down to low and simmer, stirring occasionally to break up the tomatoes, for 20 minutes.

Add the spices and maple syrup; set aside to keep warm.

To make a béchamel sauce, rinse out a medium saucepan with water, but do not dry it. Pour in the milk, add the bay leaves and peppercorns, and bring to a simmer over low heat. Turn off the heat and let it sit for 10 minutes.

Strain the milk into a bowl and wash out the saucepan. Set it over medium-low heat, melt the butter and stir in the flour. Cook until the butter is foaming and the roux is smooth.

Pour in about a third of the warm milk, turn up the heat to medium, and stir with a whisk until smooth and bubbling. Pour in the rest of the milk and whisk again until simmering and smooth.

Season with the cinnamon and salt and pepper to taste.

Preheat the oven to 350°F (180°C).

Ladle a quarter of the meat sauce into a baking dish about 14 × 9 inches (35 × 23 cm). Spoon a quarter of the béchamel sauce on top and smooth it out. Cover with a layer of lasagne noodles, breaking them to fit. Repeat the process 2 more times. Cover the top layer of noodles with the remaining sauces.

Set the dish in the middle of the preheated oven and cook for 45 minutes, until bubbling around the sides. If the lasagne becomes too brown, cover the dish loosely with a sheet of aluminum foil and turn down the temperature.

Remove from the oven and allow to firm up for 15 minutes before serving; the lasagne does not improve with reheating and is best eaten the day it is made.

Serve with a green salad. (This part of the recipe comes from me, not from Josh and Dan.)

SERVES 6
••••••••••••

1 large onion, finely chopped

2 Tbsp (30 mL) olive oil

1 lb (454 g) ground beef

½ lb (227 g) ground pork (or pork sausage)

One 28-oz (794 g) can Italian plum tomatoes

2 cups (480 mL) red wine

½ tsp (2 mL) salt + extra as needed

2 tsp (10 mL) finely chopped herbs (any of basil, thyme, rosemary, or oregano)

½ tsp (2 mL) ground nutmeg

½ tsp (2 mL) ground cinnamon

¼ cup (60 mL) maple syrup

3 cups (720 mL) milk

2 bay leaves

8 black peppercorns

3 Tbsp (45 mL) butter

3 Tbsp (45 mL) all-purpose flour

½ tsp (2 mL) ground cinnamon

Fresh ground black pepper

1 pkg oven-ready lasagne noodles

SERVES 6 TO 8

•••••••••••••••••

2 cups (480 mL) finely chopped
medium onions

3 Tbsp (45 mL) olive oil

4 medium yams, peeled and cut into
¼-inch (6 mm) rounds

3 Tbsp (45 mL) chopped sage
(preferably fresh)

1 tsp (5 mL) salt, divided + extra for
the boiling water

2 bunches spinach

6 cups (1.4 L) milk + extra 1 cup
(250 mL) if using oven-ready
noodles

1 bay leaf

8 black peppercorns

3 Tbsp (45 mL) butter

3 Tbsp (45 mL) all-purpose flour

½ tsp (2 mL) salt

Large pinch cinnamon

Large pinch nutmeg

½ lb (227 g) oven-ready lasagne
noodles (or 6 sheets fresh
lasagne noodles)

Vegetable Lasagne

••

This is a vegetable casserole and a pasta dish, an excellent addition to a buffet when you want to bolster the non-meat offerings. Oven-ready noodles will absorb more liquid during cooking, so if you use them, add the full amount of milk shown in the recipe

••

In a large saucepan, sauté the onions in olive oil until pale gold. Add the sliced yams, sage, and ½ tsp (2 mL) salt. Stir well, turn the heat down to low, cover the pan, and cook, stirring occasionally, until the yam slices are barely tender and can be pierced with a fork, about 20 minutes.

Wash and rinse the spinach. Bring a small amount of water to a boil in a medium saucepan, salt it, and add the spinach, turning it over until completely wilted. Drain it, but don't squeeze dry.

To make a béchamel sauce, rinse out a medium saucepan with water but do not dry it. Pour in the milk (including the extra 1 cup [250 mL] if using dried noodles), bay leaf, and peppercorns, and bring to a simmer over medium heat; watch it carefully toward the end. Turn off the heat and set aside to infuse.

Have a sieve ready for the next step. Set a small saucepan over medium heat, melt the butter, and add the flour; stir until the butter is foaming and the flour incorporated. Strain the infused hot milk into the pan, turn the heat to medium, and cook, stirring with a whisk, until the milk bubbles and the sauce is smooth. Remove from the heat and stir in ½ tsp (2 mL) salt, a large pinch of cinnamon, and a large pinch of nutmeg.

Preheat the oven to 350°F (180°C).

Spread a cup of the béchamel sauce on the bottom of a baking dish about 14 × 9 inches (35 × 23 cm), and cover with a layer of noodles. Spread out one-third of the spinach on top and cover with one-third of the yam slices; pour on enough béchamel sauce to cover the layer completely, about 1½ cups (360 mL). Repeat the layering twice more, finishing with the béchamel. Use more milk if there is not enough sauce to cover the top layer of noodles.

Cover the dish with aluminum foil and bake for 45 minutes in the centre of the preheated oven. Remove from the oven and let rest for 15 minutes before serving.

This recipe is good reheated.

Fusilli Pasta Salad *with* Tomato, Basil, *and* Buttermilk

Italians supposedly take a dim view of pasta salads, but this one is a different matter. It is easy to make in a large quantity and so particularly good for a party. It goes well with almost anything, particularly food cooked on the barbecue, with the creamy pasta sauce balancing the smoky flavours from the grill.

This recipe goes very well with Chicken Marbella, which you will find in the Silver Palate Cookbook. (Buddy Holly is reported to have said that "without Elvis, none of us would have made it." I think most of us who opened food shops in the 80's feel the same way about the Silver Palate).

Chop 1 tomato into neat ¼-inch (6 mm) cubes and set aside. Chop the remaining tomatoes into large chunks and transfer to the work bowl of a food processor. Process until smooth (about a minute) and add the mayonnaise, buttermilk, garlic, and salt. Process again until smooth, and set aside in a large bowl.

Boil a large pot of water; add salt to a boiling water and add the pasta. Cook until barely tender, drain, and mix the pasta into the tomato sauce while still warm. Set aside for half an hour or more, for the flavours to blend.

Stir the tomato cubes and the chopped basil into the pasta.

SERVES 8

6 large ripe tomatoes

1 cup (250 mL) Hellmann's mayonnaise

1¼ cups (300 mL) buttermilk

1½ tsp (7 mL) chopped garlic

1 tsp (5 mL) salt

1 lb (454 g) dried fusilli or rotini

½ cup (125 mL) chopped fresh basil leaves

Risotto Milanese

5 cups (1.2 L) Chicken Stock
(page 236)

0.02 oz (½ g) saffron threads

½ tsp (2 mL) salt

1 medium onion, halved and peeled

1 Tbsp (15 mL) butter

1 medium onion, finely chopped

1 clove garlic, finely chopped

1¼ cups (300 mL) Arborio,
Carnaroli, or Vialone Nano rice

1 cup (250 mL) white wine

2 Tbsp (30 mL) butter

½ cup (125 mL) Parmesan, Grana
Padano, or Pecorino cheese, finely
grated + extra for serving

This is the classic risotto flavoured with saffron and chicken stock. The quality of the chicken stock is important and homemade is definitely best, but if stock cubes are all you have, go ahead and use them—stock cube risotto is better than none at all.

On the other hand, don't make risotto (or anything else) with inferior saffron. Buying saffron is like going to the opera: all the seats are expensive, but buying the best transforms the experience. You can buy cheaper saffron from Mexico or the Himalayas and get a nice yellow colour, but only saffron from Spain or Iran will give you the true taste.

Arborio superfino is the rice most often used for risotto in North America, but it is not the best choice. Both Carnaroli (which has a large grain) and Vialone Nano (smaller; "nano" means dwarf in Italian) have a higher starch content and absorb more liquid than Arborio, giving a more intense flavour and a creamier texture. As with pasta, Italians cook their risotto much more al dente than we do. It's all about personal preference, but it is worth discovering how a culture for whom risotto is a national obsession likes it done. Just cook it less and serve with conviction.

In a saucepan over medium heat, bring the chicken stock to a boil. With a pestle and mortar, grind the saffron and salt to a fine powder; add powder to the stock along with the onion, turn the heat to very low, and leave to simmer. Adjust the seasoning: homemade stock may not be salted, but commercial stocks have more than enough.

In a larger saucepan over medium heat, melt the butter, add the chopped onion and garlic, and cook until soft. Add the rice and cook briefly to coat with the butter and onion. Pour in the wine, and stir until it has been absorbed.

Ladle a cup (250 mL) of hot stock into the rice and stir until it stops bubbling. Reduce the heat and let it cook for a minute or two, then stir again; add more stock when the first cup is almost absorbed. Keep stirring, cooking, and adding more stock. Adjust the heat so that the rice bubbles gently but does not stick to the bottom of the pan (some sticking is hard to avoid toward the end).

Add the liquid in smaller amounts as you proceed. If you run out of stock before the rice is tender, finish with plain water.

The total cooking time is about 30 minutes; it is done when there is still a slight bite at the very centre of each grain. The final consistency should be neither soupy nor dry, but just right, like Baby Bear's porridge; add stock or water if necessary.

Just before serving, stir in the butter and grated cheese, and pass around more cheese.

RISOTTO WITH PORCINI MUSHROOMS (VARIATION) A very satisfying dish, substantial and full of earthy flavours. Including some dried porcini, even when fresh mushrooms are available, adds depth and complexity. The recipe is the same as that for the Risotto Milanese with the addition of the mushrooms. The saffron is optional: beware of gilding the lily.

Soak 1 oz (28 g) dried mushrooms in a small bowl of warm water for 20 minutes. Remove, drain the liquid through a fine sieve or coffee filter, and add it to the chicken stock. Chop the soaked mushrooms coarsely and set aside.

Clean and finely slice ½ lb (227 g) fresh porcini mushrooms, if available, or white or brown mushrooms if not.

In a small frying pan, melt 1 Tbsp (15 mL) butter and 1 Tbsp (15 mL) oil, add the fresh mushrooms, and cook, stirring occasionally, until tender. Add the dried porcini and stir to mix; set aside.

Make the Risotto Milanese recipe, omitting the saffron, and adding the mushroom mix with the first addition of stock.

SALADS

....

There was a time, within living memory, when a salad was a few lettuce leaves, a tomato, and a dollop of Heinz salad cream to accompany the main course, served (in the more genteel households) on a dish with the shape of a crescent moon, fitted neatly against the rim of the main plate. This salad was simple and versatile: if you put it on a larger plate and added a slice of ham, it became a ham salad. You could do the same with chicken and make a chicken salad. And that, in those fortunately long gone days, was pretty much as far as salads went.

In the years since, salads have evolved more than any other part of dinner, to the point where now any combination of ingredients served cold or at room temperature is a salad, and will, as likely as not, turn out to be the main course of lunch or dinner. Traditionalist I may be, but I am actually okay with that. I never liked Heinz salad cream, and there's nothing in the catechism of new salads that says I can't have a plain green one if I want—as someone rightly said of same sex marriage, legalization does not mean it's compulsory.

The challenge I have with the new salads is not that they don't taste good, but in knowing when to eat them. Even breakfast, that most traditional of meals, is not safe from the incursion of lettuce, and I have to confess that it is the principle of the thing that rubs me the wrong way. Practice is another matter, and I have no trouble tackling a couple of soft poached eggs nestled on greens, raw veggies, and a nice dressing, even quite early in the morning. The fact that this combination turns out, with only minor changes, to be a *salade Lyonnaise*—one of the more delicious salads in the repertoire (recipe on page 58)—only highlights the difficulty in deciding where salads fit into a day's eating. On most days, my dance card is already full by the time the salad comes asking if I am free for the foxtrot.

The salads in this section are without exception delicious, but I will have to leave it to you to schedule their appearance. That said, if I were to be allowed one word of advice, it would be: "lunch."

Salade Lyonnaise

This is a traditional French salad, a delicious combination of bitter greens, bacon, and a soft poached egg; it makes an excellent first course. Poach the eggs ahead of time and hold them in a bowl of cold water. They can be reheated in hot water at the last minute.

SERVES 4

4 eggs

4 cups (960 mL) bitter greens (such as dandelion, curly endive, and radicchio)

4 cups (960 mL) sweet lettuces (such as leaf, Boston, and Romaine)

6 thick slices of bacon, cut into ¼-inch (6 mm) matchsticks

2 Tbsp (30 mL) olive oil

3 Tbsp (45 mL) Nancy's Vinaigrette (page 228)

Poach the eggs following the directions on page 23, keeping them soft. Lift them out into a large bowl of cold water where they will hold, unrefrigerated, for several hours.

Wash and dry the greens and lettuces and set aside in a large bowl.

Sauté the bacon in the olive oil until just starting to crisp; take the pan off the heat and set aside.

About 15 minutes before serving, bring a pan of water to a boil. Turn the heat to low and gently lower in the eggs; after 2 minutes, lift them out onto a paper towel and pat dry.

Toss the lettuces with the vinaigrette dressing, and reheat the bacon. Remove the bacon to a small dish and pour the hot bacon oil over the salad; toss together.

Set out 4 plates and divide the salad between them. Sprinkle each salad with bacon pieces.

Place an egg on top of each plate and serve immediately with crusty bread.

Essential Green Salad

••

This is your essential green salad. It has just two components, the lettuce and the dressing, and both must be top notch. Nancy's Vinaigrette (page 228) takes care of the dressing; for the lettuces it is up to you. A mixture of leaves and textures works well; radicchio is a more colourful and robust leaf, with a slightly bitter note. If romaine is part of the mix, trim off the hard spines.

••

Toss the salad with the dressing and, when the leaves are lightly coated, arrange the extras on top—avocado, green onion, or anything that does not take away from the simplicity of the whole; don't toss again before serving.

SERVES 1
(MULTIPLY RECIPE AS NEEDED)
••••••••••••••••••••••••

2 cups (480 mL) mixed lettuce

1 Tbsp (15 mL) Nancy's Vinaigrette
(page 228)

Sliced avocado (optional)

Sliced green onion (optional)

Tomato, Artichoke, *and* Feta Salad

••

An excellent salad in which the feta provides the salt to bring out the flavour of the tomatoes.

••

Cut the feta into ⅓-inch (8 mm) cubes and set aside in a large bowl.

Drain the artichokes in a colander, discarding the marinade. Transfer to a paper towel and pat dry; add to the bowl. Add the sliced red onion.

Cut the tomatoes into ½-inch (13 mm) cubes, and set aside in a colander to drain.

Whisk the vinegar, salt, and chopped garlic together in a small bowl. Gradually whisk in the olive oil to form an emulsion and thicken the dressing; stir in the oregano, pepper, basil, and parsley.

Pour the dressing over the artichokes, feta, and onions, and toss gently.

Stir in the cubed tomatoes just before serving.

SERVES 6
••••••••••••

½ lb (227 g) feta cheese

4 cups (960 mL) artichoke hearts
(canned or from a jar)

½ medium red onion, finely sliced

2 large tomatoes

2 Tbsp (30 mL) red wine vinegar

¼ tsp (1 mL) salt

½ tsp (2 mL) finely chopped garlic

½ cup (125 mL) olive oil

1 tsp (5 mL) dried oregano

½ tsp (2 mL) fresh ground black
pepper

½ cup (125 mL) finely sliced fresh
basil leaves

1 cup (250 mL) coarsely chopped
parsley (curly or Italian)

SERVES 4
• • • • • • • • • • •

4 beets, including stems
and leaves

7 oz (200 g) sheep or goat feta

¼ cup (60 mL) extra virgin
olive oil

Beets, Beet Greens, *and* Goat Feta Salad

• •

Feta is Greek for "slice" and refers to the way the blocks of cheese are cut before being stored in brine. Salt prevents the growth of bacteria, and in hot climates brining was an effective way of keeping cheese before the days of Westinghouse. The end result is definitely salty, which is the reason feta works so well with beets—it is a food marriage made in Heaven.

• •

Trim the stems, leaves, and root ends from the beets; chop the leaves and stems into 2-inch (5 cm) pieces and set aside.

Place the beets in a saucepan, cover with cold water, and bring to a boil over medium heat. Reduce the heat to a simmer and cook uncovered for up to an hour, until tender, adding water to keep the beets covered. Drain and when the beets are cool enough to handle remove their outer skins—it slips off easily. (Rubber gloves are useful.)

Half fill another saucepan with water, bring it to a boil, and add the beet greens and stems. Boil for about 8 minutes, until tender; drain in a colander and squeeze dry when cool enough to handle.

Serve the salad at room temperature. Arrange the beet greens on a platter, and slice the beets ¼ inch (6 mm) thick to arrange on top of the greens. Slice or cube the feta and arrange it on top of the beets. Drizzle with the olive oil.

Mediterranean Salad

··

This very colourful salad flavoured with sweet spices and lots of parsley was one of our most popular in the days of the Food Shops in Toronto.

··

Preheat the oven to 350°F (180°C).

Toss the bread cubes with 2 Tbsp (30 mL) oil in a large bowl. Spread them on a baking sheet and bake in the preheated oven until golden brown, turning once or twice—7 to 10 minutes. Set aside.

Put the cubed and sliced cucumber, peppers, green onion, and parsley into a large bowl.

In a small bowl, whisk together the lemon juice, salt, garlic, pepper, cinnamon, and allspice. Gradually whisk in the remaining olive oil to form an emulsion and thicken the dressing.

The recipe may be made ahead to this point. Do the final assembly 2 hours or less before serving, or the croutons will soak up the dressing and lose their crunch.

Whisk the dressing to re-establish the emulsion, pour it over the vegetables, and mix well. Add the croutons and the cubed tomatoes, and toss gently to combine.

SERVES 6

·············

2 cups (480 mL) country-style white bread, cut in ½-inch (13 mm) cubes

¾ cup (180 mL) olive oil, divided

1 cup (250 mL) English cucumber in ½-inch (13 mm) cubes

⅓ cup (80 mL) green pepper in ½-inch (13 mm) pieces

⅓ cup (80 mL) red pepper in ½-inch (13 mm) pieces

½ cup (125 mL) thinly sliced green onion

4 cups (960 mL) Italian parsley leaves, coarsely chopped

2 Tbsp (30 mL) lemon juice

¾ tsp (4 mL) salt

½ tsp (2 mL) finely chopped garlic

½ tsp (2 mL) fresh ground black pepper

1 tsp (5 mL) ground cinnamon

¼ tsp (1 mL) ground allspice

2 tomatoes, cut in ½-inch (13 mm) cubes

Caesar Salad Deconstructed

This is an elegant version of the traditional Caesar, stylish enough for a formal dinner.

SERVES 6

···········

1 baguette

2 Tbsp (30 mL) olive oil

4 hearts Romaine lettuce

1½ tsp (7 mL) peeled garlic

¼ tsp (1 mL) salt

1 anchovy filet

1 Tbsp (15 mL) Dijon mustard

2 Tbsp (30 mL) lemon juice

6 drops Tabasco sauce

8 drops Worcestershire sauce

5 Tbsp (75 mL) olive oil

1 egg

3 slices prosciutto

1 Tbsp (15 mL) olive oil

12 anchovy filets

½ lb (227 g) Parmesan cheese
(not grated)

Preheat the oven to 400°F (200°C).

To make crostini, cut the baguette on a sharp diagonal into 12 elongated slices, each about ¼ inch (6 mm) thick. Brush a large baking sheet with 1 Tbsp (15 mL) oil and arrange the bread slices on top, without overlapping, brushing them with another 1 Tbsp (15 mL) oil.

Bake in the preheated oven for 4 minutes. Turn the crostini over and bake for a further 3 minutes, until lightly browned. Set aside.

With a small sharp knife, trim each lettuce leaf along both sides of the spine, discarding the spine and leaving the leaf in 2 long pieces (which may still be joined at the top). Separate the 2 pieces, set aside in a large bowl, and trim the rest of the leaves.

In a blender (or a tall jar, using an immersion blender), combine the garlic, salt, anchovy filet, mustard, lemon juice, Tabasco, Worcestershire, and 5 Tbsp (75 mL) olive oil. Blend until completely smooth. Add the egg and blend again until thick. Set aside.

Cut the prosciutto into matchsticks and sauté in 1 Tbsp (15 mL) olive oil over medium heat until lightly crisped. Set aside.

Pour the dressing over the lettuce leaves and toss to coat; divide the leaves between the serving plates. Sprinkle with the crispy prosciutto, and cross 2 anchovy filets on each salad.

With a vegetable peeler or mandolin, shave the Parmesan cheese into thin slices and divide them between the plates.

Serve with 2 crostini on each plate.

Singapore Shrimp Noodle Salad

SERVES 6
••••••••••

1 tsp (5 mL) salt

1 lb (454 g) dried linguine

½ cup (125 mL) red pepper in julienne strips

½ cup (125 mL) green pepper in julienne strips

½ cup (125 mL) carrot in julienne strips

¼ cup (60 mL) green onion in julienne strips

½ cup (125 mL) vegetable oil

2 Tbsp (30 mL) curry powder

2 Tbsp (30 mL) oyster sauce

2 Tbsp (30 mL) lemon juice

3 cups (720 mL) cooked salad shrimp

¼ cup (60 mL) chopped coriander leaves

An excellent and colourful salad; it can be made with chicken, pork, shrimp, or any combination thereof. This recipe brings out the best in tiny salad shrimp, hand peeled if you can find them. This salad can be made ahead and stored in the fridge for a day.

Bring a large pot of water to a boil, add salt, and cook the linguine until al dente (check package timing and see the introduction to the Pasta chapter, page 37). Drain, rinse under cold water, and set aside.

Cut the vegetables into julienne strips, then put them into a large bowl.

In a small saucepan, heat the vegetable oil and curry powder until fragrant; remove from the heat and set aside.

Stir the oyster sauce, lemon juice, salad shrimp, and coriander leaves into the vegetables. Add the drained linguine and the curry oil, and mix together well.

Thai Squid Salad

···

An easy salad to prepare that makes a nice first course or summer lunch.

···

Bring a large pot of water to a boil.

Clean and rinse the squid under cold water, then cut the tubes across into ½-inch (1 cm) rings. Put the squid in the boiling water and cook for about 30 seconds, until opaque (do it in 2 batches if necessary). Drain and set aside to cool, then transfer to a large bowl.

Remove the dry top and fibrous outer leaves from the lemon grass. Coarsely chop the softer lower part and grind to a fine paste with a mortar and pestle or small grinder; add it to the squid.

Remove the stems from the coriander and mint leaves, then add the leaves to the squid along with the sliced green onions and toasted rice flour.

Set a small pan over medium-low heat and sauté the garlic and olive oil until pale gold. Remove from the heat and stir in the Spring Roll Sauce, lemon juice, and fish sauce; whisk to blend.

Pour the dressing over the squid; stir well and set aside for an hour for the flavours to blend.

SERVES 4 TO 6

··················

2 lb (900 g) squid

1 stem lemon grass

¾ cup (180 mL) coriander leaves

1 cup (250 mL) fresh mint

½ cup (125 mL) finely sliced green onions

¼ cup (60 mL) rice flour, toasted

2 tsp (10 mL) finely chopped garlic

2 Tbsp (30 mL) olive oil

½ cup (125 mL) Spring Roll Sauce (page 235 or bought)

2 Tbsp (30 mL) lemon juice

1 Tbsp (15 mL) fish sauce

Thai Beef Noodle Salad

An excellent salad for a picnic or lunch on the deck. It may be made ahead and stored in the fridge for 2 days.

Sauté the garlic and oil in a small frying pan over low heat until pale gold; remove from the heat and set aside.

Bring a large pot of water to a boil, salt it, and add the noodles. Cook until just tender; drain and transfer to a large bowl. Pour in the garlic and oil and toss to mix.

Add the Spring Roll Sauce, lemon juice, and fish sauce to the bowl and toss again.

Cut the green onions into 3-inch (8 cm) lengths, then lengthwise into thin slivers, and add to the noodles. Peel the cucumber, cut it in half, and remove the seeds with a teaspoon. Cut the halves into 2-inch (5 cm) lengths, and each length into thin strips. Add to the noodles, along with the coriander and mint leaves.

Turn the barbecue or grill to high. Rub the flank steak with oyster sauce and pepper and grill to rare or medium rare, 3 to 4 minutes per side. Set aside to rest for 10 minutes.

With a large sharp knife, cut the flank steak across the grain into very thin slices (see flank steak recipe, page 141); cut these slices into 1-inch (2½ cm) lengths and add them to the noodles.

Toss together well and serve.

SERVES 4
•••••••••••

2 tsp (10 mL) finely chopped garlic

2 Tbsp (30 mL) vegetable oil

1 tsp (5 mL) salt

½ lb (227 g) dried capellini noodles, broken in half

½ cup (125 mL) Spring Roll Sauce (page235)

2 Tbsp (30 mL) lemon juice

1 Tbsp (15 mL) Thai fish sauce

4 green onions

1 English cucumber

½ cup (125 mL) fresh coriander leaves

½ cup (125 mL) fresh mint leaves

1 lb (454 g) flank steak

1 Tbsp (15 mL) oyster sauce

1 tsp (5 mL) black pepper

SERVES 6
•••••••••••

14 oz (400 g) small new potatoes

2 tsp (10 mL) salt, divided

3 Tbsp (45 mL) Nancy's Vinaigrette Dressing (page 228)

2 Tbsp (30 mL) chopped chives

6 semi-hard boiled eggs

18 oz (500 g) fine green beans

1 lettuce (Bib, Boston, or other), washed and dried

Two 4-oz (120 g) cans tuna (Spanish is best)

9 small ripe tomatoes, quartered

Handful olives (Kalamata or Niçoise, preferably with the pits in)

½ cup (125 mL) Nancy's Vinaigrette Dressing (page 228)

Mayonnaise (page 229)

Salade Niçoise

•••

Few meals feel more like summer than Salade Niçoise, a bottle of vin rosé, and a table outdoors in the shade. This is a composed salad with no right or wrong way to serve it—you can include as many of a wide range of ingredients as you wish, and it can certainly be made without tuna or anchovy (for vegetarians). This recipe contains some tips for boiling eggs and potatoes.

•••

POTATOES This method of boiling the potatoes comes from Denmark, a country where cooks are judged on their potatoes.

The potatoes should all be roughly the same size, about 1½ inches (4 cm)—cut larger potatoes in half. Put potatoes in a saucepan, cover with cold water, add 1 tsp (5 mL) salt, and bring to a boil over medium-high heat. Set the timer and simmer, uncovered, for 12 minutes. Turn off the heat, cover the pan, and set the timer for an additional 12 minutes. At this point the potatoes should be firm but able to be pierced with a fork (leave them longer if necessary). Drain and set aside in a colander until cool enough to handle. Cut the potatoes in half and dress lightly with the vinaigrette. Sprinkle with chives (if you have them).

SEMI-HARD BOILED EGGS Place the eggs in a saucepan, cover with cold water, and bring to a boil over medium-high heat. As soon as the water boils, remove the pan from the heat, cover it, and set the timer for 5 minutes. Drain and refresh under cold water; crack the shells and leave to sit in cold water for a few minutes. Peel the eggs (there is no easy trick here), cut them in half or quarters lengthwise, and set aside.

GREEN BEANS Bring a pot of water to a boil, add 1 tsp (5 mL) of salt and the beans, bring back to a boil, and cook until tender but firm, about 3 minutes (testing after 2 minutes). Drain and refresh under cold water until cool; set aside on a cloth to dry.

ASSEMBLY There are as many ways to compose a Salade Niçoise as there are cooks, but there is only one rule—it should be a thing of beauty, and no one else's idea of what is beautiful but yours.

Once assembled, drizzle more vinaigrette over the whole salad, and pass the homemade Mayonnaise separately.

SALMON NIÇOISE (VARIATION) A nice way to give a Canadian flavour to Salade Niçoise. Simply follow the recipe above, replacing the tuna with 6 oz (180 g) barbecued or baked salmon per person. Everything else stays the same.

BEFORE DINNER

SCALLOPS *with* LEMON *and* OLIVES 74

CROSTINI *with* TOMATOES *and* HERBED GOAT CHEESE 76

CRAB DIP 76

HUMMUS 77

BLINIS *with* SMOKED SALMON *and* CRÈME FRAÎCHE 79

CARAMELIZED ONION TART 80

PISSALADIÈRE 83

SMOKED SALMON MOUSSE 84

TUNA *with* WHITE BEANS (TONNO E FAGIOLI) 84

BROCCOLINI *with* GARLIC, ANCHOVIES, *and* CHILI 85

CHERRY TOMATOES *with* CREAM 85

POLENTA *and* MUSHROOM
RAGOUT 86

....

In my house, people like to gather in the kitchen before dinner, and while peering into saucepans and sticking fingers into sauces can test my good nature, I still much prefer it to the old days when we cooks found ourselves trying to play both sides of a game of tennis—guests in the living room at one end, and dinner preparations somewhere in the back of the house at the other.

I always appreciate it when someone makes a sit-down first course, but it does not happen very often. Even a first course prepared ahead of time can be a challenge for the single-handed cook if the main course requires last minute work. Unless I can count on helpers who are not easily distracted, I would rather serve one or more small dishes in the kitchen. These "tapas" do take some time, but much of the prep can be done in advance, and there is the bonus of being with your guests.

Scallops *with* Lemon *and* Olives

••

1 Tbsp (15 mL) olive oil

2 slices of lemon, about ¼ inch
(6 mm) thick

8 large East Coast scallops (or ten
½-oz [15 g] smaller scallops)

1 cup (250 mL) white wine

16 Moroccan dried olives, pitted and
thinly sliced

12 Crostini (page 227)

These little appetizers combine intensely flavoured Moroccan dried olives with scallops. East Coast are the best, and also the most expensive, but the dish works quite well with smaller bay scallops. Reducing the wine to a glaze moderates the intense sour and bitter flavours of the olives and lemon, bringing forward the natural sweetness of the scallops.

Served on crostini, they make an excellent finger food; on a plate with crusty bread, they are a more substantial appetizer.

••

Make the crostini following the recipe on page 227, if serving that way.

Heat the olive oil in a small frying pan over medium heat, add the lemon slices, and cook until soft and lightly browned on both sides. When cool, trim the rind from the flesh, discard the flesh, and finely chop the rind; set it aside.

Dry the scallops on a paper towel. Place a frying pan with a lid over medium heat until hot enough to sear the scallops. Put the scallops in the dry pan (no oil or butter) round end up with space between. Cover the pan and cook for 3 minutes on one end only, until brown and crusty; lift them out onto a plate and cover with the lid to keep warm.

Deglaze the pan with the white wine. It will boil rapidly; if necessary, add a little water to prevent it from drying completely. Reduce to about ¼ cup (60 mL) of liquid.

If serving on crostini, stir in the olives and chopped lemon, then reduce the sauce to a glaze. Cut the scallops vertically into ¼-inch (6 mm) slices; add them to the pan and reheat. Transfer 2 scallop slices to each crostini, then spoon a little sauce on top.

If serving as a first course, add the olives and chopped lemon to the pan and cook for a minute or two. Add enough water to make up ½ cup (125 mL) of sauce, and cook briefly. Add the whole scallops to the pan just long enough to warm them—about half a minute. Place 2 to 4 scallops on each plate and spoon the sauce around them. Serve with good bread.

Crostini *with* Tomatoes *and* Herbed Goat Cheese

···

This is very colourful, attractive, and simple. Unsurprisingly I have a bias toward Salt Spring Cheese (Ruckles is a good choice), but another fresh goat cheese will be almost as good. A tomato with flavour is not easy to find in many months of the year; the hot-house tomatoes on the vine don't have much flavour in winter—the Campari or sweet salad tomatoes are a better choice.

···

In a small bowl, mix the goat cheese with the herbs; pour the oil over top and set aside.

Slice the tomatoes and sprinkle lightly with salt.

Warm the crostini and spread with the goat cheese. Place a slice or two of tomato on top of each crostini, sprinkle with salt, and decorate with a sprig of fresh herb.

SERVES 4

············

5 oz (150 g) fresh goat cheese

1 Tbsp (15 mL) fresh herbs, finely chopped + extra sprigs for garnish

2 Tbsp (30 mL) olive oil or grape seed oil

½ lb (227 g) ripe tomatoes

Salt

12 crostini (page 227)

Crab Dip

···

This is a simple dip made, unapologetically, with fake crab. Save the real crab for finer things, like the crab pasta on page 44.

···

In a large bowl, mix all ingredients together until completely blended. Taste for seasoning and add salt and pepper as needed. Serve with blue corn chips.

MAKES ABOUT 2 TO 3 CUPS (500 TO 750 ML)

····················

1 lb (454 g) fake crab

5 oz (150 g) fresh goat cheese (or cream cheese)

2 Tbsp (30 mL) Hellman's mayonnaise

1½ cups (360 mL) very finely chopped mixed red, green, and yellow peppers

2 green onions, finely sliced

1 clove garlic, mashed and finely chopped

2 Tbsp (30 mL) lemon juice

Dash Tabasco sauce

Dash Worcestershire sauce

Salt

Fresh ground black pepper

Hummus

....

Hummus is easy and inexpensive to make. You can dress it up by serving it with warm, soft pitas and whole chickpeas sautéed and tossed with ground sumac. In Canada, sumac is known for its leaves that turn a beautiful deep red in the fall; in the eastern Mediterranean it is widely used as a seasoning.

....

Drain and rinse the chickpeas; set aside ½ cup (125 mL). Put the rest of the chickpeas and the garlic, lemon juice, and tahini in the work bowl of a food processor; process until completely smooth, adding as much water as necessary for a soft texture. Taste for salt. With a spatula, spread the hummus on a wide serving platter; cover with plastic wrap and set aside until ready to serve.

Heat 1 Tbsp (15 mL) olive oil in a small pan and add the reserved chickpeas, warming them through. Sprinkle with ground sumac and pour them over the hummus.

Heat the remaining 1 Tbsp (15 mL) of oil in a small frying pan, and warm the pitas on both sides. Cut each into 8 wedges, wrapping them in a napkin to keep them warm. Serve with the hummus.

The hummus will keep for 4 days in the fridge.

SERVES 6
....

Two 14-oz (397 g) cans chickpeas or garbanzo beans

4 garlic cloves

Juice of 1 lemon

1 cup (250 mL) tahini paste

Water

Salt

2 Tbsp (30 mL) olive oil, divided

1 Tbsp (15 mL) ground sumac

4 soft-style pita or other flat bread (not pita pockets)

Blinis *with* Smoked Salmon *and* Crème Fraîche

These delicious little buckwheat pillows topped with melted butter, smoked salmon, chopped onion, and crème fraîche are a Christmas Eve tradition. They are, hands down, the best first course of all, whether standing up or sitting down. Cooking them while everyone gathers around, served hot off the griddle for each guest to do their own assembly, makes a party of a party. Food does not get any better than this—well, possibly, with the addition of a spoonful of caviar.

Buckwheat is the traditional flour for blinis (mixed here with all-purpose), but whole wheat works well. The blinis themselves are last-minute work, but all the other ingredients can be prepared in advance. Smoked tuna has been a great discovery for me, but with blinis I prefer the stronger flavour of smoked salmon. Kippers are good, too.

Make the Crème Fraîche (page 232) three days ahead, as it needs time to ripen; if you forget, it's readily available in stores.

Prepare the toppings in advance: slice the smoked fish with a sharp, narrow-blade knife (if not already sliced), and arrange on a platter. Surround with lemon wedges, cover with wrap, and set aside. Finely chop the red onion, place in a small serving bowl, cover, and set aside. Cut the butter into chunks and place in a small saucepan or microwaveable jug; set aside.

In a medium bowl, whisk the egg yolks, yogurt, and milk until smooth. In a separate bowl, whisk together the buckwheat and white flours, baking soda, baking powder, and salt. Pour most of the flour mix onto the eggs and gently mix with a spatula. Add only enough flour for a soft batter, as it will thicken as it sits. (Note that adding more flour to a soft batter is easier than adding milk to a thick one; add less flour rather than more to start.) Whisk the egg whites to stiff peaks and gently fold them into the batter; do not over mix—a little unincorporated egg white is fine.

Set a large frying pan over medium-low heat, or heat a griddle on medium. Melt a small piece of butter in the pan swirl it around and scoop small spoonfuls of batter, one for each guest, into the pan, leaving space between. Flip them when small bubbles start to appear on the top: they should be lightly browned on the cooked side, so adjust the heat up or down as required. When browned on both sides, transfer to plates and let each guest assemble their own. (If you are sitting down to eat the blinis, cook them all and keep warm in a 225°F [110°C] oven.)

Melt the butter on the stove or in the microwave; pour into a jug.

To assemble the blinis, pour melted butter over each, add a slice or two of smoked fish, sprinkle with chopped onion, top with Crème Fraîche, and add a few grinds of black pepper and a squeeze of lemon. They say you are not having a good time with blinis until the butter is running down your arm and dripping off your elbow.

SERVES 4
....

1 recipe Crème Fraîche (page 232; or store-bought)

14 oz (400 g) smoked salmon or other smoked fish

3 lemons, in wedges

1 red onion, very finely chopped

8 oz (227 g) butter

3 egg yolks

½ cup (125 mL) yogurt

1½ cups (360 mL) milk

1 cup (250 mL) buckwheat flour (or whole wheat)

1 cup (250 mL) all-purpose flour

½ tsp (2 mL) baking soda

1 tsp (5 mL) baking powder

Pinch salt

3 egg whites

Caramelized Onion Tart

2 Tbsp (30 mL) butter

6 slices bacon, chopped

4 lb (1.8 kg) onions

1 pizza crust or frozen dough,
defrosted

1 Tbsp (15 mL) cornmeal, to prevent
sticking

½ cup (125 mL) whipping cream

1 tsp (5 mL) salt

A spectacular treat for lunch or as a first course at dinner. Use a prepared pizza crust or frozen dough, for while a good crust is important, it is the caramelized onion topping that makes it memorable.

Preheat the oven to 375°F (190°C).

Melt the butter in a large pan with a lid, add the bacon, and cook until starting to crisp. Lift out the bacon and set aside, leaving the fat in the pan.

Cut the onions in half lengthwise, discard the skin, and slice them across into thin half-circles. Add the onion slices to the bacon pan, set it over medium heat, cover the pan, and reduce the heat to low, stirring every few minutes to prevent sticking. Continue to cook until the onions are golden brown, only adding water if you need it to prevent burning.

When the onions are a nice gold brown, remove the lid and cook, stirring frequently, until the moisture has evaporated and the onions are not sloppy. Remove from the heat and set aside to cool.

Roll the defrosted dough to a 12-inch (30 cm) circle. Sprinkle the pizza pan with cornmeal, set the dough on the pan, and crimp the edges to create a lip. Bake in the preheated oven for 8 minutes (or have the pre-baked crust ready).

Stir the cream into the cooled onion mixture; add salt if necessary.

Spread the onion mixture over the pizza crust and sprinkle the bacon on top. Slide it onto a pizza pan or baking sheet, set it in the middle of the pre-heated oven and bake for 20 minutes, until hot.

Remove from the oven; cool for 5 or 10 minutes, slice it, and serve.

Pissaladière

••

This tart of olives, anchovies, onions, and tomatoes captures the essence of the south of France. Accompanied by a green salad, it is a lovely summer lunch; cut into small squares, it is excellent before dinner at any time of year.

••

Defrost the puff pastry in the fridge overnight, or on the counter for 4 hours.

Cut the onions in half lengthwise, discard the outer layer and slice them across into thin (⅛ inch [3 mm]) half-circles.

Set a large pan with a lid over medium heat and add 3 Tbsp (45 mL) olive oil, onions, rosemary, and thyme, and stir until thoroughly coated with the oil. Cover the pan and reduce the heat to low, stirring regularly to prevent sticking; add a little water if needed. When the onions are very soft and pale gold, remove the lid and continue cooking to evaporate the moisture, stirring frequently to prevent browning. Remove the pan from the heat and set aside to cool; discard the herb sprigs.

Preheat the oven to 375°F (190°C).

Roll the puff pastry to a rectangle about 14 × 10 inches (35 × 25 cm) and place it on a baking sheet lined with parchment paper. With a sharp knife, cut a ½-inch (13 mm) strip from each side, moistening one side of each strip with water and laying it on top of the base, damp side down, to form a border. Run the point of a knife around the inside of the border to cut partway through the base where it joins the sides, to allow the base and the sides to puff separately.

Prick the bottom of the pastry all over with a fork—but not the border. Scallop the edges of the pastry. With the back of a small knife, draw the outside edge of the pastry border toward the centre every ½ inch (13 mm), making small indents to help keep the pastry straight as it puffs. Place in the fridge or freezer for 10 minutes to chill, then bake, uncovered, in the preheated oven for 15 minutes.

Turn the oven down to 350°F (180°C).

Gently press down the base where is has puffed up, leaving the edges at their full height. Spread the onions over the bottom of the base.

Slice the tomatoes thinly (⅛ inch [3 mm]) and arrange them on top of the onions.

Cut the anchovy fillets in half lengthwise and arrange them in a lattice pattern over the tomatoes.

Place one pitted olive in the centre of each anchovy diamond. Brush the top of the tart lightly with 1 Tbsp (15 mL) oil, and bake in the oven for 20 to 30 minutes, until the pastry is browned and the tomatoes are soft.

Cool for 10 minutes before serving.

SERVES 4 FOR LUNCH,
LOTS MORE AS AN APPETIZER
•••••••••••••••••••••••••••••••••

14 oz (400 g) puff pastry
(all-butter if possible)

3 lb (1.4 kg) sweet or yellow onions

¼ cup (60 mL) olive oil, divided

Sprig rosemary, fresh or dried

Sprig thyme, fresh or dried

Salt

½ lb (227 g) ripe tomatoes

One 1-oz (30 g) tin anchovy fillets

20 pitted black
olives

Smoked Salmon Mousse

••

A light, easy to make mousse with lots of flavour.

••

SERVES 8

••••••••••••

¼ cup (60 mL) cold water

1 Tbsp (15 mL) gelatine powder
(1 envelope)

½ cup (125 mL) boiling water

6 oz (170 g) smoked salmon,
trimmed or sliced

4 oz (113 g) cream cheese

1 Tbsp (15 mL) lemon juice

Dash Tabasco

¼ tsp (1 mL) paprika

½ tsp (2 mL) salt

2 Tbsp (30 mL) finely chopped fresh
dill + extra sprigs for serving

⅓ cup (80 mL) whipping cream

Lemon, sliced, for serving

Rye bread, thinly sliced,
for serving

Pour the cold water into a small bowl, sprinkle the gelatine on top, and allow to soften for a few minutes. Pour in the boiling water and stir until the gelatine dissolves; set aside.

In the work bowl of a food processor, process the smoked salmon, cream cheese, and lemon juice until smooth Add Tabasco, paprika, salt, and dill, and process briefly. Pour in the dissolved gelatine and process until smooth: it will be soupy. Transfer to a bowl, cover with plastic wrap, and refrigerate until cool—it does not have to be cold, and it's okay if it's starting to set around the edges. (If the whole thing has set, melt it gently over hot water and refrigerate again.)

Beat the cream to soft peaks. Whisk the mousse smooth, and fold in the cream.

Line a loaf pan with plastic wrap, with enough overhang to cover the top. Scoop the mousse into the pan, smooth the top, and cover with the plastic wrap. Refrigerate for 4 hours, or overnight.

Unmould gently onto a platter and decorate the top with sprigs of dill and slices of lemon. Serve with thinly sliced rye bread.

Tuna *with* White Beans (Tonno e Fagioli)

••

This makes a delicious summer lunch or a small plate before dinner. Use the best canned tuna you can find, from northern Spain or Portugal.

••

SERVES 4 AS A FIRST COURSE,
2 FOR LUNCH

•••••••••••••••

One 14-oz (397 g) can white beans

1 Tbsp (15 mL) lemon juice

1 tsp (5 mL) Dijon mustard

¼ cup (60 mL) good quality olive oil

1 tsp (5 mL) fresh thyme leaves

2 Tbsp (30 mL) chopped Italian
parsley

½ sweet onion, very finely sliced

One 6-oz (180 g) can best quality
tuna, in chunks

Drain and rinse the beans; set aside in a bowl. Mix the lemon juice and mustard in a small bowl, and slowly whisk in the olive oil. Pour the dressing over the beans and stir in the thyme and parsley. Divide the beans between four plates.

Arrange the finely sliced onion and the tuna on top of the beans. Serve with good bread and, for lunch, a green salad.

Broccolini *with* Garlic, Anchovies, *and* Chili

....

A simple vegetarian appetizer. Look for broccolini, rather than the lookalike broccolette, which can go mushy when cooked.

....

With a small knife, cut off the broccolini stalks at the point where the crowns branch out. Cut the stalks in half lengthwise into 2 long, thin pieces. Bring 1 inch (2½ cm) of water to a boil in a wide saucepan. Add salt and the broccolini, both stalks and crowns. Cover and cook for 4 minutes; drain thoroughly, and arrange on a serving dish.

In a small frying pan over medium heat, sauté the chopped garlic, anchovy fillets, and chili flakes in the olive oil until the garlic starts to turn pale gold. Pour over the broccolini and serve immediately.

SERVES 2 OR 3

....

1 bunch broccolini

1 tsp (5 mL) salt

½ tsp (2 mL) finely chopped garlic

4 anchovy fillets

¼ tsp (1 mL) chili flakes

3 Tbsp (45 mL) olive oil

Cherry Tomatoes *with* Cream

....

Don't knock it 'til you've tried it.

....

Cut the tomatoes in half around the waist. Melt the butter in a large frying pan over medium heat and add the tomatoes, cut side down; cook for 2 minutes. Turn the tomatoes and cook until quite soft; sprinkle with salt.

Pour in the cream, bring to a boil, and cook until the cream and tomato juices have blended, a minute or two.

Serve with French bread.

ENOUGH FOR 2

....

½ lb (227 g) cherry tomatoes

2 Tbsp (30 mL) butter

½ cup (125 mL) whipping cream

Polenta *and* Mushroom Ragout

An earthy combination of flavours.

SERVES 4 AS A FIRST COURSE,
2 AS A MAIN
•••••••••••••

½ oz (14 g) dried porcini mushrooms

1 tsp (5 mL) finely chopped garlic

2 Tbsp (30 mL) olive oil

1 lb (454 g) fresh mushrooms, sliced

One 14-oz (397 g) can diced tomatoes

½ cup (125 mL) red wine

½ tsp (2 mL) oregano

4 cups (960 mL) chicken stock or water

1 cup (250 mL) polenta

½ tsp (2 mL) salt + extra as needed

1½ cups (360 mL) thick plain Greek yogurt

2 Tbsp (30 mL) truffle oil

Soak the dried porcini in a small bowl of warm water for 30 minutes. Remove the mushrooms, squeeze dry, and coarsely chop. Strain and reserve the soaking liquid.

In a medium saucepan, sauté the garlic in oil until pale gold. Add the sliced mushrooms and cook over medium heat until they start to take on colour. Add the chopped porcini, reserved soaking liquid, tomatoes, red wine, and oregano; turn the heat down to medium low and cook, uncovered, until the sauce is reduced and thickened. Add salt to taste.

In a medium saucepan, bring the stock or water to a boil, and add the polenta and ½ tsp (2 mL) salt. Whisk until thoroughly incorporated, turn down the heat to medium low, and cook, uncovered and stirring frequently, until the polenta is tender and has the consistency of grits, about 20 minutes. Add more water if necessary.

Divide the mushrooms between 4 soup bowls; put a large scoop of yogurt on each, and ladle the polenta over top. Finish with a drizzle of truffle oil.

FISH

SEARED SALMON *in* DOLCE-FORTE SAUCE 90

HALIBUT *with* ASPARAGUS *and* LEMON RISOTTO 93

PANKO-CRUSTED HALIBUT 94

FRESH SALMON *with* HOT TARTARE SAUCE 95

ROASTED SALMON *with* DILL MAYONNAISE 95

SEARED SCALLOPS 96

CRAB CAKES 98

SPICY GARLIC SHRIMP 99

....

Take care with fish. It is very good for us and often has a wonderful flavour, but the delicate texture, one of its greatest assets, can be spoiled by overcooking. This means using either low heat or careful timing. It is perfectly fine to cook fish on high heat, even on a barbecue, as long as you make sure to remove it from the heat while the inside is still moist and tender. Barbecuing is sexy, but if you are uncertain, a more fool-proof method is to bake it in a 350°F (180°C) oven for 8 to 10 minutes, depending on the thickness.

You can test whether fish is done by pressing on the thickest part with your finger; it should be slightly firm, without the softness or "give" of raw fish. There will also be some white patches on the surface where the proteins have seeped out and coagu-lated—the fish is not ready until some of these white patches are present. A final test, which unfortunately leaves scars and betrays your lack of confidence, is to insert a knife or fork gently into the flesh and to separate the individual flakes; they should just be starting to come apart but should not, of course, be dry.

Cooking fish in moist heat at a low temperature also works well, particularly for fish with a gelatinous texture—like halibut, grouper, sea bass, and black cod—and because the heat is low, the timing is not so critical.

Seared Salmon *in* Dolce-Forte Sauce

••

This sauce, with its mix of sweet, sour, and bitter tastes, is a great way to dress up barbecued or seared salmon. Its sweetness is further emphasized by straining the sauce and reducing the liquid to a glaze before re-mixing it with the olives, capers, and raisins.

You can use salmon steaks or fillets. I prefer the fillets simply because they allow you to focus during dinner on things—such as conversation—rather than on removing the many bones concealed in the steak.

Lentils are an excellent accompaniment to salmon.

••

Pour the lentils into a medium pan; add enough water to cover and bring to a boil. Add ½ tsp (2 mL) salt, reduce the heat to a simmer, and cook for 20 to 30 minutes until tender, adding water as needed. Drain, transfer to a bowl, and stir in the chopped red onion and 2 Tbsp (30 mL) olive oil. Set aside.

Combine the raisins, balsamic vinegar, and ¼ cup (60 mL) water in a small saucepan. Bring to a boil, cover the pan, remove it from the heat, and set aside.

In a separate pan, sauté the shallots in the remaining 3 Tbsp (45 mL) olive oil over low heat until pale gold. Add them to the raisins, along with the green olives, capers, and anchovy fillet. Cook over a very low heat to amalgamate everything. Strain the sauce through a sieve; set aside the solids, return the liquid to the pan, add the maple syrup, and reduce over medium heat until syrupy. Add all the solid bits back into the sauce, and set aside to keep warm.

Barbecue, sear, or roast the salmon until just cooked.

TO SEAR Set a large heavy frying pan over medium-high heat until hot, and turn the exhaust fan to high. Add the salmon, skin side down, and cover with a lid. Reduce the heat to medium and cook the salmon, covered, for 6 minutes without turning. Remove the lid and check the salmon; it is done when there is a partial white coating on the surface, and the flesh springs back slightly to the touch.

TO ROAST Line a baking sheet with parchment paper, lay the salmon on top, and brush with olive oil. Bake in a 375°F (190°C) oven for 9 minutes, until beads of white protein start to appear on the surface.

Reheat the lentils, divide between the plates, and arrange a salmon fillet on each; spoon the sauce on top.

Halibut *with* Asparagus *and* Lemon Risotto

•••

Asparagus and lemon look and taste like spring, when halibut is at its best. Risotto is the perfect partner for halibut cooked gently over a low heat—just enough that the flakes separate, with no risk of drying out.

•••

Pour the stock into a saucepan, add the salt if the stock is homemade (commercial stocks will have more than enough already), and set it over a low heat on the back of the stove to warm.

Heat a mid-size saucepan over medium-low heat, melt 2 Tbsp (30 mL) butter (or heat the oil) and add the chopped onion. Stir and cook until translucent but not browned. Now add the rice and stir for a couple of minutes, until the butter or oil is absorbed. Pour in the white wine and cook, stirring, until it has been absorbed as well.

Turn the heat to low and add the stock, about 1 cup (250 mL) at a time; stir and cook after each addition of stock until it is almost absorbed before adding more (check the recipe for Risotto Milanese, page 54, if in doubt). Keep the mixture at a gentle bubble.

While the risotto is cooking, snap off the tough end of the asparagus stems and discard; cut the tender spears into 1½-inch (4 cm) lengths and set aside. Finely chop the lemon zest and set aside.

After 25 minutes of cooking, the rice will be soft on the outside with the centre still firm. Add the asparagus pieces to the rice, starting with the thicker ones. Stir them in, wait 2 minutes, then add the thinner stems and the spears—the aim is to have the rice and asparagus all cooked at the same time. The finished risotto should be slightly soupy, though you may need to add more stock or water to achieve it.

While the risotto is cooking, heat a frying pan—with a lid and large enough to hold the halibut comfortably—over low heat. Add the remaining 1 Tbsp (15 mL) butter or oil and add the halibut. Cover with the lid and cook on very low heat for 10 to 12 minutes; it is ready when the flakes are starting to separate from each other. Turn off the heat and set aside, covered, to keep warm.

Stir the lemon zest into the risotto and taste for seasoning. Divide the risotto between 4 warm plates and place a halibut fillet on top of each. Spoon the fish cooking juices on top.

SERVES 4
•••••••••••

5 cups (1.2 L) chicken or fish stock

1 tsp (5 mL) salt (optional)

3 Tbsp (45 mL) olive oil or butter, divided

1 medium onion, finely chopped

1½ cups (360 mL) Arborio rice

1 cup (250 mL) white wine

1 lb (454 g) asparagus

Zest of 1 lemon

4 halibut fillets (6 oz [180 g] each)

Panko-Crusted Halibut

SERVES 4
••••••••••

1 cup (250 mL) Mayonnaise
(page 229)

1 tsp (5 mL) lemon zest

1 Tbsp (15 mL) lemon juice

1 Tbsp (15 mL) freshly grated ginger

¼ cup (60 mL) whipping cream

2 lb (900 g) halibut fillet

3 Tbsp (45 mL) all-purpose flour

1 egg

1 cup (250 mL) panko crumbs

1 cup (250 mL) safflower, sunflower,
or peanut oil

Halibut has a wonderful texture but can be a bit short on flavour. Cooking it in panko (Japanese breadcrumbs) helps retain the moisture, and a lemon-ginger mayonnaise bolsters the delicate flavour.

Make the Mayonnaise following the recipe on page 229. Stir in the lemon zest, juice, and the grated ginger. Whip the cream to firm peaks and fold it into the Mayonnaise. Set aside.

Remove and discard the skin from the halibut; cut the fish into 1-inch (2½ cm) strips. Flour the fish by shaking the strips in a plastic bag with a few tablespoons of flour, or roll them on a floured plate.

In a soup plate, whisk the egg thoroughly. Spread the panko crumbs on a baking sheet; dust a second tray with panko for the finished fish.

Use one hand for the egg and the other for the breadcrumbs. Roll the fish in the egg with one hand, until completely coated, then drop it on the panko. With the other hand, sprinkle panko crumbs over the egged fish, touching only panko until the fish is covered with crumbs. Set aside on the panko-dusted tray.

Preheat the oven to 250°F (120°C).

In a medium- to high-sided saucepan, heat the oil to about 340°F (170°C). Use a thermometer or test for temperature by frying a cube of day-old bread; if it browns in about a minute, it is in the right range.

Turn the heat up to medium-high; without crowding, carefully lower in a few strips of fish using tongs. Cook for 2 minutes on one side, then turn them over with the tongs and check for colour—if they are not golden brown, turn up the heat under the oil, or down if the fish is browning too fast. Cook 1 to 1½ minutes on the other side. Remove fish with a slotted spoon and place on a baking sheet lined with paper towels, then transfer to the preheated oven to keep warm while you cook the rest.

Serve with the lemon-ginger mayonnaise.

Fresh Salmon *with* Hot Tartare Sauce

....

Salmon served for company is best with an interesting sauce.

....

Preheat the oven to 350°F (180°C).

Cover a baking sheet with parchment paper and lay out the salmon fillets. Pour the white wine or vermouth over top, cover with foil, and set in the middle of the preheated oven. Bake for 15 minutes.

In a small pan over medium heat, sauté the green onions in butter until wilted. Remove from the heat and add the chopped cornichons and the capers.

Turn off the oven and remove the salmon; transfer it to a plate, cover with the foil, and return to the turned-off oven.

Pour the juices from the baking pan into the onions and cornichons, set the pan over medium heat, and reduce the liquid to ¼ cup (60 mL). Add the crème fraîche and mustard and stir over medium-high heat until the sauce thickens. Season to taste and stir in the chopped parsley.

Serve the salmon on warm plates, and spoon the sauce around it.

SERVES 4
············

4 salmon fillets (8 oz [227 g] each)

½ cup (125 mL) white wine or dry vermouth

½ cup (125 mL) finely chopped green onions

3 Tbsp (45 mL) butter

2 Tbsp (30 mL) finely chopped cornichons

1 Tbsp (15 mL) capers

½ cup (125 mL) crème fraîche

1 Tbsp (15 mL) Dijon mustard

¼ cup (60 mL) chopped Italian parsley

Roasted Salmon *with* Dill Mayonnaise

....

Nothing looks lovelier on a buffet table than a whole salmon decorated with slices of cucumber and lemon and sprigs of dill, and few things look worse than that same salmon after half your guests have served themselves. If you cut the fish in pieces before cooking and decorate them individually, they will look as good for the last guest as they did for the first. This is a dish that deserves homemade mayonnaise.

....

Preheat the oven to 350°F (180°C).

Make the Mayonnaise following the recipe on page 229. Stir in freshly chopped dill, cover with plastic wrap, and set aside.

Line a baking sheet with parchment paper and arrange the salmon pieces on it. Brush them with the olive oil and bake in the preheated oven for 10 minutes or until white patches of protein start to appear on the surface. Remove from the oven and set aside to cool.

Peel the cucumber along one side only and slice it very thinly (a mandolin is perfect). Place in a colander, sprinkle with salt, and drain. Dry on paper towels and arrange the slices with the unpeeled side toward the tail, to look like scales.

Serve with the dill mayonnaise.

SERVES 6
············

1½ cups (360 mL) Mayonnaise (page 229)

3 Tbsp (45 mL) freshly chopped dill

4 salmon fillets (8 oz [227 g] each)

1 Tbsp (15 mL) olive oil

1 English cucumber

Salt

1 Tbsp (15 mL) butter

½ tsp (2 mL) finely chopped garlic

½ cup (125 mL) white wine or dry
vermouth

8 large scallops

½ cup (125 mL) whipping cream

Salt

Seared Scallops

••

Quick and delicious. Use the large East Coast scallops.

••

Melt the butter in a small pan over medium heat. When it foams, add the garlic and cook until pale gold; pour in the wine or vermouth, then remove the pan from the heat.

Dry the scallops on paper towels. Set a (different) frying pan over medium heat; when quite hot, set the scallops upright (round ends up and down) in the dry pan. Cover the pan and cook for 2 minutes; turn them over and cook for 1 minute more on the other end. Lift out onto a plate and keep warm.

Pour the wine and garlic mixture into the frying pan, scraping up any bits on the bottom. Reduce the liquid to half and pour in the cream. Boil until the sauce thickens; pour in any juices from the scallops, and taste for salt. Return the scallops to the pan, and reheat them briefly.

Serve with buttered spinach and good bread.

Crab Cakes

••

Not truly crab cakes since there is no real crab in them. This may be frugality carried to the point of cheapness—perhaps a different name would be better— but would a cake of fake crab by any other name taste as sweet? The base for the cakes is a very thick béchamel sauce.

••

SERVES 4
••••••••••••

1 cup (250 mL) milk

5 Tbsp (75 mL) butter

½ onion, finely chopped

3 stalks celery, finely chopped

½ cup (125 mL) all-purpose flour

2 egg yolks

12 oz (340 g) artificial crab meat

½ tsp (2 mL) fresh ground black pepper

10 drops Tabasco sauce

1 Tbsp (15 mL) finely chopped parsley

1 egg

2 Tbsp (30 mL) water

1½ cups (360 mL) panko or bread crumbs

3 cups (720 mL) safflower, sunflower, or peanut oil

Jalapeño Tartare Sauce (page 233)

Preheat the oven to 250°F (120°C).

Rinse out a small pan with water, but do not dry it. Pour in the milk and bring to a simmer over low heat. Remove from the heat and set aside.

In a heavy saucepan, melt the butter over medium heat, add the chopped onion and celery and cook, stirring frequently, as the vegetables absorb the butter and release it again—about 5 minutes.

Reduce the heat to low, add the flour and cook, stirring frequently, for 3 minutes. Pour in the hot milk and stir until a smooth thick paste has formed and the mixture boils. It may look oily, which is normal. Remove the pan from the heat and beat the egg yolks into the sauce one at a time; mix in the crab meat, pepper, Tabasco, and parsley. Set aside to cool, or spread the mixture on a large platter or plate to cool quickly.

Once cooled, use your hands to form the mixture into cakes—6 to 12, depending on size. Set aside on a floured baking sheet.

Whisk the egg and water together in a shallow bowl or soup plate until smooth.

Spread the breadcrumbs or panko on a separate bowl or plate, and spread a thin dusting on a baking sheet, for the finished cakes.

Using one hand, roll a crab cake in the egg until completely coated, then drop it on the crumbs. With the other hand, sprinkle on the crumbs; once the fish cake is covered, you can pick it up and roll it in the crumbs. Set aside on the crumb-dusted tray.

In a heavy saucepan, heat the oil to 350°F (180°C). Check with a thermometer, or test by frying a cube of day-old bread; if it browns in about a minute it is in the right range.

Gently slip the cakes into the hot oil, and cook for about 2 minutes, until browned on the bottom; turn them over carefully and brown the other side. (Don't cook more than a few cakes at a time; the oil temperature will drop and the cakes become greasy.) Drain on paper towels and transfer to a baking sheet in the preheated oven.

Serve hot with Jalapeño Tartare Sauce.

Spicy Garlic Shrimp

....

Shrimp and garlic are one of the very best food combinations, and butter makes it even better—the amount here may seem excessive, but it works. They are delicious straight from the pan with crusty bread, on crostini (page 227) as an appetizer, over rice with oriental greens, in a taco or wrap with avocado and lemon . . . the possibilities are endless.

The heart of this dish is the shrimp or prawns, and size matters: use the large 10/15s (the number it takes to make up a pound). Cutting the shrimp in half helps prevent overcooking.

Serve 2 or 3 shrimp per person for an appetizer, 4 for a first course, or 6 for a main course when served with other accompaniments.

....

Peel the shrimp, cut them in half lengthwise, and set aside on paper towels.

Heat a large frying pan over medium heat. Add the olive oil and garlic, cook briefly, add the chili flakes, and cook for 30 seconds. Add half the butter and when it foams add the shrimp, but do not crowd them—make 2 batches if necessary. As soon as they are pink on the outside they are ready.

Remove the shrimp to a serving plate and add the rest of the butter to the pan. When it foams, return the shrimp to the pan and reheat briefly.

Serve immediately with crusty bread.

SERVES 4 AS A FIRST COURSE
....

16 shrimp (10/15 size)

1 Tbsp (15 mL) olive oil

1 tsp (5 mL) finely chopped garlic

¼ tsp (1 mL) red chili flakes

¼ cup (60 mL) butter

CHICKEN

....

Growing up, when we had roast chicken at home, I could never understand why everybody else in the family was clamouring for the breast. Why would anyone want a dry and boring breast when they could have dark meat? I was a hungry (and selfish) child, and as far as I was concerned, they were welcome to fight over the breast because it meant I got what I wanted, which was the thigh. I just prayed (it was Sunday lunch, after all) that no one would realize what they were missing, and set their sights on the other thigh (I always wanted seconds).

The only way I know to cook both thighs and breasts properly while still attached to the same bird is on a rotisserie (recipe below). In all the other recipes, the legs and the breasts do much better separated.

I still have a strong preference for thighs—they taste better and will tolerate a bit of overcooking—but I have come to appreciate that a properly cooked breast can also be a lovely thing. The meat has to be treated gently, and you must not be afraid of a slightly pink centre. This is especially true if you plan to eat the chicken cold or at room temperature—an excellent way of serving it that few people do nowadays, but it was done everywhere in the far off days of my youth.

Hot chicken breasts almost always have a sauce (at least *chez moi*) and this does a grand job of concealing any pinkness in a less cooked breast. All that remains is the texture of the tender and juicy meat.

Chicken Wonderful

SERVES 2
••••••••••

3 Tbsp (45 mL) butter, divided

¼ lb (113 g) white or brown
mushrooms, sliced

1 Tbsp (15 mL) olive oil

2 chicken breasts (boneless, skin on
for preference)

¼ cup (60 mL) finely sliced green
onion

¼ cup (60 mL) white wine or
vermouth

½ cup (125 mL) whipping cream

1 Tbsp (15 mL) fresh herbs (tarragon,
chives, chervil, or parsley)

An easy and delicious recipe, this makes an excellent late night supper with a green salad and French bread.

Melt 2 Tbsp (30 mL) butter in a frying pan over medium heat, add the mushrooms, and cook until the juices have run and mostly evaporated and the mushrooms are lightly browned. Remove from the pan and set aside.

Heat the remaining 1 Tbsp (15 mL) butter and 1 Tbsp (15 mL) oil in the same pan over medium heat, add the chicken breasts skin side down, and cook until lightly browned; turn and brown the other side. Remove the chicken, add the green onion, and cook briefly. Pour in the white wine and reduce by half. Return the chicken to the pan, turn the heat down to low, cover the pan, and cook for 10 minutes.

Remove the chicken and set aside in a warm place; turn up the heat and reduce the sauce to about ¼ cup (60 mL). Pour in the cream, add the mushrooms, and reduce the sauce to about ½ cup (125 mL).

Reheat the chicken in the pan and add the fresh herbs. Adjust the seasoning.

Cut the breasts crosswise into ⅜-inch (1 cm) slices and fan them on the plates. Spoon over some of the sauce and serve with a warm baguette and a Green Salad dressed with Nancy's Vinaigrette (page 228).

Rotisserie Chicken *with* Roasted Vegetables

·····································

As few years ago, my sons and I assembled a new barbecue. It was a long job involving many small parts, and when we finally got to the last step we looked at each other and said: "Why bother? We'll never use it." Fortunately, we decided to finish what we started and we installed the rotisserie; over the years since then, we have learned that a rotisserie is, hands down, the best way to cook a chicken.

A chicken made on a home rotisserie is a world away from the supermarket bird. Even when the meat is almost falling off the bones, the breast stays moist and juicy. Most barbecues have room to slide a baking sheet under the chicken where potatoes and other root vegetables can be roasted. Basted by the juices from the chicken, they are delicious.

·····································

Tie the chicken securely in the centre of the spit so that it does not slip, and slide the spit in place. Place a baking sheet on a level surface under the chicken. Set the rotisserie burner to high, and start the bird turning. As it rotates, drizzle a few tablespoons of olive oil over the chicken followed by a generous sprinkling of coarse salt.

Cook on high heat, with the lid closed, for about an hour and a half (barbecues vary, so test by pressing the leg joint; it will become quite easy to move when done).

Cut the potatoes into 1½-inch (4 cm) chunks, place in a pot of cold water, bring to a boil, drain immediately, and arrange under the chicken, turning from time to time to coat with the chicken juices and brown them evenly; they take about 40 minutes.

Cut the carrots and parsnips into 1-inch (2½ cm) pieces and add them to the roasting pan after an hour of cooking time (they take about 30 minutes).

Risotto Milanese (page 54) is an excellent alternative to the roasted vegetables, and mixing the pan drippings into the rice at the last minute makes it even better.

SERVES 4
············

One 3 to 4 lb (1.5 to 1.8 kg) chicken (preferably organic)

Olive oil

Coarse salt

1 lb (454 g) potatoes, peeled (optional)

½ lb (227 g) carrots, scraped (optional)

½ lb (227 g) parsnips, peeled (optional)

Chicken *with* Chanterelles

. . . .

Mushrooms have a wonderful affinity with chicken, and chanterelles more than most, rivalled only by the springtime morel. Chanterelles are fluted mushrooms, white to orange in colour, harvested fresh in the fall and available dried all year. Dried mushrooms have a more intense flavour than fresh ones, and often have a smoky note when dried over an open fire; they add an intense flavour to a sauce but they lack the luscious texture of fresh ones.

Although this is a quintessentially fall dish, it is delicious in any season.

. . . .

SERVES 4

. . . .

1 oz (28 g) dried chanterelles

1 lb (454 g) fresh chanterelle mushrooms

4 large chicken breasts (skin on, wing bone attached)

2 Tbsp (30 mL) butter + extra 1 Tbsp (15 mL) for the potatoes

1 Tbsp (15 mL) finely chopped garlic

1 cup (250 mL) white wine

½ cup (125 mL) whipping cream

½ tsp (2 mL) salt (optional)

1 lb (450 g) fingerling potatoes

Soak the dried mushrooms in warm water for 30 minutes; strain and reserve the liquid, squeeze the mushrooms dry, and chop them coarsely.

Clean the fresh mushrooms, using a small brush to remove any debris. Cut them into ⅓-inch (8 mm) slices and set aside.

Cut away the chicken breast bone, leaving the wing bone in and the skin on. In a casserole large enough to hold the chicken, melt the butter over moderate heat, add the chicken skin side down (in batches if necessary), and sauté until lightly browned. Set aside.

In the same pan, cook the garlic until pale gold, adding more butter if needed. Pour in the white wine, turn up the heat, and reduce for 2 minutes. Add the chopped mushrooms, the reserved mushroom liquid, and the sliced fresh mushrooms to the pan. Cook for 5 minutes, stirring from time to time.

Add the browned chicken breasts, skin side up. Turn the heat down to very low, cover with a close-fitting lid, and simmer for 12 to 15 minutes.

Remove the lid and test for doneness—the breasts should still be slightly soft to the touch at the thickest part, as they will cook more as they sit. Remove them from the pan and keep warm.

Turn the heat up, bring the juices to a boil, and pour in the whipping cream. Cook, stirring occasionally, until the sauce thickens slightly. Check for seasoning, adding more salt if necessary—it enhances this dish. Return the chicken to the pan, reduce the heat to low, and cook, covered, until completely heated through.

Best served with fingerling potatoes cooked the Danish way: put the potatoes in a pan of cold water, bring to a boil, and cook, uncovered, for 12 minutes. Now cover the pan, turn off the heat, and let the potatoes sit for another 12 minutes. Drain and toss with 1 Tbsp (15 mL) of butter. Other potatoes are fine too, but they don't have the firm waxy texture of fingerlings; best of all are *rattes*, a potato common in France but not yet widely available here.

Pesto-Stuffed Chicken Breasts

1 lb (454 g) spinach

2 Tbsp (30 mL) finely chopped shallots

½ cup (125 mL) butter, divided

½ cup (125 mL) ricotta

2 Tbsp (30 mL) Pesto Sauce (page 223; or store-bought pesto)

1 egg yolk

Fresh ground black pepper

6 chicken breasts

3 slices prosciutto, cut in half

½ lb (227 g) mushrooms (white or brown), sliced

1 cup (250 mL) Chicken Stock (page 236; or store-bought)

¾ cup (180 mL) white wine

¼ cup (60 mL) whipping cream

3 Tbsp (45 mL) lemon juice

2 Tbsp (30 mL) chopped fresh basil

I hesitated to include this recipe from the original Food Book; *it involves a few steps, and while it is a very attractive presentation, I could not see many people attempting it. Literally at the last minute, I met a lovely couple at the market on Salt Spring who still live around the corner from where the shop used to be. This is their go-to dinner party recipe—on one occasion they made it for 70 people. Here it is again, in the hope that there are others out there as adventurous as them.*

Because of the number of steps, it is very little extra work to double the recipe, or multiply it even more. All the work, except for the final baking, can be done ahead.

Wash the spinach and remove the large stems. Add to a saucepan with the water that clings to the leaves and cook, stirring, over medium heat until wilted. Drain in a colander and, once cooled, squeeze out as much water as you can. Chop the spinach quite finely and transfer to a medium bowl.

Sauté the shallots in 2 Tbsp (30 mL) butter until soft, then add them to the spinach. Mix the ricotta, Pesto Sauce, egg yolk, and pepper into the spinach.

Bone the chicken breasts, remove the skin and trim away the fat (or buy boneless and skinless, but they are often not as good). Place the breasts, one at a time, between 2 sheets of parchment or wax paper; with a meat pounder or other blunt instrument, flatten them to almost twice their original size.

Lay out the chicken breasts with (what used to be) the skin side down, as many as will fit on the counter. Place half a slice of prosciutto in the centre of each, and divide the spinach stuffing between the breasts, on top of the prosciutto. Fold the edges of the chicken up and over, enclosing the stuffing and reshaping it into something resembling a chicken breast. Set breasts aside on a baking sheet lined with parchment paper, with the folded crease side down.

To make the sauce, place a saucepan over medium heat, melt 3 Tbsp (45 mL) butter and sauté the sliced mushrooms until the juices have run and evaporated. Once the mushrooms are starting to brown on the edges, remove them from the pan and set aside.

Pour the chicken stock into the same pan, turn the heat to high and reduce to ¼ cup (60 mL). Add the wine, bring to a boil, and reduce down to ½ cup (125 mL). Pour in the cream and cook until the sauce is lightly thickened; add the mushrooms and taste for seasoning. (Everything may be prepared up to one day ahead to this point and stored in the fridge.)

Preheat the oven to 375°F (190°C).

In a small saucepan over medium-low heat, melt the remaining 3 Tbsp (45 mL) butter and add the lemon juice; pour it over the chicken breasts.

Place the chicken in the centre of the preheated oven and bake for 25 minutes, basting once or twice. Reheat the sauce.

Remove the chicken to a warmed serving platter or plates. Pour the pan juices into the sauce, bring it to a boil, add the chopped basil, and spoon it over and around the chicken.

(Another way to serve is to slice the cooked breasts about ⅜ inch [1 cm] thick and fan them on the plates with the sauce around. Let them sit for 10 or 15 minutes in a warm spot to firm up before slicing.)

Chicken Thighs *with* Fennel, Olives, *and* Lemon

··

This is a good choice for a party because it holds well, even when guests take their time coming to the table. Boneless thighs are easier to eat in a crowd, but bone-in and skin-on have more flavour. The recipe calls for a very small amount of saffron, and grinding it in a pestle and mortar with salt makes a little go a long way. Saffron has a mildly bitter taste, as do the olives, and this brings out the sweetness in the fennel.

If the olives have pits, be sure to tell your guests.

··

Preheat the oven to 400°F (200°C).

Arrange the lemon slices on a baking sheet, preferably on parchment paper. Sprinkle lightly with salt, and bake on the top rack of the preheated oven for 12 minutes. Remove and set aside; turn the oven down to 350°F (180°C).

In a large pan, cook the chicken in 1 Tbsp (15 mL) oil and butter until the skin side is well browned and the underside lightly so; remove from the pan and set aside.

Trim the fibrous stalks from the fennel, set a bulb upright on a board, and cut it into 4 slices, each about ½ inch (13 mm) thick and held together at the root end. Cook the fennel slices over medium heat in the same pan as the previous step, until they are nicely browned on both sides, adding more oil if necessary. Set the fennel aside and wash out the pan—the dark pan scrapings will discolour the sauce.

With a pestle and mortar, grind the saffron and ½ tsp (2 mL) salt to a fine powder. Pour the chicken stock into the pan, bring to a boil, add the saffron, and cook for 1 minute. Add the chicken, skin side up, arrange the fennel around and on top, and spread the olives and lemon slices on top. Transfer to the centre of the preheated oven and bake uncovered for 30 minutes.

Sprinkle the chopped parsley on top. Serve with couscous, orzo, or rice, and a green salad.

SERVES 6 TO 8
··················

1 lemon, sliced in ¼-inch (6 mm) rounds

3 Tbsp (45 mL) olive oil, divided

12 chicken thighs

1 Tbsp (15 mL) butter

4 large fennel bulbs

Small pinch saffron threads

½ tsp (2 mL) salt + extra as needed

2 cups (480 mL) chicken stock

1 cup (250 mL) green olives (preferably pitted)

2 Tbsp (30 mL) flat leaf parsley, coarsely chopped

4 chicken breasts (bone in)

6 chicken thighs

4 cups (960 mL) chicken stock

1 cup (250 mL) white wine

2 bay leaves

5 Tbsp (75 mL) butter

10 Tbsp (148 mL) all-purpose flour

1 tsp (5 mL) salt

½ tsp (2 mL) fresh ground black
pepper

1 cup (250 mL) chopped onion
(in ½-inch [13 mm] chunks)

1 cup (250 mL) chopped carrot
(in ½-inch [13 mm] chunks)

1 cup (250 mL) chopped celery
(in ½-inch [13 mm] chunks)

½ lb (227 g) asparagus, hard stem
removed and cut into 1-inch
(2½ cm) pieces.

½ cup (125 mL) whipping cream

1 lemon

1 lb (454 g) Short Crust Pastry
(page 238)

1 egg

1 Tbsp (15 mL) water

Chicken Pot Pie

. . . .

A whole lemon supports the crust and infuses this pot pie with flavour.

. . . .

Preheat the oven to 350°F (180°C).

Arrange the chicken pieces in a large saucepan or baking dish and bake in the preheated oven for 15 minutes.

Bring the chicken stock and wine to a boil, add the bay leaves, and pour over the chicken. Cover the pan with foil and bake for a further 30 minutes.

Remove the chicken; strain the cooking liquid into a bowl and reserve. When the chicken is cool enough to handle, separate and discard the skin and bones; cut the meat into bite-size pieces and set aside.

Skim excess fat from the chicken stock and remove the bay leaves. Measure out 5 cups (1.2 L) of stock, adding water if necessary. Pour into a saucepan, bring to a simmer, and keep hot.

In a medium saucepan over low heat, cook the butter and flour together to make a roux. Using 1 cup (250 mL) at a time, add the hot stock to the roux, always whisking until the sauce is smooth before making the next addition.

Bring the sauce to a simmer, season with salt and pepper, add the chopped vegetables, and cook over low heat for 5 minutes. Turn off the heat and set aside to cool.

Prick the lemon all over with a fork and trim the base so that it stands securely on one end. Set it in the centre of the baking dish, arrange the chicken around it, pour over the sauce, and set aside to cool. (The recipe may be prepared ahead to this point and kept refrigerated.)

Preheat the oven to 400°F (200°C).

On a floured surface, roll out the pastry to a shape large enough to cover the baking dish. Brush the edges of the dish with water, roll up the pastry around your rolling pin, and unroll over the dish. Trim off any overhang, and scallop the edge by pinching and pressing the pastry onto the rim of the baking dish with the prepared chicken. Decorate the top with pastry cut-outs if you wish. Beat the egg and 1 Tbsp (15 mL) water together and glaze the pastry.

Set the dish on a baking sheet (to catch drips) and transfer to the middle of the preheated oven. Bake for 20 minutes, then reduce the heat to 350°F (180°C) and bake for a further 30 to 40 minutes, until the crust is lightly browned and the filling bubbles up around the edges.

Thai Barbecue Chicken

••

This is a great dish for summer entertaining—noodles and coriander-spiced chicken wrapped in a lettuce leaf, dipped in spring roll sauce, and eaten with your fingers. Start the day before, as the chicken is best when marinated overnight.

••

Process the coriander roots or stems to a fine paste in a food processor or blender. Add the pepper, fish sauce, oyster sauce, and garlic, and process until smooth.

Transfer the paste to a large bowl, add the chicken, and mix until well coated. Cover with plastic wrap and refrigerate overnight.

Bring a large of pot water to a boil, add salt, and cook the noodles until just tender. Drain and refresh under cold water; drain again, then toss with the toasted sesame oil.

Barbecue the chicken on low heat until done. Cool for a few minutes, then cut across into ¼-inch (6 mm) slices.

Pile the sliced chicken and the noodles in the centre of a large platter, and arrange the lettuce leaves, cucumber, coriander leaves, and mint leaves around.

Serve with Spring Roll Sauce.

SERVES 6
••••••••••••

1 bunch fresh coriander roots or stems, washed

1 tsp (5 mL) fresh ground black pepper

3 Tbsp (45 mL) fish sauce

1 Tbsp (15 mL) oyster sauce

2 garlic cloves, crushed

6 chicken breasts (skin on, bones removed) or boneless thighs

1 tsp (5 mL) salt

½ lb (227 g) rice noodles

1 Tbsp (15 mL) toasted sesame oil

2 heads leaf or butter lettuce, leaves separated, washed, and dried

1 English cucumber, peeled and thinly sliced into rounds

1 bunch coriander leaves (reserved from the roots)

1 bunch fresh mint leaves, stems removed

Spring Roll Sauce (page 235), for serving

Duck Breast *with* Cassis *and* Crispy Potatoes

4 duck breasts

Salt

4 large potatoes

½ cup (125 mL) Cassis or blackberry port

1 cup (250 mL) beef or chicken stock

½ cup (125 mL) fresh or frozen black currants (optional)

⅓ cup (80 mL) black currant jam

Juice of 1 lemon

This is a classic combination of duck with a sweet, tangy sauce of black currants. Fresh currants would be ideal, but this dish may be best in winter when even frozen currants may be hard to find. (Dried currants are not currants at all, but dried grapes—raisins de Corinthe, hence the name—and would not be a good substitute.) Use more blackcurrant jam if neither fresh nor frozen are available, with a squeeze of lemon for tartness.

It was my friend Bruce who taught me how to cook duck. He has a talent for meat, doing an excellent job with steaks, veal chops, and these duck breasts. Duck breasts stay juicy and quite tender anywhere between rare and medium, and are relatively forgiving in their cooking time.

Crispy potatoes cooked in the fat from the duck breasts are an excellent accompaniment; the Potato Pancake (page 161) would be good, and so too, somewhat to my surprise, are Scalloped Potatoes (page 162). I was expecting a fight between the creamy sauce and the blackcurrants but they are delicious together. I don't know why I was surprised. Is there anything that is not improved by scalloped potatoes?

Dry the duck breasts with paper towels. Lay them on a work surface skin side up, and with a very sharp knife score a diamond pattern on each breast, cutting through the skin and fat, but not into the meat itself. Make a series of parallel cuts ⅓ to ½ inch (8 to 13 mm) apart on one diagonal, then rotate the breast and make more cuts on the other diagonal. Rub a little salt into the diamond pattern, then set aside to dry on paper towels.

Preheat the oven to 350°F (180°C).

Heat a frying pan over medium heat without oil or butter. When quite hot, add the duck breasts, skin side down; they will spit and crackle, so have a splatter guard ready. Cook for 5 to 7 minutes until the skin is browned and crispy. Transfer the duck breasts, skin side up, to a rack set on a baking sheet and put them in the oven. (The rack lifts the duck off the pan so that it roasts instead of frying.) Cook for 15 minutes for rare or 20 minutes for medium. Remove duck from the oven, cover with aluminum foil, and keep warm.

While the duck is browning, peel the potatoes and cut them into wedges, home-fry slices, or French-fry shapes. Place them in a pan of cold water, salt it, and bring to a boil. Drain immediately and transfer to a clean bowl.

Once the duck is in the oven, pour the duck fat from the frying pan over the potatoes, toss well, and transfer to a baking sheet; place on the lower rack of the oven (the duck is on the upper rack). When the duck is done, turn up the oven to 400°F (200°C), move the potatoes to the top rack, and cook for another 15 minutes or so, turning them once, until brown and crisp. Keep them hot in the turned-off oven while you finish the sauce.

. . . recipe continued

. . . Duck Breast with Cassis and Crispy Potatoes (cont.)

Pour the cassis or port into the pan in which you cooked the duck, set it on medium heat, and reduce by half; scrape up any crispy bits sticking to the pan. Add the stock, bring it to a boil, and reduce by half.

Add the fresh or frozen currants to the pan (if you have them), then reduce the heat and add the blackcurrant jam. Stir until melted, then leave to simmer on very low heat, adding water if necessary to prevent it from burning. Taste for salt; if your stock is homemade it will probably need it.

To serve, slice the duck breasts across into ¼-inch (6 mm) slices, fan them out (overlapping slightly) on warm plates, and spoon some of the sauce around and over them. Accompany with the crispy potatoes or Green Beans with Garlic and Tomatoes (page 149).

Chicken Fat Rice

••

This is Southeast Asian comfort food at its best. It is surprisingly delicious.

••

SERVES 6
••••••••••••

1 large chicken or 12 chicken pieces

6 Tbsp (90 mL) thinly sliced shallots (or onion)

2 Tbsp (30 mL) chicken fat or butter

1 Tbsp (15 mL) finely chopped garlic

2½ cups (600 mL) short grain Oriental rice

5 cups (1.2 L) chicken stock

2 Tbsp (30 mL) oyster sauce

1 tsp (5 mL) salt

2 Tbsp (30 mL) chopped green onions

2 Tbsp (30 mL) chopped fresh coriander

Spring Roll Sauce (page 235), for serving

Cut the chicken into 10 or 12 pieces: remove the legs and separate the drumsticks, cut off the wings with a piece of the breast attached, and split the breasts in half, cutting each half into 2 or 3 pieces.

Preheat the oven to 350°F (180°C).

Set a large pan that can go in the oven over medium heat and sauté the shallots in the butter or fat until pale gold. Add the garlic and continue cooking until lightly browned. Add the chicken pieces and cook until they lose their raw look—they do not need to be browned.

Add the rice to the pan, stir until coated with fat, then pour in the chicken stock, oyster sauce, and salt. Bring it to a boil, cover tightly with a lid or foil, and transfer to the preheated oven. Bake for 15 minutes, remove the lid, stir well, and return to the oven for 15 minutes more. Remove from the oven and allow the pan to sit, covered, for another 10 minutes.

Sprinkle with the green onions and coriander, and pass around the Spring Roll Sauce.

MEAT

OXTAILS *with* AMARONE 119

BEEF POT ROAST *with* SAFFRON NOODLES 120

GINGER GARLIC SHORT RIBS 122

OSSO BUCCO 123

STEAK AND MUSHROOM PIE *with* CHEDDAR
BISCUIT TOPPING 125

TOURTIÈRE 127

LAMB SHANKS *with* FIGS, RED WINE, *and* QUINCE 128

MOUSSAKA 130

PRIME RIB *of* BEEF 132

RACK *of* LAMB 133

BEEF TENDERLOIN *with* MORELS *and* MADEIRA 134

GRILLED LAMB RIBS *with* TZATZIKI, HUMMUS, *and* PITA 136

BEEF WELLINGTON 137

BUTTERFLIED LEG *of* LAMB *with* LIME, MUSTARD,
and BASIL BUTTER 138

LAMB TENDERLOIN *in* PUFF PASTRY 139

FLANK STEAK *with* ANCHOVY AIOLI 141

CASHEW-BREADED PORK TENDERLOIN *with* BITTER
GREENS 142

STEAK *with* RED WINE *and* PEPPERCORN
SAUCE 144

....

I divide meat into three groups: the tender cuts, the tougher cuts, and the innards. The tougher cuts come from the hard-working parts of the animal and respond best to long, slow cooking. The tender cuts are the parts getting a free ride from their chewier colleagues; they are tender because they don't work so hard and can be cooked at a higher temperature for a shorter time. In the third category, ignored by most and disdained by many, are the interesting inner parts of the animal known as "offal," a word that does them no justice.

You might think these two approaches to cooking—high heat for a short time, and low heat for a long time—would add up to the same thing, but it doesn't work that way. High temperatures harden proteins, and a tough cut cooked at a high temperature will come out like an old boot; only long slow cooking will bring out its best.

For each cut of meat there is a combination of time and temperature that will give us the best results, and that is what we have to find. The tender cuts can be cooked anywhere from very rare all the way to well-done, if that is how you like it, and they will still be tender. The tougher cuts need long, slow cooking, but they are redeemed by the wonderful gelatinous texture that this cooking will produce—in fact they can be elevated to heights that a tender cut, however nicely cooked, may never achieve. There are not many cooks who would trade away a nicely cooked oxtail for a loin of veal, or indeed for almost anything else.

RECIPES *for* SLOW COOKED MEAT

....

Slowness is a virtue when cooking temperatures are very low (225°F to 250°F [110°C to 120°C]). Cooking times are correspondingly long, but there is a logic to them: high heat toughens proteins and dissolves gelatine, while low heat keeps the proteins tender and the gelatine intact, allowing lovely textures to develop. Whether it is on the stovetop or in the oven (where it is easier to control the temperature), you should aim to keep the cooking at more than a simmer, and you will be rewarded with remarkable flavour and texture.

Oxtails *with* Amarone

••

As anyone who has spent time looking at cows in a field knows, their tails are in constant motion, curling around and swatting at things. There is not a lot of meat on a tail, and what there is can be tougher than an old boot—until you apply long, slow, and moist heat to it, when its true glory is revealed.

I strongly recommended that you drink the Amarone, and let the oxtails bathe in some lesser wine—they will not mind.

••

Preheat the oven to 225°F (110°C).

Set an ovenproof pan with a lid, or a Dutch oven large enough to hold all the oxtails (preferably in 1 layer), over medium heat; add the olive oil and brown the oxtails on all sides. Set aside the meat and add the onion, celery, carrot, and garlic to the pan. Cook and stir until lightly browned, then remove and set aside with the oxtails.

Remove and discard most of the seeds from the canned tomatoes, cut them into a small dice, and pour into the pan along with the red wine and stock. Bring to a boil, scraping any bits from the bottom of the pan, and add the rosemary and salt. Turn the heat to low and put the oxtails and vegetables back in the pan. Bring to a simmer, cover the pan, and transfer to the centre of the preheated oven.

Bake in the oven for 1 hour; uncover the pan and check that the liquid is barely simmering. Return to the oven and cook for another 2 hours. Take out the pan again and check for doneness by feel or by cutting off a small piece and tasting. If it needs a bit more time, let it have it; it's best not to turn the heat up to speed things along.

When done, remove the meat from the pan and set aside in a bowl to retain the liquid. Pour the sauce through a sieve into a second bowl, pressing down to squeeze all the liquid out of the vegetables before discarding them. Let the liquid rest until the fat has risen to the surface and skim off as much of it as you can.

Set the pan over medium heat and add the sauce. Add the juices from the meat, bring to a simmer, then reduce the sauce until it is slightly syrupy. Taste for seasoning and adjust if necessary. Return the oxtails to the covered pan and gently reheat the meat. (You can set it aside in the fridge once it has cooled and reheat it later.)

Serve on warm plates with mashed potatoes made with plenty of cream. If there is any sauce left over, it is far from correct—but delicious nonetheless—to warm it up and pour a little over a green salad made with Nancy's Vinaigrette (page 228).

SERVES 4
••••••••••••

6 to 8 pieces oxtail (depending on size)

2 Tbsp (30 mL) olive oil

1 cup (250 mL) finely sliced onion

½ cup (125 mL) finely sliced celery

½ cup (125 mL) finely sliced carrot

1 Tbsp (15 mL) finely chopped garlic

1 14-oz (397 g) can whole or diced tomatoes

3 cups (720 mL) Amarone or other robust red wine

2 cups (480 mL) beef or chicken stock

½ tsp (2 mL) salt

2 sprigs rosemary

Beef Pot Roast *with* Saffron Noodles

· ·

SERVES 6

· · · · · · · · · · · ·

2 Tbsp (30 mL) olive oil

3 to 4 lb (1.4 to 1.8 kg) pot roast
of beef (preferably chuck, top or
bottom round)

12 peeled garlic cloves

½ cup (125 mL) thinly sliced carrots

1 cup (250 mL) thinly sliced onions

1½ cups (360 mL) red wine

4 cups (960 mL) beef or chicken
stock

A pot roast can be a lovely thing, and this is Karen the Chef's version. The noodles in this recipe are actually saffron crêpes rolled up and cut into strips, which sounds like a lot of work, but really isn't. I am not just saying that—I was pleasantly surprised by how easy it is—and the crêpe noodles do make the dish more interesting and have a much lighter texture. You can of course use pasta noodles (with or without saffron) and it will still taste good. The meat is served on top of the noodles, and the spicy crème fraîche and tomato sauce make a delicious combination.

The cooking time for the meat is a little hard to estimate, and it may be a good idea to cook it ahead of time, even the day before. That way you can be sure it will be completely cooked, and the flavour will be better for sitting longer in the sauce.

· ·

Preheat the oven to 250°F (120°C).

In a heavy pan set over medium-high heat, heat the oil and sear the meat until nicely browned all over. Remove the meat and set aside in a saucepan or ovenproof dish with a lid. Add the garlic, carrots, and onions to the hot pan and sauté, stirring from time to time, until the onions are softened and lightly browned, then remove and add to the pot roast.

Deglaze the pan with the wine, scraping up any bits on the bottom. Reduce slightly, then add the stock and bring to a boil. Pour the sauce over the pot roast, set the pan over medium heat, and bring it back to a simmer. Cover the pan and transfer to the centre of the preheated oven.

Bake for 3 hours. It should bubble very gently, so check it after 45 minutes to make sure, adjusting the oven temperature as necessary.

The meat is ready when it feels a little softer to the touch than it did at the beginning of cooking; there should still be a bit of spring-back to it, and getting to know just what that feels like takes practice. Perhaps the best test is to cut a small piece off the end with a sharp knife and taste: it should be soft and tender, and not dry. Give it as much extra time as it needs, resisting the temptation to turn up the heat.

SAFFRON NOODLES Make the noodles while the meat is cooking. Mix the saffron and boiling water in a small bowl and set aside for half an hour to infuse.

In a large bowl, beat together the eggs, salt, milk, water, and saffron threads and water. Whisk together until well combined, add the flour, and whisk just enough to make a smooth batter.

Set a crêpe pan over medium-low heat. When it is hot, add a dot of butter: it should foam up but not burn quickly, so adjust the heat if necessary. Ladle enough batter into the pan to just cover the bottom, tilting the pan to swirl it around. Cook until the top is starting to dry and it is firm enough to lift with a palette knife or spatula, then turn it over (or flip it). Cook briefly on the other side then slide onto a plate. Keep going until all the batter has been used, stacking the crêpes to keep them warm—they won't stick together.

To make the crêpes into noodles, roll up a stack of 3 crêpes and cut them into ⅓-inch (8 mm) slices; set aside, still rolled up, on a plate or baking sheet.

HORSERADISH CREAM In a small bowl, mix together the crème fraîche, horseradish, tomatoes, salt and pepper; set aside until serving.

SERVING If the meat has been cooked ahead, reheat it in the sauce over medium heat. When it simmers, cover the pan and reduce the heat to very low, or return to the 250°F (120°C) oven. It will take about 40 minutes to warm up.

Remove the meat from the sauce and place it in the turned-off oven, loosely covered with foil. Warm the serving plates as well.

Strain the sauce through a sieve, pressing down to get all the liquid. Return to the pan, bring to a boil over high heat, and reduce until it is slightly syrupy—you want about 2 cups (480 mL). Taste and adjust the seasoning.

With a sharp knife, cut the meat across the grain into ¼- to ½-inch (6 to 13 mm) slices. Set out the warm plates and divide the noodles between them, arranging them in a ring around the edge. Lay 2 slices of meat in the centre of each plate and spoon the sauce on top. Spoon horseradish cream over the noodles.

SAFFRON NOODLES
Small pinch saffron threads

2 Tbsp (30 mL) boiling water

4 eggs

½ tsp (2 mL) salt

1 cup (250 mL) milk

1 cup (250 mL) water

1⅓ cups (320 mL) all-purpose flour

⅓ cup (80 mL) butter

HORSERADISH CREAM
1 cup (250 mL) crème fraîche

2 Tbsp (30 mL) prepared horse-radish sauce

2 large tomatoes, remove most seeds and cut into a ¼-inch (6 mm) dice

¼ tsp (1 mL) salt

½ tsp (2 mL) fresh ground black pepper

SERVES 4

• • • • • • • • • • • •

4 large beef short ribs

2 Tbsp (30 mL) olive oil

6 finely chopped garlic cloves

2 Tbsp (30 mL) freshly grated
ginger

½ tsp (2 mL) hot chili flakes

1 Tbsp (15 mL) orange zest

½ cup (125 mL) orange juice

¼ cup (60 mL) maple syrup

¼ cup (60 mL) hoisin sauce

½ cup (125 mL) red wine

¼ cup (60 mL) soy sauce
or tamari

½ cup (125 mL)
water

Ginger Garlic Short Ribs

This recipe goes very well with Polenta (page 227), with a spicy ginger sauce that is perfect for short ribs.

Preheat the oven to 235°F (115°C).

Set an ovenproof pan with a lid or a Dutch oven (large enough to hold the ribs) over medium heat and brown the ribs on all sides in the olive oil. Remove and set aside.

In the oil left in the pan, cook the garlic, ginger, and chili flakes for 2 or 3 minutes, stirring to prevent them from sticking.

Add the orange zest and juice, maple syrup, hoisin sauce, red wine, tamari, and water. Bring to a boil, turn the heat down, and add the short ribs. When it simmers, cover the pan and transfer to the centre of the preheated oven.

Cook for 3 hours, or until tender. Once or twice during the cooking, lift the lid to make sure the liquid is barely bubbling at a gentle simmer. Adjust the oven temperature cautiously; it's easy to increase the cooking time, not so easy to shorten it, so keep it long and slow.

The ribs are done when the meat is tender to the touch and starts to separate from the bone. You can check for doneness by feel, or cut off a small piece from one of the ribs and taste for that melt-in-your-mouth feel.

When the ribs are ready, remove the pan from the oven. (Leave an oven mitt on the handle so you don't burn yourself when you go to move the still-hot pan 5 minutes later and automatically grab for the handle!)

Remove the ribs and keep them warm while you finish the sauce. Pour the juices into a measuring jug or other tall, narrow container, and allow the fat to rise to the surface. Skim off as much as you can and set it aside. Return the liquid to the pan and bring to a boil; reduce over medium-high heat for a few minutes until it becomes slightly syrupy. It is a highly flavoured, sweet, spicy, garlicky, and gingery sauce and probably does not need any more seasoning, but check it anyway and add anything you think is missing.

Serve with Polenta (page 227) or Scalloped Potatoes (page 162).

Osso Bucco

One of the great dishes of Italian cooking, the classic example of long, slow cooking producing perfect texture and flavour. The traditional accompaniments are Risotto Milanese (page 54) and gremolata, a mixture of garlic, parsley, and lemon zest—see the recipe below.

Preheat the oven to 250°F (120°C).

Shake together the flour and veal shanks in a plastic bag to coat them nicely.

Set an ovenproof pan with a lid or a Dutch oven (large enough to hold the veal in 2 layers) over medium heat, pour in the olive oil, and brown the veal shanks on both sides in batches. Remove the veal and set aside.

In the same pan, cook the onion, celery, carrot, and garlic until lightly browned, adding more oil if needed. Set aside with the veal.

Remove and discard most of the seeds from the canned tomatoes, cut them into a small dice and add them to the pan, along with the wine and chicken stock. Bring to a boil, scraping up any bits on the bottom of the pan. Turn the heat to low and add the salt. Return the veal to the pan, spooning the vegetables on top and between the layers.

Arrange the lemon peel and herbs on top. Bring back to a boil, then cover the pan and transfer to the centre of the preheated oven. Bake in the oven for 1 hour, then take out the pan and turn the veal shanks over (moving the top layer to the bottom if there are two layers). Bake for another hour, then take out the pan and check for doneness either by feel or by cutting off a small piece and tasting. It may well need a bit more time, this recipe errs on the side of caution; if so, give it the extra time it needs.

While the meat is cooking, prepare the gremolata: in a small bowl, mix together the parsley, garlic, and lemon zest; set aside for the flavours to blend.

Take the veal out of the pan and set aside in a bowl to catch the juices. Pour the sauce through a sieve into a second bowl, pressing to squeeze all the liquid out of the vegetables (which can then be discarded). Leave the sauce to sit until the fat has risen to the surface and skim off as much as you can.

Place the pan over medium heat, add the sauce and the juices from the veal bowl, and bring to a simmer. Taste for seasoning and adjust as needed. Return the veal to the pan, turn the heat to low, and gently reheat the meat. (Turn it off if you are not serving right away, and allow to cool. May be done 2 or 3 days ahead to this point; keep refrigerated.)

Serve on warm plates. Pass the gremolata separately. Risotto Milanese (page 54) goes very well with it.

SERVES 6

¼ cup (60 mL) all-purpose flour

6 pieces centre-cut veal shank (1 inch [2½ cm] thick)

2 Tbsp (30 mL) olive oil

1 cup (250 mL) finely sliced onion

½ cup (125 mL) finely sliced celery

½ cup (125 mL) finely sliced carrot

1 tsp (5 mL) finely chopped garlic

One 14-oz (397 g) can whole tomatoes

2 cups (480 mL) white wine

1 cup (250 mL) chicken stock

½ tsp (2 mL) salt

2 bay leaves

2 strips lemon peel

1 sprig thyme

8 basil leaves

GREMOLATA

3 Tbsp (45 mL) finely chopped parsley

1½ tsp (7 mL) finely chopped garlic

1 Tbsp (15 mL) grated lemon zest

Steak *and* Mushroom Pie *with* Cheddar Biscuit Topping

···

This is a good dish for a winter buffet. The biscuit topping makes a welcome change from the usual short crust pastry; it's very easy to make and very satisfying. It's hard to get the underside of the biscuit topping fully cooked when baked on top of the filling, and the answer is to bake it separately from the meat.

You can make the filling a day or two ahead, and like all recipes for slow-cooked meat, the flavour will get better as it rests.

Chuck is from the front end of the animal and is an excellent choice for stewing and pot roasts; it has more flavour than the hip, but also more fat—hence the flavour—and is less prone to drying out.

···

Preheat the oven to 235°F (115°C).

Set a large frying pan over medium-high heat, add the oil, and briefly sear the meat all over; set aside in a bowl. Turn the heat down to medium and, in the same pan, sauté the mushrooms, adding more oil if necessary. When the juices are released and have mostly evaporated, add them to the bowl with the seared steak. Deglaze the pan with the beer; let it come to a boil and reduce slightly. Add the stock to the pan, bring to a boil, and set aside.

Set a medium ovenproof pan with a lid over medium-low heat. Melt the butter, add the flour, and stir to make a roux. Whisk in half of the hot beer and stock; keep whisking until smooth, then add the rest of the beer and whisk again. The sauce should be a little thicker than whipping cream.

Add the Worcestershire sauce, soy sauce, salt, and pepper. Add the steak and mushrooms to the sauce and bring it all to a gentle simmer, stirring from time to time. Cover the pan with its lid and place in the centre of the preheated oven. Bake for 2 hours, checking once or twice that the liquid is barely bubbling.

Remove the pan from the oven and test a piece of meat for doneness. If it needs more cooking, add half an hour and then test again. When done, set aside to cool. (May be done ahead to this point.)

If baking the biscuit topping on the stew:

About an hour and a half before serving, heat the stew until it feels warm to your finger, then transfer to a baking dish about 9 × 12 inches (20 cm × 30 cm), and proceed with the biscuit topping.

Preheat the oven to 400°F (200°C).

In a small bowl, mix the buttermilk and egg yolk together.

In a medium bowl, mix together the sugar, salt, flour, baking powder, and baking soda, and 1 cup (250 mL) grated cheese. A stand mixer fitted with the paddle attachment is a good way to mix the dough, but it can also be done in a food processor or by hand. When blended, add the cubes of cold

... recipe continued

SERVES 4
············

2 Tbsp (30 mL) olive or other vegetable oil

2 lb (900 g) chuck steak, cut into 1-inch (2½ cm) cubes

1 lb (454 g) white or Cremini mushrooms, quartered

11 oz (330 mL) dark beer

1 cup (250 mL) beef stock (or chicken stock or water)

1½ Tbsp (22 g) butter

2 Tbsp (30 mL) all-purpose flour

½ Tbsp (7 mL) Worcestershire sauce

½ Tbsp (7 mL) soy sauce

½ tsp (2 mL) salt

¼ tsp (1 mL) fresh ground black pepper

CHEDDAR CHEESE BISCUIT TOPPING

⅔ cup (160 mL) buttermilk (or half-and-half yogurt and milk in a pinch)

1 egg yolk

1 tsp (5 mL) sugar

¼ tsp (1 mL) salt

2 cups (480 mL) all-purpose flour

1½ tsp (7 mL) baking powder

½ tsp (2 mL) baking soda

2 cups (480 mL) aged Cheddar cheese, grated, divided

½ cup (125 mL) cold butter, cut into small pieces

. . . Steak and Mushroom Pie with Cheddar Biscuit Topping (cont.)

butter and mix to the consistency of coarse crumbs, taking care not to over mix if using a machine.

Now add the buttermilk into the dry ingredients and mix just enough to bring it together. Turn out the dough onto a lightly floured work surface and knead until nearly smooth—no more than half a minute.

Roll out the dough to the size of your baking dish, about ½ inch (13 mm) thick. With a sharp knife, cut the dough into serving-size pieces and arrange them, without overlapping, on top of the stew in the baking dish, covering the filling. Bake in the centre of the preheated 400°F (200°C) oven for 10 minutes.

Remove from the oven and sprinkle the remaining 1 cup (250 mL) grated Cheddar on top of the biscuits. Return to the oven and bake for a further 10 minutes, at which point the biscuit should be risen and the cheese melted and golden.

If baking the biscuit separately:

Prepare the biscuit topping as above, baking them on a baking sheet lined with parchment for the same time and temperature. Reheat the stew in the pan just before serving; spoon onto individual plates and set a square of biscuit on each.

INDIVIDUAL BISCUITS (VARIATION) To make 20 individual biscuits instead of the pie topping, roll out the dough and use a 2-inch (5 cm) cookie cutter (or a glass) to cut them out. Arrange them on a baking sheet lined with parchment and bake as above.

Tourtière

···

A traditional dish on Christmas Eve in Quebec, and just as comforting and satisfying on any other winter night. It can be made with all pork, as here, or a mixture of pork with veal and/or beef. While it is the spices that make the dish, some pork is necessary for a juicy filling.

···

Make the pastry and store it in the fridge. Take it out half an hour before you need it.

Put the ground meat, onions, ginger, cloves, and allspice, salt and pepper in a large saucepan over medium heat and cook, stirring to break up the meat, until it loses its raw colour. Add ½ cup (125 mL) water, bring to a boil, reduce the heat to low, and simmer for half an hour. Stir in the breadcrumbs, remove the pan from the heat, and set aside to cool.

Lightly flour your work surface, and divide the pastry in 2 almost equal parts; roll out the bigger one to a circle slightly larger than your pie dish, roll it up around your rolling pin, and unroll it over the dish. Spoon the cooked meat onto the pastry and smooth it out.

Roll the other piece of dough to a slightly smaller circle. Brush the edges of the bottom crust with water, set the second circle on top, and pinch the 2 layers firmly together around the edge. Trim away any excess with a sharp knife, and cut 8 vents in the top to allow steam to escape. (May be made ahead to this point.)

Preheat the oven to 425°F (220°C).

Beat the egg yolk and 1 tsp (5 mL) water together to make a glaze and brush it over the pastry. Place the pie in the centre of the preheated oven and bake for 15 minutes; reduce the heat to 350°F (180°C) and bake a further 40 minutes, until the pastry is golden brown.

Remove from the oven and allow to cool for 20 minutes before cutting. This is a good time to bring out some of those interesting chutneys hiding in the back of the fridge.

SERVES 8
············

1 recipe Short Crust Pastry
(page 238)

2 lb (900 g) ground pork (or a
combination of pork, beef, and veal)

1½ cups (360 mL) finely chopped
onions

1 tsp (5 mL) ground ginger

¼ tsp (1 mL) ground cloves

¼ tsp (1 mL) ground allspice

1 tsp (5 mL) salt

½ tsp (2 mL) fresh ground pepper

½ cup + 1 tsp (130 mL) water,
divided

1 cup (250 mL) fine dry breadcrumbs

1 egg yolk

Lamb Shanks *with* Figs, Red Wine, *and* Quince

SERVES 4

···········

2 Tbsp (30 mL) olive oil

4 lamb shanks

2 cups (480 mL) red wine

8 dried figs (Greek or Turkish), cut in half

2 cups (480 mL) chicken stock

¼ cup (60 mL) balsamic vinegar

½ tsp (2 mL) ground cardamom

½ tsp (2 mL) ground cinnamon

2 Tbsp (30 mL) quince paste

There is no question that for a long time, the shanks of a lamb have been looked down on when compared to the chops and legs, and in the physical world of up and down, lambs share that point of view. But they have never doubted the value of their shanks, and nor have diners who set taste and texture above fashion. Not only are lamb shanks every bit as delicious as other cuts, I find it comforting to know that all the parts of an animal, for whose demise I am partly responsible, are being used and appreciated, and nothing is going to waste. I cannot be sure lambs feels the same way, but if I were in their shanks, I think I would want every last bit of me to be enjoyed.

The Scots of course have taken this philosophy of waste-not-want-not to another level and created, if that is the right word, haggis. My concession to haggis extends to eating it once a year on Burns Night. I fear it will be a long time before haggis achieves the veneration that R. Burns believed it deserved. Not so with lamb shanks; they are, as the sheep lying on its back would agree, superior. (Sheep have broad backs and really can get stuck the wrong way up, unable to right themselves, sometimes with fatal consequences.)

It's worth seeking out the lighter brown Greek or Turkish figs rather than the dark Mission.

Preheat the oven to 225°F (110°C).

Set a large ovenproof pan over medium heat, add the oil, and brown the shanks on all sides. Set them aside, pour off the oil, and deglaze the pan with the red wine. Bring the wine to a boil until slightly reduced; add the figs, stock, balsamic vinegar, cardamom, and cinnamon. Bring to a boil again, turn the heat down to medium low, put the shanks in the pan, bring the liquid to a simmer, cover the pan, and set it in the middle of the preheated oven for 2½ hours. Remove the lid after an hour to make sure the heat is not too high and the liquid is barely bubbling; adjust the oven temperature if necessary.

The meat will shrink away from the bone as it cooks; some shrinkage is fine but a lot may be a sign the oven is too hot. Test the meat with a fork and by pressing with your finger—when it is ready, it will be tender and quite easy to pull off the bone.

Remove the pan from the oven, take out the shanks, and set aside. Place the pan over medium-high heat and reduce the sauce to about 2 cups (480 mL). Add the quince paste to the pan, stirring until melted. Return the shanks to the pan and reheat on low.

Mashed potatoes or orzo work well with the sauce; couscous also, if you want to emphasize the North African combination of lamb and fruit.

SERVES 4
· · · · · · · · · ·

2 large eggplants, cut across into
⅓-inch (8 mm) rounds

⅔ cup (160 mL) olive oil, divided

1 large onion, finely chopped

1 lb (454 g) ground lamb

One 28-oz (794 g) can diced
tomatoes

1 tsp (5 mL) oregano

1 tsp (5 mL) ground cinnamon

Salt

Fresh ground black pepper

1 recipe Béchamel Sauce (page 234)

2 eggs

Pinch nutmeg

Moussaka

A Greek variation on the shepherd's pie theme that takes only a bit more work and repays it handsomely. Baking the eggplant in the oven is easier than frying, and uses much less oil.

Preheat the oven to 400° F (200°C).

In a large bowl, toss the eggplant slices with ½ cup (125 mL) oil until well coated. Arrange them in 1 layer on a large baking sheet. (You may need a second sheet, or 2 batches.)

Bake for 10 minutes, then check for browning; the eggplant should be starting to turn light brown on the underside—if not, give them 2 minutes more. Turn and cook for 7 minutes on the other side, until very lightly browned.

Turn the oven down to 350° F (180°C).

Sauté the chopped onion in 2 Tbsp (30 mL) oil over medium heat until softened. Add the ground lamb, turn up the heat to medium-high, and cook until it is no longer pink.

Add the tomatoes, oregano, cinnamon, salt and pepper. Bring to a simmer, reduce heat to low, and cook, stirring occasionally, for 30 minutes.

Make the Béchamel Sauce. When it is ready, beat the eggs very well in a separate bowl, pour in ¼ cup (60 mL) of the sauce and beat again; beat in a second ¼ cup (60 mL) to temper the eggs and stop them from curdling. Remove the pan from the heat and pour the egg and sauce mixture back into the rest of the Béchamel; add the nutmeg and stir well. Adjust the seasoning.

Choose a baking dish, about 6 × 8 inches (15 × 20 cm) and 2 inches (5 cm) or more deep. Spread a third of the meat mixture over the bottom, cover with a third of the eggplant slices, then continue with 2 more layers of meat and eggplant. Pour the Béchamel over the top. (May be done ahead to this point.)

Bake in the preheated oven for 40 minutes. Check after 25 minutes; if it is browning too much, cover loosely with aluminum foil. It is done when heated through and nicely browned on top.

Moussaka, like many dishes that combine meat with vegetables and other flavourings, is just as good when reheated the next day.

THE TENDER CUTS

···

These cuts are the bankers of the animal's anatomy, living the easy life while the rest of the muscles do the work. They don't require long, slow cooking because they are already tender. They may not have the flavour of the tougher cuts, but they make up for it in tenderness—some, like the tenderloin, so tender that they can be eaten raw. That does not mean they do not require care in cooking, but it is care of a different kind than the tougher cuts.

Tender cuts (apart from the prime rib [page 132] and tenderloin recipes [page 134, 142]) are cooked at a relatively high temperature, and the longer they cook the more the proteins harden and the tougher the meat becomes. From the point of view of tenderness, it makes sense to cook them as little as possible, and if your tastes run to four minute eggs and raw oysters, that means medium-rare or less.

MARINADES FOR MEAT
·····························

OIL-BASED MARINADES, with garlic, herbs, and olive oil, can add delicious flavours to meat. They will not change the texture of the meat, and they are a good choice for tender cuts where you want to enhance the flavour.

WET MARINADES, which contain wine or vinegar, are different: they do help to tenderize the meat. They also change the taste and, depending on what is in the marinade, they can change the colour, too. If you like the pinks and reds of a nicely cooked steak, it is best to avoid wet marinades, particularly on a barbecue where the liquid gets in the way of charring the outside.

DRY RUBS modify taste and add flavour; usually they do not affect colour. They can be a good addition when the cooking is long and slow, allowing the uniform flavour of the rub time to blend with the other cooking flavours.

With a tender piece of meat, I prefer to serve a sauce with the meat that will complement its natural flavour.

Prime Rib of Beef

··

SERVES 1 PER EACH
¾ LB (340 G)

···············

1 prime rib of beef (on the bone)

Salt

Fresh ground black pepper

In this recipe, a tender and very flavourful cut of meat is roasted for a long time at a low temperature. Karen the Chef introduced me to this method, and I would not cook a prime rib any other way. The result is a roast that is evenly cooked from one end to the other, as pink at the outside as it is in the centre. The timing is important, but the method is simple.

A prime rib is a special occasion kind of meat. It is big and expensive, and although you don't have to buy the full seven ribs, it should be at least as long as it is thick, which means four ribs weighing 4 lb (1.8 kg) or more, enough for six people. (When the bones are included in the weight, as they are with a prime rib, the normal allowance of ½ lb [227 g] per person before cooking is increased to ¾ lb [340 g].)

Plan your timing backwards from the time you plan to serve. It is always a good idea to bring meat to room temperature before putting it in the oven, but it is absolutely essential when cooking a large roast at a low temperature. Take it out of the fridge at least 3 hours before it goes in the oven. When you add the cooking time of about half an hour per 1 lb (454 g)—see below—and half an hour of resting time before carving, a 6-lb (2.7 kg) prime rib needs to come out of the fridge about 7 hours before you plan to serve.

Despite the low oven temperature, you can still roast the potatoes around the beef while it is cooking, if there is space under or around the rack. They do not mind slow cooking, and can be crisped at a high temperature—along with Yorkshire pudding (if you like, and who does not?)—once the beef is ready.

··

Preheat the oven to 225°F (110°C).

Rub salt and pepper over the meat.

Place a rack in the roasting pan to raise the meat off the bottom and prevent the underside from overcooking.

Roast in the preheated oven 30 minutes per 1 lb (454 g) for medium-rare, or 35 minutes per 1 lb (454 g) for medium. When the cooking time is up (or when an internal thermometer reads 127°F [53°C] for medium-rare) take the roast out, cover it with foil, and set it aside in a warm place for up to 30 minutes. Reserve the pan juices for the gravy (recipe follows). Make sure to warm the serving plates.

Serve with Yorkshire Pudding (page 164) and Perfect Roast Potatoes (page 159).

THE GRAVY

···

This is not a purist's gravy, but it is full of flavour, and quickly made.

···

Pour off the fat and juices from the roasting pan into a glass measuring jug or small bowl. Skim 3 Tbsp (45 mL) of fat from the top and add to the roasting pan. Skim as much of the rest of the fat as you can and, if the timing works, use it for Yorkshire puddings or roast potatoes—it adds more flavour than vegetable oil; reserve the meat juices for the gravy.

Place the roasting pan over 2 burners on the stove, over very low heat. Add the flour to the fat, stirring to make a roux; brown the flour a little. Pour in the red wine, stock, and reserved meat juices, bring to a boil, and stir or whisk until quite smooth.

Pour in the soy sauce, Worcestershire, and balsamic vinegar. Continue to cook until slightly reduced and smooth. Taste, add more flavourings, and dilute with stock if necessary. Strain into a gravy boat or jug, and pass around with the beef.

Reserved fat and juices from Prime Rib of Beef (previous page)

2 Tbsp (30 mL) all-purpose flour

½ cup (125 L) red wine

2 cups (480 mL) beef or chicken stock

1 Tbsp (15 mL) soy sauce

½ tsp (2 mL) Worcestershire sauce

1 tsp (5 mL) balsamic vinegar

Salt

Fresh ground black pepper

Rack *of* Lamb

···

This is a delicious cut of lamb, and best served simply: rubbed with Dijon mustard and rosemary, roasted medium-rare, and served with pan juices. Accompany with a vegetable or potato that has some sauce of its own: Scalloped Potatoes (page 162), Swiss Chard (page 154), or creamed spinach.

Each rack has nine ribs; three per person is a fair serving.

···

Preheat the oven to 400°F (200°C).

In a small bowl, combine the mustard, rosemary, and garlic; rub the mixture over the lamb.

Place the lamb on a rack on a baking sheet. Place in the centre of the preheated oven with the bones or thinner end of the rack toward the door.

Bake 20 minutes for rare or 25 minutes for medium-rare. (Much as I like rare meat, I think lamb has more flavour and better texture cooked medium-rare.) Remove from the oven and keep warm. About 5 minutes before serving, warm the plates in the turned-off oven.

SERVES 6

············

2 Tbsp (30 mL) Dijon mustard

1 Tbsp (15 mL) finely chopped rosemary

1 tsp (5 mL) finely chopped garlic

2 racks of lamb, trimmed

SERVES 8
. . . .

1 beef tenderloin, 2½ to 3 lb (1.13 to
1.4 kg) trimmed weight

2 Tbsp (30 mL) softened butter

Salt

Fresh ground black pepper

1 oz (30 g) dried morels

1 lb (454 g) fresh white or cremini
mushrooms

2 Tbsp (30 mL) butter

1 cup (250 mL) stock, veal or beef

1 cup (250 mL) Madeira

1 cup (250 mL) whipping
cream

Beef Tenderloin *with* Morels *and* Madeira

This is the most luxurious of meat dishes, combining a traditional sauce with a cooking temperature that is just the opposite. The normal practice (myself included) has been to cook tenderloin at 425°F (220°C) for 30 to 35 minutes. Not so here: the meat is cooked at 300°F (150°C) for an hour, and it comes out perfectly cooked, evenly coloured, and beautifully tender.

Mushrooms and Madeira are perfect for a sauce that must not overpower the mild flavoured beef. The sweet wine brings out the sweetness of the meat, and the smokiness of the dried mushrooms adds a slight bitter note.

A tenderloin is thicker at the butt end than the tail end, making it difficult to cook the whole thing to the same degree of doneness. The best approach is to cut off the thin tail and the thick butt, leaving the evenly thick centre cut (known as Chateaubriand in France). It will weigh between 1½ and almost 3 lb (680 to 1400 g); a large one is more than enough for eight.

The butt can be tied and roasted in the same way at 300°F (150°C), but will take longer—75 minutes rather than the 60 in this recipe; or it can be cut into steaks and grilled. The tail end is best kept for beef stroganoff or stir fry.

Take the meat out of the fridge at least 2 hours before cooking and bring it to room temperature.

With a sharp knife, trim the sinew and fat from the outside of the tenderloin until it is neat and even. If there is enough meat to allow it, cut off the thinner tail end of the tenderloin and keep it for another use. If not, turn the tail under and tie it with kitchen string, in such a way that the roast is roughly the same thickness throughout. If necessary, tie the meat in other places to make a neat package. Rub with softened butter and season with salt and pepper.

Preheat the oven to 300°F (150°C).

About 1 hour and 20 or 30 minutes before serving, place the tenderloin on a rack sitting on a roasting pan or baking sheet (to lift the meat off the bottom of the pan). Roast in the preheated oven for 60 minutes, without opening the door (or cook to an internal temperature of 130°F [54°C] on a meat thermometer). Remove the meat from the oven, cover with foil, and set aside to keep warm for 20 to 30 minutes. Heat the plates in the turned-off oven.

While the meat is cooking, soak the dried morels in a small bowl of warm water for 30 minutes. Squeeze them dry and slice into pieces large enough that they are still recognizably morels; strain and reserve the soaking liquid.

Slice the fresh mushrooms ³⁄₁₆ of an inch (5 mm) thick. Melt the butter in a saucepan over medium heat, add the fresh mushrooms, and sauté until the liquid is released and mostly evaporated. Add the morels and cook them together for a few minutes; pour in the strained soaking liquid and the stock

. . . recipe continued

. . . Beef Tenderloin with Morels and Madeira (cont.)

and stir until reduced to about 1 cup (250 mL) of liquid. Add the Madeira and reduce again to about 1½ cups (360 mL). Pour in half of the cream, bring to a boil, and reduce slightly; add the rest of the cream (or more if necessary and reduce again to about 2 cups (480 mL). Season to taste with salt and pepper.

Carve the meat into nice thick slices (½ inch [13 mm]). Serve on warm plates with a spoonful or two of sauce and pass the rest around. Serve with Scalloped Potatoes (page 162) or Potato Pancake (page 161); spinach or green beans would be good, too.

Grilled Lamb Ribs *with* Tzatziki, Hummus, *and* Pita

Rib chops are a rack of lamb separated into individual chops, marinated in garlic, herbs, and olive oil. You can cut a whole rack into chops, or buy them already cut: allow three chops per person. Tzatziki is a good accompaniment.

Mix the olive oil, herbs, garlic, salt, and pepper in a bowl large enough to hold the chops; add the chops and mix well to coat. Cover with plastic wrap—or put everything in a large freezer bag—and refrigerate overnight.

Preheat the barbecue to moderately hot.

Remove the chops from the marinade and pat dry with paper towels. Barbecue for 2½ minutes on the first side, then 1½ minutes for medium-rare on the second side, or 2 minutes more for medium.

Remove from the barbecue and keep warm for 5 or 10 minutes. Serve with tzatziki (recipe follows), hummus (page 77), and pita warmed on the barbecue.

TZATZIKI

Place the yogurt in a sieve lined with cheesecloth or paper towel, and drain for at least 2 hours. Turn into a bowl and add salt, mint, parsley, and garlic. Mix well, cover with wrap, and set aside in the fridge.

SERVES 4
• • • • • • • •

2 Tbsp (30 mL) olive oil

1 Tbsp (15 mL) chopped fresh rosemary

1 Tbsp (15 mL) chopped Italian parsley

1 tsp (5 mL) chopped thyme

½ tsp (2 mL) finely chopped garlic

½ tsp (2 mL) salt

¼ tsp (1 mL) fresh ground pepper

12 lamb rib chops

MAKES ABOUT 2¼ CUPS (560 ML)
• • • • • • • • •

2 cups (480 mL) full fat plain yogurt

½ tsp (2 mL) salt

2 Tbsp (30 mL) finely chopped mint (fresh or dried)

2 Tbsp (30 mL) fresh Italian parsley leaves, coarsely chopped

½ tsp (2 mL) finely chopped garlic

Beef Wellington

••

No connection, it seems, to the hero of Waterloo, but still enormously popular The beef is not seared before being wrapped in pastry because, contrary to popular belief, it is not effective at sealing in the meat juices—all it does is create a grey ring of overcooked meat on the outside of the beef, and that is not something we want.

Chanterelle mushrooms are a nice change from the regular white mushrooms.

••

Take the tenderloin out of the fridge 2 hours before cooking, to bring it to room temperature.

Cut the bread into cubes, place in a small bowl and pour over the stock; set aside to soak.

Cook onion in the butter over medium heat until soft and translucent. Add the mushrooms and the water and continue to cook, stirring frequently, until the water has evaporated and the mixture is quite dry. Squeeze the bread dry (reserve stock for Madeira sauce) and add it to the mushrooms. Add the egg, salt and pepper, and work the mixture with your hands until completely incorporated.

Divide the pastry in two and roll each half into a rectangle, ¼ to ⅜ of an inch (6 to 10 mm) thick, on which the meat will fit comfortably, with a 1½-inch (4 cm) border all around.

Line a baking sheet with parchment paper; lay this smaller pastry rectangle on it, and centre the tenderloin on top. Spread the beef with mustard, then cover it evenly with the mushroom mixture.

Roll out the second half of the pastry to a slightly larger rectangle, brush the exposed border on the bottom layer lightly with water, then drape the second sheet of pastry over the first, pressing down gently to make a seal where the 2 sheets meet. With a small knife, trim away excess pastry, leaving a ¾-inch (2 cm) border all around. Scallop the edges by drawing the back of the knife gently inwards (toward the meat) every ¾ inch (2 cm) or so around the perimeter—this helps the pastry rise straight as it puffs. Cut 2 small round vents in the top for steam to escape, and decorate with pastry cutouts if you wish. Set aside in a cool spot until you are ready to bake, but you don't want to make the meat cold.

To make the Madeira sauce, sauté the 1 Tbsp (15 mL) butter and shallots until starting to brown. Add the flour and cook briefly, then pour in the red wine and cook until reduced and quite thick. Add the stock, thyme, and crushed peppercorns, and reduce again, to about 1½ cups (360 mL). Strain through a fine sieve into a bowl, pressing to extract all the juices. Return the sauce to the pan and add the Madeira and salt and pepper to taste.

Preheat the oven to 425°F (220°C). About 1 hour before dinner, brush the pastry with the egg glaze.

Put the beef in the centre of the preheated oven and bake for 15 minutes. Turn the oven down to 350°F (180°C) and bake for a further 25 minutes

. . . recipe continued

. . . Beef Wellington (cont.)

for medium-rare, or 30 minutes for medium. Remove from the oven, cover loosely with foil, and set aside to keep warm—it will be fine for 15 or 20 minutes. Turn the oven off and put in the serving plates to heat.

A serrated knife is the best way to cut the pastry on a Beef Wellington, and if it is sharp, it will cut the tender meat as well. Carve into ½- to ¾-inch (13 to 19 mm) slices, lay them on the warmed plates, and spoon over the Madeira sauce.

Butterflied Leg *of* Lamb *with* Lime, Mustard, *and* Basil Butter

Removing the bone from a leg of lamb makes carving much easier, and the actual boning is not hard. Ask the butcher to do it for you if you are uncertain. For the best flavour, start cooking on the barbecue then finish in the oven.

SERVES 6 TO 8
•••••••••••••••••

1 tsp (5 mL) finely chopped garlic

1 Tbsp (15 mL) olive oil

½ tsp (2 mL) salt

1 leg of lamb, bone removed

LIME, MUSTARD, AND BASIL BUTTER

½ cup (125 mL) butter, at room temperature

2 Tbsp (30 mL) chopped fresh basil

1 Tbsp (15 mL) finely chopped shallots (or onion)

1 Tbsp (15 mL) finely chopped chives

Juice of 1 lime

½ tsp (2 mL) finely chopped garlic

1 Tbsp (15 mL) Dijon mustard

½ tsp (2 mL) salt

½ tsp (2 mL) fresh ground black pepper

Mix the garlic, olive oil, and salt in a large bowl; add the lamb and rub the mixture into the meat. Cover with plastic wrap and set aside for a few hours at room temperature, or overnight in the fridge. Bring it out a few hours before cooking to allow the meat to come to room temperature.

To make the lime butter, cream the butter until light and fluffy. Add all the herbs and seasonings, mix it together well, and scoop onto a sheet of waxed paper. Roll the paper up and around the butter to make a log about 1½ inches (4 cm) in diameter. Enclose in plastic wrap and refrigerate until firm. (May be done 2 days ahead to this point.)

Cooking the lamb will take about 40 minutes, plus another 10 or 15 minutes resting time, so start about an hour before you plan to serve. Set the barbecue on medium-low. Preheat the oven to 300°F (150°C).

Place the lamb flat on the grill, skin side down, close the cover, and cook butterflied for 15 minutes, checking after a few minutes to make sure the meat is not browning too fast (after 15 minutes you want it to be lightly browned on the first side). Turn the meat over and cook for another 15 minutes at the same temperature.

Remove from the grill and place on a rack in a roasting pan; set the pan in the middle of the preheated oven and cook 15 minutes more.

Remove the lamb from the oven and set it aside, covered with foil. Turn off the oven and put in the plates to warm.

Slice the lamb across the grain into ¼-inch (6 mm) slices. Cut the herb butter into ¼-inch (6 mm) rounds and arrange 2 on each serving of lamb.

Both the lamb and the lime butter go well with Green Beans with Garlic and Tomatoes (page 149).

Lamb Tenderloin *in* Puff Pastry

....

This recipe (and Beef Wellington, page 137) are an echo from another age, but people still love them and are very appreciative of cooks who take the trouble to make them.

....

Trim the fat and sinew from the lamb loins. Heat a frying pan over medium-high heat. Once hot, add 1 tsp (5 mL) oil and sear the lamb loins quickly on all sides. Remove and set aside to cool.

Remove the stems from the spinach and wash it thoroughly. Bring ½ an inch (13 mm) of water to a boil in a medium pan, add the salt and spinach, and cook until just wilted. Drain and (once cooled) squeeze out as much water as you can. Chop the spinach coarsely.

Melt the butter in a small pan and cook the spinach gently until the butter is absorbed. Season with salt, pepper, and nutmeg, then set aside to cool.

Divide the puff pastry in two. Roll each half into a rectangle about 14 × 8 inches (35 × 24 cm). Lay the tenderloins side by side in the centre of one of the rectangles, with the thinner end of one alongside the thicker end of the other, leaving a ½-inch (13 mm) gap between them. Spoon the spinach over and between the loins, leaving a 1-inch (2½ cm) border of pastry uncovered.

Brush the exposed border with water, lay the second pastry rectangle on top, and press together. With a sharp knife, trim the border to ½ inch (13 cm) all around, then scallop the edge by drawing the back of the knife gently into the pastry every ¾ inch (8 mm) or so; this helps the pastry to rise straight as it puffs up during cooking. Transfer to a baking sheet lined with parchment paper and cover loosely with plastic wrap, then refrigerate until ready to use.

Preheat the oven to 425°F (220°C). About 45 minutes before you want to serve, brush the pastry with a well-beaten egg.

Transfer the lamb to the middle of the preheated oven and bake for 15 minutes. Turn the oven down to 375°F (190°C) and bake 15 minutes more. Remove from the oven, cover loosely with foil, and set aside to keep warm—it will be fine for 15 minutes.

Slice the lamb into ½-inch (13 mm) slices with a sharp serrated knife. The creamy sauce of Scalloped Potatoes (page 162) makes them a great accompaniment for this dish.

SERVES 4
....

2 large lamb tenderloins

1 tsp (5 mL) vegetable oil

1 lb (454 g) fresh spinach

½ tsp (2 mL) salt

2 Tbsp (30 mL) butter

Fresh ground black pepper

Pinch nutmeg

1¼ lb (567 g) puff pastry

Flank Steak *with* Anchovy Aioli

Flank steak remains something of a bargain in the world of tender cuts of meat. It has excellent flavour but is chewy if treated like a regular steak. Cooking it rare and slicing thinly across the grain are the secrets to success.

The salty sweetness of the anchovy aioli works very well with the steak, and frankly the garlic is not necessary—it's nice to have a break from it now and then. Homemade Mayonnaise (page 229) is best.

Take the flank steak out of the fridge a couple of hours before cooking to allow it to come to room temperature.

With the flat side of a kitchen knife, mash the anchovies (and garlic if you are using it) to a paste on your work surface, then chop them thoroughly. Stir into the mayonnaise and set aside.

Preheat the barbecue to high. Season the steak generously with salt and pepper.

Lay the flank steak in the middle of the hot grill, close the lid, and cook for 4 minutes (5 minutes if thicker than 1 inch [2½ cm]); turn it over and cook for a further 3 minutes (4 for a thick steak). Remove from the heat and rest for 15 minutes in a warm place.

Cut the flank steak with a sharp knife across the grain (at right angles to the clearly visible long, narrow, lengthwise fibres) into slices ⅛ inch or so (3 or 4 mm) thick. Serve with the anchovy aioli and Oven Fries (page 158).

SERVES 6
············

1 flank steak (about 2 lb [900 g])

ANCHOVY AIOLI

One 2-oz (50 g) tin anchovies

1 clove garlic (optional)

2 cups (480 mL) Mayonnaise (page 229)

Cashew-Breaded Pork Tenderloin *with* Bitter Greens

SERVES 4
••••••••••

1½ lb (680 g) rapini (bitter) or broccolini (milder)

2 Tbsp (30 mL) dry sherry

1 Tbsp (15 mL) Dijon mustard

1 egg white

3 Tbsp (45 mL) cornstarch

¼ tsp (1 mL) salt

¼ tsp (1 mL) fresh ground black pepper

1 Tbsp (15 mL) oyster sauce

1 large pork tenderloin (about 1½ lb [680 g])

2 cups (480 mL) cashew pieces

2 cups (480 mL) white breadcrumbs or panko

2 cups + 2 Tbsp (530 mL) vegetable oil, divided

2 cloves garlic, crushed

5 thin slices fresh ginger

Fleur de sel, for serving

In Babe, one of my all-time favourite movies, as Pig is being eyed as the centrepiece of Christmas dinner, the mice, playing the Greek chorus, break into song with "Pork is a nice sweet meat"—true enough of the slow-cooked cuts, but the more tender cuts can be a bit bland. In this recipe, the loin is flattened like a schnitzel, then coated with crushed cashews and breadcrumbs. The pork and cashews are indeed nice and sweet, the bitter greens spiced with sherry, and mustard are the perfect foil.

Wash and drain the rapini or broccolini.

In a small bowl, mix together the sherry and mustard.

In a medium bowl, mix together the egg white, cornstarch, salt, pepper, and oyster sauce.

Cut the pork loin into 1¼-inch (3 cm) pieces. One at a time, place them flat on a sheet of waxed or parchment paper, one cut end on the paper with the other facing up. Cover with a second sheet of paper and, with a rolling pin or other blunt instrument, flatten to ¼ inch (6 mm) or slightly thinner. Transfer to the egg and oyster sauce mixture and coat thoroughly. When all are done, cover and set aside at room temperature for an hour, or overnight in the fridge.

Bring a small pan of water to a boil and blanch the cashews for 1 minute; this stops them burning when deep-fried. Drain, transfer to a cutting board, chop coarsely, and crush with a rolling pin to an even crumb. Transfer to a baking sheet and mix thoroughly with the bread crumbs.

One at a time, take the pork slices and coat them with the cashew mixture, pressing it into the meat, then set them aside on a second baking sheet sprinkled with more bread crumbs.

Preheat the oven to 180°F (82°C).

Heat 2 cups (480 mL) of oil in a medium frying pan or saucepan on medium-low heat to 350°F (180°C); test by dropping in a small cube of bread—it should take about a minute to turn medium brown.

With a pair of tongs, transfer the pork to the hot oil one piece at a time and cook for 45 to 60 seconds per side. The meat will cool the oil, so you may have to turn up the heat to maintain the temperature. When nicely browned, transfer the pork to a baking sheet and keep it warm in the preheated oven. Continue until all the slices are done.

In a wok or large frying pan over medium-high heat, cook garlic and ginger in 2 Tbsp (30 mL) oil until well browned. Remove them and discard, but leave the oil in the pan; add the greens and stir-fry for 30 seconds, add the sherry-mustard mixture, and continue to stir-fry until the greens are wilted and slightly softened. Add water if necessary.

Divide the pork and the greens between 4 plates. Sprinkle with fleur de sel.

COOKING STEAK

Allow about ½ lb (227 g) per person, or a little less for flank steak and tenderloin. Take the steaks out of the fridge at least an hour before cooking and allow them to come to room temperature.

Cook steaks on a hot grill; give them a little longer (about 60 percent of the total time) on the first side than the second. Grill temperature varies widely from one barbecue to another, but 10 minutes per 1 inch (2½ cm) of thickness is a good starting point for a medium-rare steak. The actual time required may be different, ranging from 8 minutes per 1 inch (2½ cm) for rare to 12 minutes for medium or 15 minutes for well done.

Learning to judge a steak by feel while it is cooking is a useful skill. Press with your thumb or finger on the thickest part of the meat—with experience you will learn to associate the feel with how the steak looks when eventually cut.

A steak that's 1 inch (2½ cm) or more thick and served sliced (rather than as a whole steak) will usually be juicier than a thinner steak.

Let the steaks rest at room temperature—not in the oven—for 5 to 10 minutes after they come off the grill. This allows time for the juices displaced by the heat of cooking to permeate the meat, and it makes a big difference to the texture. A longer resting period is better, provided the meat stays warm, and serving on hot plates is always a good idea..

Steak *with* Red Wine *and* Peppercorn Sauce

SERVES 4
• • • • • • • • • •

1 cup (250 mL) red wine

2 cups (480 mL) stock (beef or chicken)

2 Tbsp (30 mL) peppercorns (pink and green)

2 cups (480 mL) whipping cream

Salt

2 lb (900 g) grilling steak (see Cooking Steak, page 143)

1 recipe Potato Pancake (page 161)
Ground black pepper

Ever since the children were teenagers we have sold cheese together at the Salt Spring Saturday market. Over the years, I have had the pleasure of their company and they have learned practical math skills. It is inspiring to work alongside the other vendors, watching their self-reliance, optimistic view of the world, and their ability to navigate the slings and arrows of small business life. The market could not exist without our customers who have made a conscious decision to buy at the market, willingly paying a bit more to support the community. As well as being the most important attraction for visitors to the island, the market provides some of the glue that holds Salt Spring together.

During the season, Saturday night dinner seldom varies from steak with red wine peppercorn sauce and potato pancakes. The steaks are usually rib steaks (with the bone), rib-eyes (no bone), or strip loin, but sometimes top sirloin, and particularly the cap steaks, with a cover of fat on one side (which some butchers say is their favourite cut), and sometimes even flank steak. We don't buy tenderloins, partly because of price, but mostly because the red wine sauce would overpower their more delicate flavour.

Preheat the oven to 175°F (80°C).

Set a wide pan over medium heat, add the wine, and reduce to ⅓ cup (80 mL). Add the stock and reduce again, to about 1 cup (250 mL). Crush the peppercorns in a grinder or mortar and add to the wine mixture. Add half the cream and reduce again to 1 cup (250 mL); taste for salt, add the remaining cream, reduce the heat, and leave to simmer while the steaks are cooking.

Cook the steaks on a very hot barbecue or frying pan (see page 143 for timing). Remove from the heat, cover with foil, and keep warm, but not in the oven.

While the meat is resting, warm the plates in the preheated oven.

Add any steak juices to the sauce, and check for seasoning.

When the steaks have rested for at least 5 minutes, transfer to a cutting board and carve in slices about ¼ inch (6 mm) thick.

Cut the pancake into quarters, arrange 1 on each plate, pour some sauce onto the plate and arrange the steak slices on top of the sauce. Serve with a leafy green vegetable like spinach or chard.

VEGETABLES *and* POTATOES

....

I am far from vegetarian, but when I sit down to dinner, the vegetables are what I go for first. They may not be the stars of the show, but they provide the balance for everything else, making harmony of the whole.

Eggplant *in* Spicy Tomato Sauce

....

Excellent with grilled meat.

....

2 medium eggplants

5 Tbsp (75 mL) olive oil, divided

½ tsp (2 mL) chili flakes

1 tsp (5 mL) turmeric

1 tsp (5 mL) finely chopped garlic

½ cup (125 mL) finely chopped onion

One 28-oz (794 g) tin diced tomatoes

1 tsp (5 mL) salt

Fresh ground black pepper

Preheat the oven to 375°F (190°C).

Cut the eggplants into 2-inch (5 cm) thick rounds; lay each round on one of its flat ends and cut into wedges, as if it was a cake—4, 6, or 8 pieces, depending on the size of the eggplant.

Toss the wedges with about 3 Tbsp (45 mL) olive oil in a large bowl, until the oil has been absorbed.

Arrange the wedges in a single layer on a large baking sheet; bake in the preheated oven for 5 minutes, or until medium brown on the underside. Take the pan out of the oven and turn the wedges over with kitchen tongs; return to the oven and cook the other side, about 4 minutes. Remove from the oven and set aside.

In a medium saucepan over medium heat, combine the remaining 2 Tbsp (30 mL) olive oil with the chili flakes and turmeric. Stir and cook for 1 minute; add the finely chopped garlic and onion, and continue cooking until soft and translucent.

Add the canned tomatoes and salt, bring to a boil, cover the pan, and cook over very low heat for 30 minutes. Add the fresh ground pepper, and more salt if needed. Stir the eggplant wedges into the tomato sauce and heat through.

It is good hot or at room temperature.

Green Beans *with* Garlic *and* Tomatoes

One of my early cooking heroes was Madeleine Kamman, a French woman of strong opinions who was not shy about expressing them. She maintained that green beans should be fully cooked to avoid what she disdained as the grassy quality favoured by English cooks. Why the English should have been singled out for disapproval I am not sure (except that she was French), but on the question of green beans, she got it right.

Bring a large pan of water to a boil, salt it, add the beans, bring it back to a boil, and cook until almost tender, about 6 minutes.

Drain and refresh under cold water; set aside to drain completely.

Sauté the garlic and butter in a saucepan over medium heat until pale gold. Add the tomatoes and tomato concentrate and cook until soft. Stir in the beans and cook until heated through and nicely coated with the tomatoes.

Serve with grilled or roasted meat.

SERVES 4
....

Salt

1 lb (454 g) fine green beans, stem ends trimmed

1 tsp (5 mL) garlic, finely chopped

2 Tbsp (30 mL) butter

1 cup (250 mL) coarsely chopped tomatoes (fresh or canned)

1 Tbsp (15 mL) tomato concentrate (from a tube)

Belgian Endive *with* Bacon *and* Cream

··

This exceptional combination of endives, bacon, and cream makes a wonderful accompaniment to a meat or chicken dish that has no sauce of its own. It is also excellent by itself.

··

Set a large saucepan over medium heat, add the butter and bacon, and cook, stirring occasionally, until the bacon is almost crispy. Scoop out the bacon and set it aside in a small bowl.

Put as many endives as will fit in a layer into the same pan, reduce the heat to medium low, cover the pan, and braise them in the remaining fat. Cook for 10 minutes, then turn and braise on the other side. Take them out and braise the remaining endives, adding more butter if needed.

Layer all the endives in the pan, turn the heat to very low, cover with the lid, and braise for at least an hour or up to an hour and a half (or bake in a 275°F [135°C] oven for the same amount of time). After 30 minutes, switch the endives on the top layer to the bottom and vice versa, adding a little water if needed to prevent them burning. They are ready when a fork pierces them easily. Remove the endives from the pan and into a bowl.

Put the cream and bacon pieces into the pan and bring to a boil, stirring to incorporate any bits on the bottom. Taste for seasoning and adjust it, then return the endives to the pan, cover it, and cook over low heat for 5 or 10 minutes.

SERVES 6
············

1 Tbsp (15 mL) butter

½ lb (227 g) smoked side bacon, cut into thick matchsticks

10 Belgian endives

1½ cups (360 mL) whipping cream

Braised Leeks

SERVES 4

••••••••••

4 medium leeks

2 Tbsp (30 mL) butter

½ cup (125 mL) whipping cream

Pinch nutmeg

Salt (optional)

Simple and perhaps already one of your standbys (as it is one of mine). The final step of reducing the cream sauce until it is thick enough to coat the leeks greatly improves the dish.

Trim the tops and outer layer from the leeks and cut into 1-inch (2½ cm) rounds.

Melt the butter in a medium saucepan, add the leeks, turn the heat to low, cover the pan, and braise for 10 to 15 minutes, until very lightly browned.

Pour in the whipping cream and add a pinch of nutmeg. Cook for 5 minutes over low heat, covered, then remove the lid, turn up the heat, and reduce the cream until it is thick enough to coat the leeks. Add salt if needed.

Braised Fennel

SERVES 4

••••••••••

2 large fennel bulbs

1 Tbsp (15 mL) butter

1 Tbsp (15 mL) olive oil

¼ cup (60 mL) chicken stock or
water

½ tsp (2 mL) salt

¼ cup (60 mL) ouzo or
anisette

Braising softens the crunch of raw fennel, takes the edge off the anise taste, and creates a quite unexpectedly rich accompaniment for grilled meat or chicken.

Trim the fennel stalks to about 1 inch (2½ cm) above the bulb. Cut the fennel vertically toward the root into slices about ½ inch (13 mm) thick, with each slice held together at the root end.

In a large frying pan or a wide saucepan with a lid, melt the butter in the olive oil over medium heat; add the sliced fennel in a single layer, or in 2 batches if necessary. Cover the pan, reduce the heat to medium low, and cook for 7 or 8 minutes, until lightly browned; turn and brown the other side.

Return all the slices to the pan, in 2 layers if necessary, and add the chicken stock (or water), salt, and ouzo (or anisette). Cover the pan tightly, reduce the heat to low, and braise for 20 minutes. Check for tenderness by piercing with a fork—there should be very little resistance—and serve immediately.

Swiss Chard *with* Prosciutto and Parmesan

2 bunches Swiss chard

¼ cup (60 mL) finely diced prosciutto

1 tsp (5 mL) finely chopped garlic

2 Tbsp (30 mL) olive oil

¼ tsp (1 mL) fresh ground black pepper

½ cup (125 mL) grated Parmesan cheese

A Mediterranean treatment of chard, a good partner to grilled meat.

Trim the stems from the leaves of the chard by cutting along the sides of the stem with a small sharp knife. Chop the stems into ¼-inch (6 mm) slices on the diagonal, and coarsely chop the leaves.

Sauté the prosciutto and garlic in the olive oil in a large frying pan until the garlic turns pale gold; add the chard stems and cook until they start to wilt.

Turn the heat up to high and add the chopped leaves; sauté, stirring constantly, until completely wilted. Sprinkle with pepper and grated Parmesan.

Grilled Radicchio

2 heads radicchio

2 Tbsp (30 mL) olive oil

½ tsp (2 mL) salt

½ tsp (2 mL) fresh ground black pepper

2 Tbsp (30 mL) full flavoured olive oil for finishing

Radicchio is a great addition to a salad, and excellent on the grill. Cooking does not destroy its distinctive bitter edge, while the grill imparts a pleasantly smoky flavour. Choose medium radicchio that are heavy for their size, and serve drizzled with a peppery olive oil.

Cut the radicchio in half lengthwise, and the halves into 2 or 3 wedges. Toss them in a bowl with olive oil, salt, and pepper.

Heat the barbecue grill to medium. Arrange the radicchio wedges on the grill, one flat side down. Cook for 2 or 3 minutes, flip to the other flat side, and cook 2 or 3 minutes longer, until the radicchio is tender, wilted, and a little charred around the edges.

Remove from the grill and serve warm with a finishing olive oil. They are excellent with steak.

Barbecued Ratatouille

For this ratatouille, the vegetables are grilled separately and combined just before serving. The textures are firmer than when the vegetables are cooked together, and the flavours more distinct. If you can find tomatoes that are red, ripe, and full of flavour, chop them and stir in at the end without any precooking.

Perforated steel barbecue trays or baskets make simple work of grilling vegetables—and are great for barbecuing fish.

Cut the eggplants into 1½-inch (4 cm) thick rounds; lay each piece on one of its flat ends and cut it into wedges, as if it was a pizza—4, 6, or 8 wedges, depending on the diameter of the eggplant. Sprinkle with salt and set aside to drain in a colander.

Cut the zucchini like the eggplant, into slightly smaller wedges; set aside in a bowl and sprinkle with salt. Cut the onions into 1-inch (2½ cm) chunks; set aside in a bowl. Cut the peppers in half, trim off the membranes, and remove the seeds. Cut the flesh into 1-inch (2½ cm) squares and add to the onions. Cut the tomatoes into ½-inch (13 mm) chunks (canned tomatoes in quarters), put them in a sieve set over a bowl, and leave to drain.

Turn on the barbecue and set a large perforated pan on the grill.

In a medium bowl, toss the onions and peppers in 1 Tbsp (15 mL) olive oil and transfer to the grill pan (set the bowl aside to toss the other vegetables). Grill for 7 to 10 minutes, stirring occasionally to brown them evenly. Remove from the grill while on the firm side—they will soften as they cool—and set aside in a clean bowl.

Dry the eggplant with paper towels, toss in olive oil, and grill until lightly browned. Repeat with the zucchini, adding both to the onions when still slightly underdone.

Place a large saucepan on low heat. Add 2 Tbsp (30 mL) of olive oil and the finely chopped garlic, and cook until pale gold. Add the grilled vegetables to the pan, turn up the heat to medium, and heat them through, stirring gently.

Fold in the diced tomatoes, taste for seasoning, and adjust as needed.

Remove the pan from the heat and set aside to cool.

Serve at room temperature, or even cold from the fridge, with grated Parmesan cheese and extra olive oil.

SERVES 6

2 medium eggplants

3 small zucchini

Salt

2 medium onions

3 sweet red peppers

Olive oil

1 lb (454 g) ripe tomatoes (or 1 large can of plum tomatoes)

1 large clove garlic, finely chopped

Parmesan cheese, grated, for serving

Spinach *with* Balsamic Vinegar

··

The sweet balsamic balances the earthiness of the spinach; it's good with salmon.

··

SERVES 2
············

1 bunch spinach

½ tsp (2 mL) salt

¼ cup (60 mL) butter

1 Tbsp (15 mL) finely chopped
shallots

1 tsp (5 mL) finely chopped garlic

2 Tbsp (30 mL) chopped sundried
tomatoes

2 Tbsp (30 mL) balsamic vinegar

½ tsp (2 mL) salt

¼ tsp (1 mL) fresh ground black
pepper

Cut the stems from the spinach and rinse the leaves.

Pour 1 inch (2½ cm) of water into a saucepan, bring it to a boil and salt it. Add the spinach leaves, stirring and cooking until they are wilted. Drain, and when it is cool enough to handle, squeeze out most of the water with your hands. Set aside.

Melt the butter in a saucepan over medium heat, add the finely chopped shallot and garlic, and sauté until soft but not brown. Add the drained spinach to the pan and stir in the sundried tomatoes; cook until heated through.

Finish with the balsamic vinegar, salt, and fresh ground pepper.

DANISH BOILED POTATOES

Seriously? A recipe for boiled potatoes? Yes, indeed, and it comes from the Danes, people who really care about their potatoes. I can't swear they all cook them this way, but I know a few who do, and it actually makes a difference. The result is a potato that is evenly cooked throughout and is less likely to split the skin or crumble when cut. (For how to boil an egg, see page 21; still working on how to boil water).

Choose potatoes of much the same size, or cut them into equal chunks. The timing here is for potatoes about 1½ inches (4 cm) in diameter.

Fill a saucepan with cold water and add the potatoes. Add 1 tsp (5 mL) salt and bring to a boil over medium-high heat. Turn the heat down to a gentle boil and cook, uncovered, for 12 minutes (set a timer). Remove the pan from the heat, cover with a lid, and set the timer for another 12 minutes. The potatoes should be firm, but tender enough to be pierced with a fork. Exact timing depends on the potatoes; if not quite done, re-cover with the lid and leave another 5 minutes. Drain and serve.

Oven Fries

These are not real French fries, but they are much better than the frozen ones, and excellent with grilled meat. Use large potatoes, of any variety

SERVES 4

4 large or 6 medium potatoes

1 tsp (5 mL) salt

2 Tbsp (30 mL) duck or goose fat (or vegetable oil)

Turn on the oven to 400°F (200°C).

Peel the potatoes, cut them in half lengthwise, then cut each half into 3 or 4 wedges, again lengthwise. Place them in a saucepan of cold water, add the salt, and set over high heat. As soon as they come to a boil, drain them, and spread on a baking sheet to cool.

Toss the potatoes with the fat or oil in a large bowl until well coated. Turn them out onto the baking sheet and arrange in a single layer; bake in the pre-heated oven for 15 minutes, turn them over (with tongs), and bake another 15 minutes until brown and crisp.

Serve immediately, or transfer to a serving dish lined with paper towels, sprinkle with salt, and keep warm in the turned-off oven.

Warm New Potato Salad

Excellent with cold meat or fish—but not straight from the fridge, as flavours are more pronounced at room temperature. The potato salad is also best warm.

SERVES 6

2 lb (900 g) small new potatoes

1½ tsp (7 mL) salt, divided

¼ cup (60 mL) red wine vinegar

1 Tbsp (15 mL) finely chopped fresh tarragon

¼ cup (60 mL) finely chopped shallots

4 egg yolks

¾ cup (180 mL) crème fraîche

Put the potatoes in a saucepan, cover with cold water, add 1 tsp (5 mL) salt, and bring to a boil. Boil for 12 minutes (set a timer), remove the pan from the heat, cover it, and let it sit for a further 12 minutes. Test for doneness—a fork should pierce the potatoes, but not too easily. Cover and leave them to sit longer, if necessary.

Whisk together the vinegar, tarragon, chopped shallots, and ½ tsp (2 mL) salt in a large bowl to combine. When the potatoes are ready, drain them well and, when cool enough to handle, cut them in half and toss with the dressing until well coated.

Combine the egg yolks and crème fraîche in a small saucepan; set it over low heat and cook, stirring constantly, until slightly thickened. Pour over the potatoes and mix thoroughly. Serve warm.

Sweet Potato *and* Gorgonzola Purée

···

This is the humble sweet potato elevated to aristocracy. It makes a wonderful accompaniment to chicken and turkey. Use the orange-fleshed sweet potatoes, usually called yams in grocery stores (even though they really aren't—yams are a different species, rarely available in North America).

···

Peel and slice (or cube) the sweet potatoes; place them in a saucepan, cover with cold water, bring to a boil, and cook over medium heat for 15 to 20 minutes until tender. Drain in a colander and return to the pan. Mash them to a smooth purée with a potato masher or immersion blender; add the crème fraîche, butter, salt, and pepper, and mix thoroughly.

Cut the blue cheese into small pieces and stir it in until almost melted; add the finely chopped sage and stir again. Serve hot.

SERVES 6 TO 8
·················

3 large orange sweet potatoes

¼ cup (60 mL) crème fraîche

1 Tbsp (15 mL) butter

½ tsp (2 mL) salt

¼ tsp (1 mL) fresh ground black pepper

4 oz (113 g) Gorgonzola or other blue cheese

1 Tbsp (15 mL) finely chopped sage

Perfect Roast Potatoes

···

These are crisp, slightly crunchy, salty, and tender on the inside. They need a hot oven, and can be a bit of a challenge to cook alongside roast beef using the slow method (i.e., the preferred method, see Prime Rib of Beef [page 132]). This is where you need to practise serial cooking: the meat first and then the potatoes. It works because the roast will stay warm covered with foil while the potatoes are in the oven—and provided, as always, that the dinner plates are warm.

···

Preheat the oven to 450°F (230°C).

Peel the potatoes and cut them into 1½-inch (4 cm) chunks. Put them in a pan of cold water on medium-high heat, add the salt, and bring to a boil. Drain them immediately and spread on a baking sheet to cool quickly and evenly.

When cool enough to handle, rough up the surface with a fork, making ridges to create a crispy exterior as they cook. Toss them with the oil in a large bowl and arrange on the baking sheet in 1 layer, with a little space between each potato.

Transfer to the middle of the preheated oven and bake for 15 minutes. Remove the potatoes from the oven and turn them over with tongs. Bake another 15 minutes (longer if necessary) until crisp and brown.

Transfer to a serving dish lined with paper towels, sprinkle with salt, and keep warm in the turned-off oven.

SERVES 4
···········

2 lb (900 g) potatoes

2 tsp (10 mL) salt

3 Tbsp (45 mL) olive oil (or other vegetable oil)

Potato Pancake

••

This is a large frying pan-size pancake served in wedges, like a cake, that's crispy on the outside and soft on the inside. It goes well with meat or chicken that has a sauce of its own, or simply with grilled meat if your vegetable is on the saucy side, like the Belgian Endive with Bacon and Cream (page 151).

Baking potatoes are a good choice here; they tend to have less moisture than the waxy varieties.

••

SERVES 4
•••••••••••

3 large baking potatoes

2 Tbsp (30 mL) olive oil

2 Tbsp (30 mL) butter

1 tsp (5 mL) salt

Peel the potatoes if necessary, which it will be if you use baking potatoes; thin-skinned potatoes are fine as they are. Put them in a bowl of cold water.

In 2 batches (to stop browning when exposed to air) dry and coarsely grate the potatoes, using a hand grater or a food processor. Wrap them in a clean dishcloth and squeeze out any excess moisture, but don't rinse them in water as it will remove the potato starch that holds the pancake together.

Set a 10- or 11-inch (25 or 27 cm) frying pan over a medium-low heat and add half of the oil and butter. When it foams, add a batch of grated and squeezed potatoes. Spread them evenly and sprinkle with salt. Grate the second batch, squeeze dry, and add them to the pan. Spread out and smooth the top to form 1 pancake.

Let the potatoes cook for 10 minutes; lift the edge with a spatula and check for browning. The bottom should be a mottled medium-brown and a little crispy; give it a little longer if necessary.

To flip the pancake, slide a spatula or palette knife underneath to make sure it is not stuck to the pan, and place a large lid or plate over the pancake. Turn both the pan and the lid/plate over together so that the pancake is now resting on the lid, cooked side up. Set the empty frying pan back on the heat and add the rest of the oil and butter. When it foams, slide the pancake back into the pan and cook another 10 to 15 minutes, until browned and crispy on both sides.

These pancakes are best straight from the pan, but can be kept warm in a 225°F (110°C) oven, placed directly on the rack (the underside becomes soggy on a baking sheet).

Scalloped Potatoes

One of the great dishes of the potato world and perfect with grilled or roast meat, scalloped potatoes are very rich, very comforting, and completely delicious. This recipe is easy and reliable, and you can use any type of potato you like.

SERVES 6 IN A 9 × 6 INCH (23 × 15 CM) BAKING DISH

1 cup (250 mL) whipping cream

¼ cup (60 mL) butter

¼ tsp (1 mL) freshly grated nutmeg

1 tsp (5 mL) salt

1 tsp (5 mL) fresh ground black pepper

8 large potatoes

Preheat the oven to 350°F (180°C)

Rinse out a large saucepan with water (do not dry it) and pour in the cream; add the butter, nutmeg, salt, and pepper. Set the pan on medium-low and heat just until the butter melts; set aside while you prepare the potatoes.

It is not essential to peel the potatoes if the skins are clean and thin, but I think the dish looks better if they are, and it's not much more work—so peel them and put in a bowl of cold water.

Using a mandolin or a food processor fitted with the slicing blade, cut the potatoes into slices ³⁄₁₆ of an inch (5 mm) thick. A sharp knife will work, but cutting consistent slices this thin can be a bit of a challenge.

Put the potato slices in a large bowl, whisk the warm cream and butter together and pour over the potatoes. Mix until all the slices are separated and coated with cream. Layer the potato slices evenly in the dish until they are all used up or the dish is three-quarters full. Pour in the remaining cream—it should be almost up to the top of the potatoes; hold some back or add more as needed

Put the dish on a baking sheet to catch any overflow during cooking. Transfer to the centre of the preheated oven and bake for 1 hour, until a fork easily pierces the potatoes and the top is lightly browned. If it is browning too quickly, turn the heat down and cover the dish loosely with foil.

Let the potatoes sit in a warm place (such as the turned-off oven) for 15 minutes to absorb the cream before cutting into portions. Potatoes may be cooled completely and reheated later in a 275°F (135°C) oven for 30 to 45 minutes (depending on the size of the dish).

SERVES 6

••••••••••

1¼ cups (300 mL) milk

2 whole eggs

1 egg yolk

1 cup (250 mL) all-purpose flour

½ tsp (2 mL) salt

¼ cup (60 mL) duck fat or
other oil

Yorkshire Pudding

••

For many of us, Yorkshire pudding is the best thing about roast beef. We all take it for granted that it's the eggs, milk, and flour that give Yorkshire pudding its lovely puffy texture. But did you ever wonder where the flavour comes from? Well, nor did I, until Helen suggested we bake it in some leftover duck fat. The difference in taste was remarkable, and the light bulb went on: the flavour of Yorkshire pudding comes from the fat it's cooked in. Of course you don't need to use duck fat as the recipe suggests—it will puff just as well with any oil or fat— but it does give it a great flavour, as would fat skimmed from the drippings of the roast beef.

The batter can be baked in muffin cups for individual Yorkshires, or in a large pan, for a pudding with a variety of textures: puffed up and crispy around the edges, softer and heavier in the middle. You can make it in the pan in which the meat was cooked, but I think it's better to keep that for making the gravy— which, of course, is the other best part about roast beef (see gravy recipe with the Prime Rib of Beef, page 133).

Mix the pudding ingredients an hour or more before baking and let the batter rest at room temperature to relax the glutens. If made further ahead and stored in the fridge, take it out an hour before baking—the warmer it is when it goes in the oven, the better.

••

Whisk the milk, eggs, and yolk in a large bowl; add the flour and salt and whisk again, until completely smooth. Cover with plastic wrap and set aside for an hour or more at room temperature—it should be warm when it goes in the oven. (Put it in the fridge if more than 2 hours, and give it time to warm to room temperature before baking.)

Preheat the oven to 425°F (220°C).

Pour ½ tsp (2 mL) fat into each muffin cup for 12 individual puddings, or all of it into a large baking pan, about 14 × 9 inches (35 × 22 cm). Put the pan(s) in the hot oven for 5 minutes; take them out and pour in the batter, return to the oven, and bake, without opening the door, for 15 minutes.

Turn the oven down to 350°F (180°C) and cook another 5 to 10 minutes for the small ones, or 20 to 30 minutes for a large pan.

The Yorkshire puddings will stay warm in the turned-off oven for quite a while.

Toad *in the* Hole

....

For most of us, Toad in the Hole belongs to the mythology of childhood—a delicious and intensely satisfying food that grown-ups talked nostalgically about, but which always existed somewhere just over the horizon, out of reach, and never something we actually had for supper. This is a pity because it really is as good as it sounds, and dead easy to make.

....

Make the Yorkshire pudding batter following the recipe and set aside to rest.

Preheat the oven to 425°F (220°C).

When the batter has rested, pour the fat into a baking dish about 10 × 7 inches (25 × 18 cm), add the sausages, and set in the centre of the preheated oven. Bake for 7 minutes.

Stir the batter gently. Remove the dish from the oven, pour in the batter, and return to the oven. Bake for 15 minutes, then reduce the heat to 350°F (180°C) and bake for another 15 minutes, until puffed and golden.

This would be good with the Gravy on page 133.

SERVES 4

....

1 recipe Yorkshire Pudding (page 164)

6 large sausages (or 12 small)

EASY BAKING

....

These are the baked goods that beckon to us from the display cases of every coffee shop in the country. They are popular not just with customers, but with café owners too, as they are easy to make and the ingredients are readily available and inexpensive—all good reasons to make them yourself at home.

Blueberry Muffins

MAKES ABOUT 15 MUFFINS
....

2 cups (480 mL) all-purpose flour +
extra for dusting the muffin tin

¾ cup (180 mL) granulated sugar

1½ tsp (7 mL) baking powder

½ tsp (2 mL) salt

2 eggs

⅔ cup (160 mL) milk

1 tsp (5 mL) vanilla extract

½ cup (125 mL) melted butter

2 to 3 cups (500 to 720 mL)
blueberries (fresh or frozen)

This was one of the two most popular variety of muffins at our shop in Toronto (the other was Apple Pie, page 169). Each morning, the first one in would make the muffins, and in the days before we were able to afford a real pastry chef, that was often me. We had placed the baking oven beside the front door, hoping that carrying the fresh baking through the store would create good aromas and a feeling of freshness and bustle; in fact, all it did was make a longer walk for the baker.

Preheat the oven to 350°F (180°C).

Grease the muffin tin and dust with flour, or line with paper cups.

Whisk together 2 cups (480 mL) flour with the sugar, baking powder, and salt; set aside.

Warm the milk (cold milk will solidify the butter) and, in a large bowl, combine the eggs, milk, vanilla, and melted butter; whisk together.

Pour all the dry ingredients into the wet and gently mix until combined. Fold in the blueberries, working carefully with frozen berries so they do not bleed and turn the batter purple. Scoop the batter into the muffin cups.

Bake in the preheated oven for 25 minutes, until the top springs back when pressed.

Remove from the oven and cool briefly before taking out of the tin.

Apple Pie Muffins

....

Muffins are among the simplest of baked goods. All it takes is two bowls, one for the wet ingredients (milk, eggs, sour cream, etc.), the other for the dry (flour, sugar, baking powder, etc.). Whisk up the ingredients in each bowl, add the dry to the wet, add some fruit, scoop into a muffin tin, and bake.

This was our all-time most popular muffin, and it is easy to taste why. The streusel topping makes a more interesting muffin with little extra work.

....

Preheat the oven to 325°F (160°C).

Prepare the streusel topping by mixing together ½ cup (125 mL) brown sugar, 6 Tbsp (90 mL) flour, the melted butter, and the cinnamon in a small bowl. Set aside.

In a large bowl, mix together the egg, vegetable oil, vanilla, the remaining 1½ cups (360 mL) brown sugar, and the buttermilk. Set aside.

In a second bowl, mix together the remaining 2½ cups (600 mL) flour with the baking soda and salt. Pour these dry ingredients into the wet ingredients and gently mix; fold in the diced apple.

Scoop the batter into the muffins cups, divide the streusel topping between them, and bake in the preheated oven for 30 minutes, until the tops spring back when pressed.

Remove from the oven and cool slightly before turning out.

MAKES ABOUT 15 MUFFINS
....

2 cups (480 mL) brown sugar, divided

2½ cups + 6 Tbsp (690 mL) all-purpose flour, divided

¼ cup (60 mL) melted butter

1 tsp (5 mL) ground cinnamon

1 large egg

⅔ cup (160 mL) vegetable oil

1 tsp (5 mL) vanilla extract

1 cup (250 mL) buttermilk (or milk mixed with 2 Tbsp [30 mL] plain yogurt, to make 1 cup [250 mL] total)

1 tsp (5 mL) baking soda

½ tsp (2 mL) salt

2 apples, peeled, cored, and diced into ½-inch (13 mm) chunks (about 2 cups [480 mL] total)

Coffee Cake Muffins

....

These look like a muffin, but the method is more like a cake. No denying they taste good, though.

....

MAKES 16 MUFFINS
••••••••••••••••••••

¾ cup (180 mL) brown sugar

½ cup (125 mL) finely chopped dried apricots

½ cup (125 mL) chopped walnuts

⅓ cup (80 mL) semi-sweet chocolate chips

2 Tbsp (30 mL) cocoa powder

1 Tbsp (15 mL) instant coffee powder

2 tsp (10 mL) ground cinnamon

1 cup (250 mL) unsalted butter

2 cups (480 mL) granulated sugar

4 eggs

2 tsp (10 mL) vanilla extract

1 cup (250 mL) all-purpose flour

2 cups (480 mL) cake and pastry flour (or all-purpose)

1 tsp (5 mL) baking soda

2 tsp (10 mL) baking powder

½ tsp (2 mL) salt

2 cups (480 mL) sour cream

Preheat the oven to 350°F (180°C).

Grease 16 muffin cups, or line with paper.

To make the filling, mix together the brown sugar, chopped apricots, walnuts, chocolate chips, cocoa powder, coffee powder, and cinnamon in a small bowl; set aside.

Cream together the butter and sugar in the bowl of a stand mixer (or by hand in a medium bowl) until light and fluffy. Add the eggs one at a time, mixing well between each, then add the vanilla extract.

In a separate bowl, whisk together the 2 flours, baking soda, baking powder, and salt.

With the mixer on its lowest speed (or by hand), add half the flour to the creamed butter mixture and gently incorporate. Fold in half of the sour cream, then the rest of the flour, followed by the rest of the sour cream. Mix gently until there are just a few pockets of unincorporated flour.

Scoop half of the mixture into the muffin cups, layer with half the filling, then top with another layer of the muffin mix and the remainder of the filling.

Bake in the preheated oven for 20 to 30 minutes, until the muffins are golden brown and spring back to the touch.

Christmas Coffee Cake

....

Heidi was the buyer for our Food Shops in Toronto, and a great friend. She was the one who created the atmosphere of overwhelming abundance in the stores. Each Christmas, at our busiest season, she would find the time to make this coffee cake for my family.

....

Preheat the oven to 350°F (180°C).

Lightly butter and flour an 8½-inch (22 cm) spring-form pan.

Make the topping by mixing together the cinnamon, brown sugar, and coffee powder in a small bowl. Set aside.

Make the filling by mixing together the walnuts, cranberries, and coconut in a small bowl. Set aside.

In a medium bowl, whisk together the 2 flours, the baking powder, and baking soda until well blended. Set aside.

Cream ½ cup (125 mL) butter and the sugar together in the work bowl of an electric mixer (or by hand), until light and fluffy. Add the eggs one at a time, mixing well after each addition. Beat in the vanilla extract.

Doing the final mixing by hand gives the cake a finer crumb: gently fold the flour mixture into the batter, then carefully blend in the sour cream until there are almost no pockets of unincorporated flour.

Spoon half the batter into the prepared spring-form pan. Sprinkle with half the topping (the brown sugar and cinnamon mix), followed by all of the cranberry-and-walnut filling. Scoop in the remaining batter and finish with the last of the topping.

Bake in the preheated oven for 40 to 45 minutes, until a cake tester comes out clean. Cool in the spring-form pan and serve when still slightly warm from the oven.

SERVES 8 TO 10
....

1½ tsp (7 mL) ground cinnamon

¾ cup (180 mL) light brown sugar

2½ Tbsp (37 mL) instant coffee powder

½ cup (125 mL) walnut pieces

1 cup (250 mL) fresh cranberries

6 Tbsp (90 mL) unsweetened coconut

1 cup (250 mL) cake and pastry flour

½ cup (125 mL) all-purpose flour + extra for dusting the pan

1½ tsp (7 mL) baking powder

1 tsp (5 mL) baking soda

½ cup (125 mL) unsalted butter + extra for greasing the pan

1 cup (250 mL) granulated sugar

2 eggs

½ tsp (2 mL) vanilla extract

1 cup (250 mL) sour cream

Blueberry Lemon Loaf

· ·

A quick and easy loaf.

· ·

MAKES 8 SLICES

· · · · · · · · · · · · · · · · ·

½ cup + 2 Tbsp (155 mL) granulated sugar, divided

2 Tbsp (30 mL) light brown sugar

1¼ cups (300 mL) all-purpose flour, divided

2 Tbsp (30 mL) cold unsalted butter

1 tsp (5 mL) baking powder

¼ tsp (1 mL) salt

¼ cup (60 mL) unsalted butter, softened + extra for greasing the pan

1 egg

1 tsp (5 mL) vanilla extract

⅓ cup (80 mL) milk

1 Tbsp (15 mL) grated lemon zest

¼ cup (60 mL) blueberries, fresh or frozen

Preheat the oven to 350°F (180°C).

Lightly butter and flour a small loaf pan, about 6 × 3 inches (15 × 8 cm) on the base, and 2 inches (5 cm) deep.

In a medium bowl, make the streusel topping by whisking together the 2 Tbsp (30 mL) granulated sugar, the brown sugar, and ¼ cup (60 mL) flour. Using the coarse side of a box grater, grate the frozen butter into the bowl and lightly stir together. Set the topping aside.

In a large bowl, whisk together the remaining 1 cup (250 mL) flour, baking powder, and salt, and set aside.

In the bowl of a stand mixer (or by hand), cream together the softened butter and remaining ½ cup (125 mL) sugar until light and fluffy; add the egg and vanilla and mix until completely incorporated.

Add half the milk and half the flour mixture and mix well; mix in the rest of the milk and flour.

Finally, fold in the grated lemon zest and the ¼ cup (60 mL) of blueberries.

Pour the batter into the prepared pan and top with the ½ cup (125 mL) of blueberries and the streusel topping.

Bake in the preheated oven for 40 to 50 minutes, until the top is pale golden and a toothpick comes out clean.

Carrot Cake

· ·

An easy and delicious cake.

· ·

Preheat the oven to 325°F (160°C).

Lightly butter and flour an 8½-inch (22 cm) spring-form pan.

Wash and scrub the carrots and cut into 2-inch (5 cm) chunks. With the motor running, drop the carrots down the feed tube of a food processor and process until finely chopped. Scrape them into a bowl and set aside.

In the same food processor bowl, combine the sugar, vegetable oil, eggs, and vanilla, and process for 30 seconds. Add the carrots and the flour, baking soda, cinnamon, and pineapple, and process for another 30 seconds until completely blended.

Scrape the batter into the prepared spring-form pan and bake in the centre of the preheated oven for 50 to 60 minutes. When a tester comes out clean, remove the cake from the oven and cool it completely.

To make the icing, beat the soft butter in a stand mixer until light and fluffy. Gradually add the icing sugar and mix until incorporated; add the cream cheese or fresh goat cheese and beat until smooth.

Once the cake is cool, spread the icing over the top and sides. Press the ground pecans into the sides, and arrange the halves on top.

SERVES 8 TO 10
· · · · · · · · · · · · · · · · ·

2 cups (480 mL) carrots

2 cups (480 mL) granulated sugar

1½ cups (360 mL) mild vegetable oil

3 eggs

1 tsp (5 mL) vanilla extract

2 cups (480 mL) all-purpose flour + extra for dusting the pan

2 tsp (10 mL) baking soda

2 tsp (10 mL) ground cinnamon

½ cup (125 mL) crushed pineapple (canned is fine, of course)

1 lb (454 g) unsalted butter, softened to room temperature + extra for greasing the pan

1 cup + 2 Tbsp (280 mL) icing sugar

1 lb (454 g) cream cheese or fresh goat cheese

½ cup (125 mL) ground pecans

12 pecan halves

Chocolate Bundt Cake

....

An easy, dense cake with excellent flavour. Slightly under-baking it gives the best result.

....

3 cups (720 mL) all-purpose flour +
extra for dusting the pan

3 cups (720 mL) granulated sugar

1 cup (250 mL) unsweetened cocoa
powder

1 Tbsp (15 mL) baking powder

1 tsp (5 mL) salt

1½ cups (360 mL) milk

1 cup (250 mL) unsalted butter,
softened + extra for greasing the pan

1 Tbsp (15 mL) vanilla extract

3 eggs

¼ cup (60 mL) light cream (or half-
and-half milk and cream)

Preheat the oven to 325°F (160°C).

Thoroughly butter and flour a 10-inch (25 cm) tube or Bundt pan.

In the work bowl of a stand mixer, whisk together the flour, sugar, cocoa, baking powder, and salt.

Make a well in the centre of the flour mixture; pour in the milk, soft butter, and vanilla, and mix with the paddle attachment on medium speed for 5 minutes. Now add the eggs, one at a time, mixing well between each. Finally add the cream and beat until smooth.

Pour the batter into the prepared pan and bake in the preheated oven for up to 1½ hours. Check the cake after an hour, and then every 10 minutes; it is ready when a skewer comes out almost clean, with just a few crumbs sticking to it.

Chocolate Reversal Cookies

···

Chunks of white chocolate provide little pockets of sweetness in the dark chocolate batter. Better not to ask how any self-respecting chocolate manages to be white.

···

Preheat the oven to 375°F (190°C).

Butter and flour a cookie sheet, or line it with parchment paper (which works better).

In a medium bowl, whisk together the flour, baking soda, and cocoa powder; set aside.

With a stand mixer (or by hand), cream the butter until light and fluffy; add the egg and vanilla and mix until smooth. Stir in the cocoa-and-flour mixture by hand (it will fly everywhere if you do it by machine), then mix in the chunks of white chocolate.

Scoop up the batter with a tablespoon, using a second spoon to scrape the dough onto the baking sheet. Leave some space between the mounds and flatten them slightly with a fork or the heel of your hand.

Bake in the preheated oven for 12 to 14 minutes. The cookies are done when the edges are slightly firm to the touch and the centre is still quite soft. Remove from the oven and cool on the baking sheet for a couple of minutes before transferring to a rack to cool completely.

MAKES 16 COOKIES

·······················

1 cup (250 mL) all-purpose flour + extra for dusting the cookie sheet

1 tsp (5 mL) baking soda

½ cup (125 mL) unsweetened cocoa powder

¾ cup (180 mL) unsalted butter + extra for greasing the cookie sheet

1 egg

1 tsp (5 mL) vanilla extract

1½ cups (360 mL) white chocolate chunks (or chips)

Lemon Squares

···

2 cups (480 mL) all-purpose flour

⅔ cup (160 mL) powdered
(icing) sugar

1 cup (250 mL) cold unsalted butter,
cut into small pieces

6 eggs

3 cups (720 mL) granulated sugar

½ cup (125 mL) all-purpose flour

1 cup (250 mL) lemon juice

5 cups (1200 mL) shredded,
unsweetened coconut

This recipe, with its intense lemony flavour, was given to us by Sarah Band, a long-time friend from Toronto. We included it in the original Food Book, *but without the credit she deserved for her kind gesture. So here is that credit now, way past its due date, but with sincere gratitude.*

···

Combine the flour and icing sugar in the work bowl of a food processor fitted with the steel blade. Pulse once or twice to mix, then spread the butter pieces over the flour and process until the mixture resembles fine crumbs. Set aside to rest at room temperature for 30 minutes.

Preheat the oven to 375°F (190°C).

Working with your hands, press the dough into the bottom of a 12 × 18 inch (30 × 45 cm) cookie sheet. Chill it for 5 minutes, then bake in the centre of the preheated oven for 15 to 20 minutes, until pale golden brown on top. Set aside to cool.

Whisk the eggs in a large bowl until completely mixed, and keep on whisking while you add the sugar. When the sugar is dissolved, gently whisk in the flour and lemon juice. Finally, stir in the shredded coconut.

Give the lemon mixture a final stir to distribute the coconut evenly, and pour it onto the pre-baked base. Bake for another 25 to 30 minutes until very lightly browned around the edges and the centre is no longer wobbly. Remove from the oven and cool completely before cutting into bars.

Store in an airtight container or zip-lock bag.

Chocolate Chunk Cookies

....

To ensure these cookies are both tender and chewy, mix the batter as little as possible after adding the flour, and slightly under-bake them. Make the dough 6 hours or more before you plan to bake them to give the glutens time to relax. If you are using chocolate chips, the ones made by Ghirardelli are bigger than most and have a great flavour.

....

In a medium bowl, whisk together the flour, sugar, salt, and baking soda; set aside.

In a stand mixer (or by hand), cream the butter and brown sugar together, scraping down the sides of the bowl once or twice. When light and fluffy, turn the mixer to slow and add the eggs one at a time. When well beaten, add the flour mix all at once on the slowest speed, immediately followed by the chocolate chunks. Mix just enough to bring everything together.

Cover with plastic wrap and refrigerate for 6 hours or overnight. Unbaked dough will keep for at least 4 days in the fridge.

Preheat the oven to 350°F (180°C).

Lightly butter a baking sheet, or better still, line it with parchment paper.

Scoop out balls of dough about 2 oz (60 grams) each—the size of a small ice cream scoop—and place them about 3 inches (8 cm) apart from one another on the cookie sheet, leaving room to spread as they bake.

Bake in the preheated oven for 10 to 12 minutes until lightly browned around the edges and still slightly underdone in the centre. Transfer to a rack and leave to cool. Store in an airtight container.

MAKES 18 COOKIES

....

2 cups (480 mL) all-purpose flour

1 cup (250 mL) granulated sugar

¼ tsp (1 mL) salt

¼ tsp (1 mL) baking soda

1 cup (250 mL) unsalted butter, softened to room temperature + extra for greasing the pan

1 cup (250 mL) light brown sugar

2 large eggs

10 oz (283 g) semi-sweet chocolate, chopped into small chunks (or 1½ cups [360 mL] chocolate chips)

EVERYDAY DESSERTS

....

This may be a bit of an oxymoron since some people, God help them, don't eat dessert every day—a missed opportunity to be sure, but perhaps not altogether surprising given the barrage of warnings about fat, sugar, and white flour. Disappointing though, because dinner without dessert has no form; it's just a single course with a focus on nourishment. Including even the simplest dessert in a normal weekday dinner elevates the experience—and cooking, above all, is about how food can enhance experience.

What you will find here are recipes that don't take a lot of preparation time; most of them can be made while the rest of dinner is cooking. A couple—zabaglione and caramelized oranges—are more sophisticated and can hold their own in any company; they are included here because they are quick to make, and delicious to boot.

SERVES 6

••••••••••••

1 loaf raisin bread

¾ cup (180 mL) whipping cream

¾ cup (180 mL) milk

4 eggs

½ cup (125 mL) granulated sugar

½ cup (125 mL) icing sugar

½ cup (125 mL) raisins or sultanas

½ cup (125 mL) bourbon (or brandy)

2 tsp (10 mL) vanilla extract

½ tsp (2 mL) ground cinnamon

½ tsp (2 mL) ground ginger

¼ cup (60 mL) butter, in small
pieces + extra for greasing the
baking dish

1 recipe Custard or Crème Anglaise
(page 239)

½ cup (125 mL) bourbon

Bread Pudding *with* Bourbon Sauce

Raisin bread, raisins, and bourbon elevate the bread pudding of our youth to a rich and delicious dessert. If time allows, let both the bread and the soaking liquid sit, separately, before baking; but if you are in a hurry, just go ahead with the recipe.

Cut the bread into 1-inch (2½ cm) cubes (or squares if the bread is pre-sliced) and set aside.

In a large bowl, combine the cream, milk, eggs, sugars, raisins, bourbon, vanilla, and the cinnamon and ginger; mix everything together well. (If you have time, set the bread and the soaking liquid aside separately and allow to sit for 2 hours—or proceed directly with the recipe.)

Preheat the oven to 375°F (190°C).

Generously butter a 7 × 10 inch (18 × 25 cm) baking dish.

Stir the bread cubes into the liquid, mix well, and transfer to the buttered baking dish. Dot the top with the remaining butter, and bake in the preheated oven for 35 to 40 minutes, until the pudding has risen and the top is nicely browned.

Serve with Bourbon Sauce (recipe follows).

BOURBON SAUCE

Make the Custard, following the recipe on page 239.

When the custard is cool, or just before serving, warm the bourbon in a small saucepan over low heat. Allow the alcohol to evaporate, but it is not necessary to bring it to a boil. On a gas stove the alcohol may ignite, so keep your face averted—it will not affect the taste. Cool slightly, then stir into the custard until completely mixed.

Fruit Crumble

···

This is a good last-minute dessert—it can be ready in less than an hour and the actual preparation time is only 25 minutes. Make it a day or two ahead—it will be just as good, if not better, re-heated—and be sure to include some berries in the fruit selection (frozen are fine); their juice makes a big difference.

···

Preheat the oven to 375°F (190°C).

Cut the fruit into bite-size pieces, transfer to the baking dish, and toss with the lemon juice. If there are no berries among the fruit, add a few table-spoons of water to the dish along with the lemon juice.

Combine the oats, both kinds of flour, ½ cup (125 mL) granulated sugar, the brown sugar, and the melted butter in a large bowl. Mix together with your hands until the butter is completely absorbed and the mixture has an even, crumbly texture.

Spread the crumble mix evenly on top of the fruit and press down to smooth it out. Mix the cinnamon and the remaining 2 Tbsp (30 mL) sugar together in a small bowl; sprinkle it over the crumble.

Bake in the preheated oven for 30 to 40 minutes until the topping is golden and the juices from the fruit bubble up around the edges.

Serve with ice cream (good), whipped cream (better), or Greek yogurt (best).

CRANBERRY PEAR CRUMBLE (VARIATION) This is a winter variation on the regu-lar Fruit Crumble, in which everything remains the same except for the fruit. Replace the traditional mixed fruit with 1 cup (250 mL) pear (peeled, cored, and diced) and 2 cups (480 mL) fresh or frozen cranberries. If the cranber-ries are frozen, allow a little extra cooking time.

SERVES 4 TO 6
··················

3 cups (720 mL) mixed fruit (including some berries)

1 Tbsp (15 mL) lemon juice

1 cup (250 mL) rolled oats

½ cup (125 mL) whole wheat flour

¼ cup (60 mL) all-purpose flour

½ cup + 2 Tbsp (155 mL) granulated sugar, divided

¼ cup (60 mL) light brown sugar

3 oz (85 g) melted butter

1 Tbsp (15 mL) ground cinnamon

Caramelized Oranges

SERVES 6

•••••••••

6 oranges

½ cup (125 mL) granulated sugar

2 Tbsp (30 mL) water

Served with caramel sauce, these oranges make a light and elegant finish to a rich meal. Without the caramel, simply sliced, they are a wonderfully fresh accompaniment to richer desserts—Crème Brulée (page 198), Crème Caramel (page 200), and particularly Zabaglione (page 187).

With a very small sharp knife, peel the oranges in a spiral from top to bottom, as you would an apple, and remove all the pith. Slice them across into ¼-inch (6 mm) rounds, and arrange in a serving dish, or on individual plates.

Make the caramel with the sugar and water following the instructions on page 200. When ready, remove the pan from the heat and set it in a shallow pan of cold water to stop the cooking. Pour the caramel over the oranges; it will melt in the juice from the oranges and form a delicious sauce for the fruit.

Chocolate Mousse

SERVES 4

•••••••••

½ lb (227 g) dark chocolate, in small chunks

¼ lb (113 g) unsalted butter

4 eggs, yolks and whites separated

1 Tbsp (15 mL) granulated sugar

½ cup (125 mL) whipping cream

This is an easy dessert to make at the last minute, and everyone loves it.

Make a bain-marie by pouring 1 inch (2½ cm) of water into a pan over which a stainless steel bowl will sit comfortably without touching the water. Set the pan over medium heat; when it boils, turn the heat to very low, place the bowl over the pan, and add the chocolate and butter. Stir regularly until melted and quite smooth.

Remove the pan from the heat and stir in the egg yolks, one at a time. Set the whites aside in a separate, clean bowl.

In a stand mixer or by hand, whisk the egg whites vigorously, adding the sugar once they become white and frothy. Continue beating until they hold a stiff peak, but don't overbeat. Gently fold the whites into the still-warm chocolate until incorporated. Divide the mousse between 4 glasses or small dishes.

To decorate the mousse with whipped cream, beat the whipping cream to soft peaks, and spoon on top of each mousse.

What could be simpler?

Fruit Clafouti

....

A clafouti is a dessert of fruit baked in a batter that falls somewhere between a custard and a sponge. This recipe, created by Roxanna Palcu (who is one of the stars of our market stand on Salt Spring), is gluten- and dairy-free: it uses fresh goat cheese, and ground or powdered almonds (either will work) replace the flour.

Any summer fruit in season will do: peaches, apricots, figs, berries, or pitted cherries and plums.

....

Preheat the oven to 375°F (190°C).

Butter a 6-cup (1.4 L) gratin dish generously.

In the bowl of a stand mixer (or by hand), cream the almonds, sugar, and goat cheese until thoroughly mixed. Add the eggs one at a time, beating each until completely incorporated before adding the next. Add the salt, nutmeg, and vanilla and almond extracts, then mix again to create a smooth batter.

Arrange the fruit on the bottom of the buttered gratin dish. Pour the batter over it, transfer to the middle of the preheated oven, and bake for 30 to 40 minutes, until puffed and lightly browned—it may even take a little longer.

Serve warm from the oven with lightly whipped cream.

SERVES 6
....

Butter

⅓ cup (80 mL) powdered almonds

½ cup (125 mL) granulated sugar

5 oz (150 g) soft fresh goat cheese

3 large whole eggs

¼ tsp (1 mL) salt

¼ tsp (1 mL) grated nutmeg

2 tsp (10 mL) vanilla extract

1 tsp (5 mL) almond extract

3 cups (720 mL) sliced soft fruit

Lemon Possets

....

"Posset" was an old English drink favoured by the likes of Henry VIII, of hot milk curdled with ale or wine, and flavoured with sweet spices. These days the cream is not curdled, lemon is the flavour of choice, and it is no longer a drink. It is as delicious as lemon mousse, and much easier to make.

....

Zest the lemons (or grate the lemon skins) and chop finely. Squeeze the lemon and reserve ½ cup (125 mL) of the juice. Set both the zest and the juice aside.

Rinse out a saucepan with water and do not dry the inside. Set it over a medium-low heat. Pour in the cream and bring to a simmer; let it cook gently for 1 minute. Remove from the heat, add the sugar, and stir until dissolved. Add the lemon juice and zest and stir well.

Pour the posset into individual ramekins or glasses. Refrigerate for 4 hours or overnight—it will firm up as it cools.

SERVES 6
....

3 lemons

3 cups (720 mL) whipping cream

1 cup (250 mL) berry or granulated sugar

Baked Apples *and* Custard

SERVES 4
············

4 large apples

1 cup (250 mL) raisins, currants,
dried cranberries, or blueberries

½ cup (125 mL) brown sugar

Butter

1 recipe Custard *or* Crème Anglaise
(page 239; or Bird's Custard)

Nostalgia can cloud our judgment. Not everything from childhood was wonderful: Nanny was no saint and most nursery food was appalling. But when it comes to baked apples and custard, nostalgia gets it right—even if (maybe especially if) the custard is Bird's.

I am not a fan of Macintosh apples for eating—I find them soft and mushy—but they are a very good choice for baking. Crisp apples like Jazz, Braeburn, and Pink Lady are perfect for eating and for apple tarts and pies, but they do not soften up enough to make a good baked apple.

These apples can be prepared in 10 minutes (another 10 if you go for the homemade custard), and cooked in an hour.

Preheat the oven to 350°F (180°C).

Core the apples from the stem end: with a melon baller, scoop out a series of small balls from the stem down the centre of the apple until the core has been removed, stopping before you break through the bottom. With a small sharp knife, cut through the skin around the waist of each apple, like the Equator around the Earth; this allows the apple to expand during cooking without bursting the skin.

Fill the hollowed core with a mixture of the dried fruit and brown sugar, pressing down firmly. Set the apples in a baking pan, top with a knob of butter, and pour a little water into the pan to stop them sticking. Bake in the preheated oven for 45 minutes to an hour, depending on the size of the apples.

Make the custard while the apples are baking, or follow the instructions on the Bird's Custard Powder tin.

Serve the apples in a dessert bowl, and pass the custard separately.

Zabaglione

••

This is a completely delicious dessert, invaluable when you need to pull some-thing out of your hat on short notice. Marsala is the alcohol of choice, and this recipe alone is a good reason to always keep a bottle on hand. However, almost any liquor will substitute perfectly well, a sweet sherry perhaps best of all. (In a pinch I have used Drambuie, which may indeed be the best use for this liqueur capable of producing the mother of all awful hangovers.)

You can serve Zabaglione on its own, or on top of fruit: sliced oranges are very good, or fresh raspberries or strawberries.

••

Set out a glass for each person, with the fruit arranged on the bottom.

Prepare a bain-marie by bringing 1 inch (2½ cm) of water to a simmer in a saucepan over which a stainless steel bowl will sit without touching the water. Whisk the egg yolk, sugar, and wine together in the bowl and set it on top of the simmering water.

Whisk constantly while heating; in Italy they say whisking should always be in the same direction, which sounds bizarre, but perhaps they are just confirming what we do naturally. Keep whisking until the mixture becomes warm, thick, and "forms a ribbon"—as the Zabaglione falls off the whisk back into the bowl, it is thick enough to draw a slowly dissolving pattern on the surface.

Divide the warm Zabaglione between the prepared glasses, and serve immediately.

SERVES 1
ALTHOUGH IT TASTES SO GOOD MOST PEOPLE WILL HAPPILY EAT MORE. YOU MIGHT WANT TO INCREASE THE QUANTITIES BY A THIRD TO A HALF, AND MAKE EVERYBODY HAPPY
•••••••••••••••••••

½ cup (125 mL) fresh fruit

1 egg yolk

1 Tbsp (15 mL) granulated sugar

1 Tbsp (15 mL) Marsala or other liqueur

SPECIAL OCCASION DESSERTS

....

Most of us have long understood that any meal that deserves the name of dinner always involves dessert. My friend Tony believed in eating dessert first, in case he should be too full for it at the end. But as my mother warned (as I'm sure yours did, too) any time I ate unscheduled sweets, I would not, in the Scots expression, "be able for my dinner."

It turns out that our mothers were right (no surprise there), but Tony was wrong: eating sugar satisfies our craving, but it dulls our appetite. Sweetness at the beginning of dinner will interfere with our enjoyment of the food that is to come; served at the end, it sends us from the table pleasantly satiated and satisfied.

Dessert is often the most memorable part of the meal, in part because it is the taste that lingers with us at the end of the evening. It seems to me this is as good a reason as any to give it the attention it needs. It may be true that the fancier ones have a reputation for being more challenging, but I am not pulling your leg when I say most of them are not complicated, and don't require any special culinary skills. Making desserts calls for some knowledge, a bit of experience, and judgment—the same qualities we would bring to anything that matters to us.

That said, it has to be acknowledged that cooks who like making desserts are a little different, and perhaps the best way to put it is that we take pleasure in the details. With desserts, small things can make a big difference, and a cook who is drawn to the details, as I am, may be more likely to get pleasure out of making desserts.

Approached with care, there is no recipe here you cannot make. All the details you need are carefully explained. Take heart and go for it; as my friend Ole likes to point out, "What could possibly go wrong?"

Tart Lemon Tart

•••

This is an intensely lemony tart which can be served simple and unadorned, or with a decoration of candied lemon slices for a more professional look. Perhaps best of all, it can become the base for Lemon Meringue Pie (page 192).

•••

Make the Sweet Short Crust Pastry following the recipe on page 240. Wrap in plastic and refrigerate.

You will need an 8- or 9-inch (20 to 23 cm) tart pan with a removable bottom.

Sprinkle the work surface generously with flour. Place the pastry in the centre and beat it a few times with a rolling pin to soften. Roll out the pastry a little larger than the pan, about ³⁄₁₆ of an inch (5 mm) thick; roll it around the rolling pin, lift, and unroll over the tart pan. Press the pastry firmly onto the base and against the sides; trim the excess from the rim with a small knife, and use it to plug any holes. Refrigerate the pastry-lined pan for 30 minutes.

Preheat the oven to 375°F (190°C).

In the bowl of a stand mixer (or by hand), cream the butter, sugar, and cornstarch together until fluffy. Add the eggs one at a time, beating between each one. Add the lemon zest and then, with the mixer on low speed, add the lemon and orange juices. The mixture may separate, but it does not matter.

Remove the pastry shell from the fridge, prick the base all over with a fork, and set in the upper part of the preheated oven. Bake, as is and uncovered, for 15 minutes, until dry but not brown. Remove and set aside.

Turn down the oven to 325°F (160°C).

Plug any holes in the tart shell with leftover trim. Mix the filling thoroughly and pour it into the warm tart shell. Transfer to the oven and bake for 25 to 30 minutes, or until set. Check after 15 minutes and, if the top is browning, reduce the heat to 300°F (150°C) and cover loosely with aluminum foil. When set, remove from the oven and set aside to cool.

To make the candied lemon slices, bring the sugar and water to a boil in a small saucepan. Turn the heat to low, add the lemon slices, and cook for 10 minutes. Add more water if the syrup becomes too thick or the sugar crystallizes, but this should not happen if the heat is low.

Remove the lemon slices to a sheet of wax paper to drain; while still warm, arrange them on top of the tart.

The tart is best eaten at room temperature, but may be refrigerated for 3 days.

SERVES 6
•••••••••••

1 recipe Sweet Short Crust Pastry (page 240)

¼ cup (60 mL) unsalted butter

¾ cup (180 mL) granulated sugar

1 tsp (5 mL) cornstarch

4 eggs

Zest of 1 lemon

¾ cup (180 mL) fresh lemon juice

¼ cup (60 mL) fresh orange juice

CANDIED LEMON SLICES

½ cup (125 mL) granulated sugar

½ cup (125 mL) water

1 lemon, cut into 6 thin slices

Lemon Meringue Pie

•••

This pie takes the Tart Lemon Tart (page 191) recipe the next step and to another level.

I have no principles when it comes to lemon meringue pie. I eat it anywhere and everywhere. Sometimes it is good, other times not very good, but even when it is not good it is always better than none at all.

It will not surprise you that this one is excellent. The meringue can take the form either of the regular one you see in old-fashioned diners, or an Italian meringue—piped in rosettes—as seen in up-market pastry shops. One is no more correct than the other, but the regular meringue is easier if you don't have a stand mixer.

•••

Follow the recipe for Tart Lemon Tart to the point where the tart is fully baked, out of the oven, and set aside to cool. (You can also make it in an 8- or 9-inch [20 to 23 cm] pie plate rather than the tart pan.) Now make either the Regular or Italian Meringue, spread or pipe it over the pie, and bake as described in the recipes below.

REGULAR MERINGUE Preheat the oven to 350°F (180°C).

Beat the egg whites to medium peaks, adding 2 Tbsp (30 mL) sugar halfway through, then stir in the rest of the sugar until well incorporated. While the pie is still warm, spread the meringue on top of the pie with a large spoon or spatula, mounding it up toward the centre. Bake in the middle of the preheated oven for 15 minutes, until golden brown.

Cool before serving.

ITALIAN MERINGUE Turn up the oven to 450°F (230°C).

In the bowl of a stand mixer, beat the egg whites until foamy; add 2 Tbsp (30 mL) granulated sugar and continue whisking to medium peaks. Turn the mixer to its lowest speed and let it stir gently while you prepare the sugar syrup.

Bring the water and ¾ of a cup (180 mL) sugar to a boil in a small clean saucepan without stirring (swirling the pan is fine); reduce the heat to low and cook for 5 minutes, until the surface is covered with bubbles. Remove the pan from the heat, increase the mixer speed to medium, and pour the hot syrup into the egg whites in a slow, steady stream.

Turn the mixer to low and leave it to whisk until the meringue has cooled (the bowl may still feel slightly warm to your hand). It is ready when the meringue inside the cage of the whisk rises into a rounded peak.

Scoop the meringue into a piping bag fitted with a large star tip. Pipe rosettes about 1½ inches (4 cm) high over the surface of the pie, completely covering it; fill in the empty spaces between the rosettes until there is no meringue left.

Bake in the centre of the preheated oven for 10 minutes, checking frequently, until the meringue is browned and the tips of the rosettes are almost burned.

SERVES 6 TO 8
··················

¾ cup (180 mL) icing
(confectioner's) sugar

¼ cup (60 mL) unsweetened
cocoa powder

5 egg whites

¾ cup (180 mL) granulated sugar,
divided

8 oz (227 g) semi-sweet chocolate,
in chunks

5 oz (150 g) butter

6 eggs

Chocolate, for grating

Fresh raspberries,
for garnish

Death by Chocolate

There are many desserts with this wonderful name, but this cake with layers of chocolate meringue and chocolate mousse stands alone. It was one of the first desserts we made at the Shop, and we supplied them to Panache, the restaurant next door. Freddie, its flamboyant chef and co-owner, came up with the name, maybe not original but well deserved nonetheless.

Bake and assemble the cake at least half a day before serving to give the meringue time to soften.

Preheat the oven to 300°F (150°C).

Line 2 baking sheets with parchment paper (one is not big enough), and draw (but do not cut) three 9-inch (23 cm) diameter circles as templates for the meringues, with space between them. Fit a pastry bag with a large plain tip, at least ½ inch (13 mm) wide.

Whisk together the icing sugar and cocoa powder, and set aside.

In a stand mixer, or by hand, beat 5 egg whites to stiff peaks, whisking in 2 Tbsp (30 mL) of granulated sugar halfway through. Stir in another 6 Tbsp (90 mL) sugar, then gently fold in the cocoa and sugar mixture by hand until incorporated, being careful not to deflate the egg whites.

Scoop about half the mixture into the pastry bag. Using the circle as a guide and starting at the outside, pipe the meringue in a long spiral, working toward the centre. Continue with the rest of the meringue until all the circles are covered.

Bake in the preheated oven for 1 hour, switching the top tray for the bottom halfway through. The finished meringues should be firm and dry to the touch, and quite easily separated from the parchment paper. Give them more time in the oven as necessary, turning the temperature down if the meringue is browning.

When they are cool and firm, stack the 3 circles one on top of the other, turning the top circle upside down so the smooth underside is facing up. With a serrated knife, trim the edges so that the sides of the stack are fairly smooth and even. Set aside.

To make the chocolate mousse, place a stainless steel bowl over a large pan of simmering water (but not touching the water). Add the chocolate chunks to the bowl and cut in the butter so that it's in pieces. Stir over low heat until both are completely melted, then remove the bowl from the pan and leave to cool for 5 minutes.

One at a time, separate 6 eggs, putting 5 yolks in the chocolate—stirring in each yolk thoroughly before adding the next. Set aside. Put the 6 whites in a large clean bowl (or the bowl of a stand mixer).

Beat the 6 egg whites to stiff peaks, adding the remaining ¼ cup (60 mL) sugar halfway through. Gently fold them into the warm chocolate; the mousse will be quite soft at this point, but will firm up as it cools.

Place the bottom meringue circle on a cake stand or a piece of parchment paper on a clean surface on which it can rotate (it makes icing the sides easier). With a palette knife, spread a quarter of the mousse evenly over the meringue; set the middle meringue on top of the mousse, aligning it the same way it was when trimmed. Spread with another quarter of the mousse, and top with the final upside-down meringue.

Spread the remaining mousse over the top and sides of the cake. The mousse should by now have firmed up enough to stick to the sides, and will become firmer as you work with it. Dipping the palette knife in hot water during the final stages helps to give the cake a smooth finish.

Set the cake aside to firm up, and when it is firm, cover very loosely with plastic wrap and leave in a cool place for at least 4 hours, or up to 2 days.

With a vegetable peeler or coarse grater, peel or grate chocolate shavings from a chunk of chocolate and decorate the top of the cake. Serve with whipped cream and decorate with fresh raspberries.

Oeufs à la Neige (Snow Eggs)

SERVES 6

••••••••••

1 recipe Custard *or* Crème Anglaise (page 239)

6 egg whites

¼ cup (60 mL) granulated sugar

SPUN SUGAR

2 Tbsp (30 mL) water

½ cup (125 mL) granulated sugar

For a long time I thought Floating Islands and Oeufs à la Neige were the same thing, but it turns out that I was wrong (and perhaps not alone). A Floating Island is a larger meringue baked in a soufflé dish, unmoulded, surrounded with custard, and cut in slices like a cake. Oeufs à la Neige (snow eggs) are individual meringues poached in simmering water, drained, floated on a sea of custard, and decorated with strands of caramel. They are both delicious, but I prefer the presentation of the snow eggs, where everyone gets their own individual island; this is the recipe that follows. Children love them.

Make the custard ahead of time, to give it time to cool. Cover with plastic wrap and set aside. Before poaching the meringue, pour the custard into a wide, shallow serving dish.

Bring a wide, shallow pan (a frying or sauté pan), half filled with water, to a gentle simmer over medium heat. Lay out paper towels or a clean cloth for draining.

Beat the egg whites until frothy; continue beating as you add the sugar 2 Tbsp (30 mL) at a time, until the meringue is thick and glossy.

To form individual meringues, dip 2 large spoons in water, scoop a spoonful of meringue with one, then use the other, facing the first, to form an egg shape. Remove the top spoon, lower the bottom one with the egg white attached into the water, and let it float off. Repeat until the pan is full but not crowded.

Poach for 7 minutes on one side, then turn them over with a slotted spoon (easier said than done—they want to float the other way) and poach 3 minutes on the other. Lift meringues out onto the paper towels or cloth to drain. Finally, gently transfer to the serving dish and "float" them on top of the custard. Keep going until all the meringues are cooked and afloat.

SPUN SUGAR A spun sugar decoration is not essential, but the slightly bitter flavour of the caramelized sugar nicely balances the sweet meringue and custard.

Pour 2 inches (5 cm) of cold water into a large saucepan or sink, ready to cool the sugar pan.

Scrub out the inside of a small saucepan thoroughly. Pour in the water and the sugar and set over medium heat. Bring to a boil, increase the heat to medium-high, and cook until it reaches a mid-brown caramel colour. You can shake the pan to ensure even colouring, but best not to stir it (see instructions on page 200 for details).

When the caramel reaches medium brown, hold the pan handle with an oven mitt, take it off the heat, and set it in the cold water bath. Avert your face, as the very hot pan will make the water spit vigorously. (If the colour is not dark enough, return the pan to the heat and cook a bit longer, with no harm done.)

Cool for a minute or two, then lift the caramel with a fork (stirring is okay now) and let the strands fall back into the pot. As the caramel cools, these strands form long flexible threads that you can lift and drag over the floating islands. The caramel will melt in the custard but stick to the meringues and make an attractive decoration.

SERVES 6
············

2½ cups (600 mL) whipping cream

3 egg yolks

1 cup (250 mL) granulated sugar,
divided

Crème Brulée

···

Crème Brulée is one of the truly great desserts, and not hard to make. The texture of the custard is critical, and if the ratio of egg yolks to cream is out of balance, the smooth creaminess will be lost; follow the measurements carefully.

Burning the sugar with a blowtorch (or the purpose-made kitchen version) is standard practice nowadays, and it gives much better control than the old method of placing the dish under the broiler.

Bake the custard at least 6 hours ahead, and caramelize the sugar 2 hours or more before serving, to allow the custard to cool and firm up.

···

Preheat the oven to 300°F (150°C).

You will need an ovenproof serving dish with a 4-cup (1 L) or greater capacity that is at least 2 inches (5 cm) deep. You will also need a roasting pan into which the serving dish will fit comfortably for the water bath.

Bring a kettle of water to a boil and have it ready.

Rinse out a medium saucepan with water but do not dry it; this helps prevent milk solids sticking to the pan. Pour in the cream and bring it almost to a simmer over medium heat. Remove from the heat and set aside.

In a large bowl (or the work bowl of a stand mixer) combine the egg yolks and ½ cup (125 mL) sugar. Whisk for 2 minutes until thoroughly mixed, then pour in the hot cream in a slow, steady stream. Mix just enough to combine—beating longer will make it frothy.

Strain the custard into the ovenproof dish, using a sieve to remove any egg or milk solids that may have coagulated.

Set the custard dish in the roasting pan and slide it onto the middle rack of the preheated oven. Pull the rack out a short distance (to make pouring easier) and pour at least 1 inch (2½ cm) of hot water from the kettle into the roasting pan. Carefully slide the rack back in.

The baking time may vary, so check for doneness after an hour. It is ready when the custard is set around the edges but not completely firm all over. The centre will be a little wobbly when the dish is gently jiggled, and a tester will still come out creamy—it will firm up as it cools. If not done, continue baking and check every 10 minutes until ready. If the top is browning too much, turn the oven down to 275°F (135°C) and cover the dish loosely with foil.

Remove the roasting pan from the oven and leave to cool for 10 minutes. Lift the custard dish out of the water bath, and when completely cool, cover with plastic wrap and refrigerate until cold.

About 2 hours or more before serving, sprinkle the remaining ½ cup (125 mL) sugar evenly over the top of the custard.

Turn on the blowtorch and aim it, from quite close range, at an area of sugar. It takes a considerable amount of heat to melt and burn the sugar, but the blowtorch gives you excellent control. It can be nerve-wracking at first, but once you have the confidence that the dish will not crack, and the burning of the sugar will not get out of control, it is quite straightforward. So far I have managed not to crack any serving dishes—when they say ovenproof, it seems that ovenproof is what they mean.

Return the Crème Brulée to the fridge and keep cold until ready to serve.

SERVES 6

•••••••••••

2 cups (480 mL) granulated sugar, divided

2 Tbsp (30 mL) water, for the caramel

2 cups (480 mL) milk

½ cup (125 mL) whipping cream

1 vanilla bean (or 1 tsp [5 mL] vanilla extract)

2 large eggs

2 egg yolks

Crème Caramel

There are two parts to a crème caramel—the custard and the caramel, one providing the texture, the other a combination of bitter and sweet that gives sophistication to the more bland sweetness of the custard. The custard should be luscious and creamy, yet firm enough to hold its shape, and this comes from the right ratio of eggs to milk and cream. A good caramel should be dark without being burnt; the key to success is care (and a little courage) in browning the sugar.

Crème Caramel goes well with sliced oranges or strawberries or raspberries—any fruit with enough acidity and flavour to balance the silky sweetness of the dish.

Preheat the oven to 325°F (160°C).

You will need a straight-sided 4- or 6-cup (960 to 1400 mL) soufflé dish, or 6 individual ramekins, as well as a roasting pan in which the soufflé dish or ramekins will sit comfortably, to use as a water bath.

Bring a large kettle of water to a boil and have it ready. Fill a large pan or sink with 2 inches (5 cm) of cold water.

To make the caramel, scrub out the inside of a small saucepan, add 2 Tbsp (30 mL) water and 1 cup (250 mL) sugar and set it over medium heat. Swirl the pan to help mix and dissolve the sugar, but do not stir. Watch it carefully once the syrup boils; the surface will become covered with bubbles as the water evaporates, then gradually start to take on a golden colour. Bear in mind that while it is cooking, the caramel appears darker than it really is; courage is required to keep going when it already looks dark. The worst that can happen is that you brown it too far, it burns, and you have to start over; on the flip side, if you pull the pan off the heat and cool it too soon and find the caramel is not dark enough, simply return the pan to the heat and continue cooking.

As soon as the caramel reaches a rich medium brown, dip the base of the pan briefly in cold water to stop further cooking, and pour it all at once into the soufflé dish or ramekins. Immediately rotate the dish(es) and swirl the caramel around to coat the bottom and the lower part of the sides. It will harden quite quickly, but evenness is not essential.

To make the custard, combine the milk, cream, and vanilla bean (but not the extract, if using) in a small saucepan; set it over medium heat and bring it almost to a boil. Remove from the heat and set aside for the vanilla bean to infuse (or add vanilla extract now).

In the bowl of a stand mixer, or by hand, whisk together the eggs, egg yolks, and the remaining 1 cup (250 mL) granulated sugar.

When thoroughly mixed, pour in the hot milk mixture in a slow stream, whisking steadily. Strain the custard through a sieve into the soufflé dish (or ramekins) to remove any lumps.

Set the dish or ramekins in the roasting pan and transfer to the middle of the preheated oven. Pull out the oven rack a short distance (to make room to pour in the water), bring the kettle back to a boil and gently pour hot water around the dishes, about halfway up the sides. Slide the oven rack back in and close the oven door.

Bake for 50 to 60 minutes, until a tester comes out almost clean (individual ramekins will be done in about 20 minutes).

Remove from the oven, lift the dish(es) out of the roasting pan and set aside; the custard will firm up a bit as it cools. Refrigerate it if you plan on serving later, but give it some time to warm up before serving as the texture at room temperature is superior.

Release the custard by running a knife around the inside of the dish. Set a serving plate (with a small lip) upside down over the dish, and flip them both over together. Allow the custard to slide out, then lift off the dish. The melted caramel makes a delicious sauce for the custard, even better if there is an edge of bitterness in the caramelized sugar.

4 egg whites

¼ tsp (1 mL) salt

¼ tsp (1 mL) cream of tartar

1 cup minus 1 Tbsp (235 mL)
granulated sugar

1 Tbsp (15 mL) cornstarch

1 tsp (5 mL) white wine vinegar

½ tsp (2 mL) vanilla extract

3 cups (720 mL) fresh fruit (a mix
of berries and tropical fruit—kiwi,
pineapple, star fruit, mango, passion
fruit), in chunks

1½ cups (360 mL) whipping
cream

Pavlova

This is a great dessert for a party—it looks fantastic, is completely delicious, and despite the mountain of cream, it is light and fresh. It is as popular as chocolate, and makes a great birthday cake, too.

On the underside of the world, Australia and New Zealand have a fierce debate over which country deserves the credit for this dessert. The Aussies believe a chef in Perth, inspired by Anna Pavlova's performance in Swan Lake, recreated the dying swan's cloud of white feathers out of meringue, white sugar, and cream. Maybe not, say the Kiwis, backed up by the OED, which recently awarded them the credit. It turns out neither of them is right—"pavlova" is the prosaic evolution (in England, or perhaps America) of an old German torte; sometimes fiction is much more interesting than the truth.

The cream of tartar, vinegar, and cornstarch in the egg whites makes a softer and chewier meringue than the crunchy French one.

Preheat the oven to 275°F (135°C).

Line a large flat baking sheet, at least 12 inches (30 cm) squared, with parchment paper. Use a cake pan, bowl, or plate as a guide to draw a circle approx. 9 inches (23 cm) in diameter.

In a stand mixer (or by hand) beat together the egg whites, salt, and cream of tartar to medium peaks. Continue whisking until thick and glossy, adding the granulated sugar 2 Tbsp (30 mL) at a time. Stir in the cornstarch, white wine vinegar, and vanilla extract.

Scoop the meringue onto the parchment paper inside the pencilled circle, mounding it up in the centre.

Bake in the preheated oven for 1½ to 2 hours, until very lightly browned, crisp on the outside, and still soft in the centre. Check after an hour, and if it is already starting to brown, turn the temperature down to 225°F (110°C).

When done, remove from the oven and cool completely. It may collapse in the centre as it cools, which is normal.

Cut the fruit in bite-size pieces and set aside.

When ready to serve, beat the whipping cream to soft peaks. Spread half the fruit over the meringue, cover with the cream, and finish with the remaining fruit.

Raspberry *and* Fig Gratin

••

A hard-to-resist dessert that combines the best of Crème Brulée (page 198) with fresh raspberries and cream. When figs are not in season, use raspberries or strawberries on their own.

••

Arrange the raspberries on the bottom of a wide ovenproof serving dish that is 6 cups (1.4 L) or more in size.

Combine the egg yolks and sugar in the bowl of an electric mixer (or stainless steel bowl, if by hand), and whisk until pale yellow and quite thick.

Set the bowl over a pan of simmering water (not touching the water), pour in the whipping cream, and stir until the mixture becomes almost too hot for your finger.

Remove the bowl from the water bath, fit it into the stand mixer with the whisk attached, and beat on medium speed until cool; it will be light and frothy, and will have increased volume. Stir in the vanilla and set aside.

Preheat the oven to 375°F (190°C).

Cut each of the figs across into 4 rounds. Pour half the custard over the raspberries, arrange the slices of fig on top, and finish with the remaining custard.

Just before serving, set the dish in the middle of the oven and bake until warmed through—about 6 minutes from room temperature, 10 minutes if refrigerated. Remove the dish from the oven and turn on the broiler. When very hot, return the dish to the oven and lightly brown the top. Watch it carefully and serve immediately.

SERVES 6
••••••••••••

2 cups (480 mL) fresh raspberries

3 egg yolks

¼ cup (60 mL) granulated sugar

1 cup (250 mL) whipping cream

¼ tsp (1 mL) vanilla extract

5 fresh figs

Aunt Dorothy's Cheesecake

SERVES 10
••••••••••

Butter

1 cup (250 mL) Graham cracker crumbs

3 Tbsp (45 mL) melted butter

2 lb (900 g) cream cheese (or fresh goat cheese)

¾ cup (180 mL) granulated sugar

4 large eggs

Zest of 1 lemon, finely chopped

1 cup (250 mL) 18% cream (or half milk and half whipping cream)

3 Tbsp (45 mL) lemon juice

½ cup (125 mL) fresh berries (or berry coulis), for serving

Lisa Shamai was one of the first cooks at the Yonge Street shop, and her Aunt Dorothy became a strong supporter of our fledgling business. She was kind enough to give us her cheesecake recipe, which we used for as long as the business survived. She was a lovely woman, and this is a lovely cake. Using fresh goat cheese gives the cake a wonderfully smooth texture. Like cheese itself, dishes made with cheese will have a smoother and creamier texture if brought to room temperature before serving.

Preheat the oven to 350°F (180°C).

Cut a circle of parchment paper to cover the base of an 8½-inch (22 cm) spring-form pan. Make a collar by cutting 2 strips of parchment about 3 inches (8 cm) wide by 15 inches (38 cm) long. Butter the base and sides of the pan, as well as the parchment paper base and strips (the double buttering gives much better adhesion). Press the paper onto the base and against the buttered sides.

In a small bowl, mix together the Graham cracker crumbs and melted butter; press the mix firmly onto the base of the spring-form pan, using a flat disc to tamp it down. Bake in the preheated oven for 10 minutes; remove and set aside to cool. Turn the oven down to 325°F (160°C).

In a stand mixer fitted with the paddle (or by hand, but it's a lot more work), beat the cream cheese until fluffy. Add the granulated sugar and beat until smooth. Scrape down the sides and bottom of the bowl. With the mixer on medium speed, add the eggs one at a time, beating well after each one.

Turn the mixer to low, add the lemon zest and cream, and mix until completely smooth. Stir in the lemon juice.

Set the spring-form pan on a baking sheet, pour in the cheesecake mixture, and transfer the baking sheet to the middle rack of the oven.

Bake for 45 to 60 minutes, until almost set. Slower is better. It will puff up slightly around the edges; it is done when the centre also rises and the surface is level. It may still be slightly wobbly, but it will firm up as it cools. If in doubt, turn off the oven and leave it for another 10 minutes.

Remove from the oven and cool to room temperature before removing the cake from the pan and sliding it off the base onto a flat plate.

Decorate with fresh berries or fruit coulis before serving.

Birthday Cake

....

This is an impressive way to celebrate friends who appreciate the finer things in life, but there is no point pretending that it is a piece of cake. It brings together three classic elements: hazelnut meringue, French buttercream, and chocolate ganache, all requiring care but none of them difficult. Making it a few times will give you confidence and put fear to flight.

The recipe is split into three parts to make it easier to follow. It is best to make the meringue and the buttercream the day before serving; the ganache icing can be made on the day. A stand mixer is just about essential for making the buttercream.

....

HAZELNUT MERINGUE Preheat the oven to 350°F (180°C).

Spread the hazelnuts on a cookie sheet and toast them for 8 minutes. Remove and set aside to cool briefly, then wrap in a clean kitchen towel and rub them together to remove the papery skins; they will not all come off, and that is fine. Transfer to the work bowl of a food processor, add 1 Tbsp (15 mL) of sugar, and pulse to a coarse powder, taking care not to over-process and turn it into paste. Toss with the cornstarch and flour, and set aside.

Turn the oven down to 300 °F (150°C).

Line 2 large baking sheets with parchment paper and, using a plate or cake base as a guide, draw three 8- to 9-inch (20 to 23 cm) circles.

In a stand mixer or by hand, whisk the egg whites, adding 2 Tbsp (30 mL) sugar when they become foamy. Continue beating to firm peaks, then add ¼ cup (60 mL) sugar and whisk briefly. Finally, fold in the icing sugar.

Gently fold the hazelnuts into the meringue, and scoop it into a pastry bag fitted with a ½-inch (13 mm) plain tip. Starting at the outside, cover each circle on the parchment paper by piping the meringue in a long spiral toward the centre. (May also be done by dividing the meringue between the circles and spreading it with a palette knife).

Bake in the preheated oven for 1 hour and 20 minutes, or until dry enough to be separated from the parchment. Remove from the oven and leave to cool on the paper, or leave them to cool in the turned-off oven.

Stack the meringues one on top of the other, with the top one upside down. With a serrated knife, trim the edges until the sides of the stack are even. Set aside.

ORANGE BUTTERCREAM Cut the butter into ½-inch (13 mm) cubes and set aside to come to room temperature—it will take at least an hour.

Cut the orange into ³⁄₁₆-inch (4 mm) slices. Combine ¼ cup (60 mL) water and ½ cup (125 mL) sugar in a small pan set over medium heat; when the sugar has melted and the syrup bubbles, turn the heat to low, add the orange slices, and cook for 10 minutes. Lift out the orange slices onto a plate, to drain and cool. Discard the syrup.

. . . recipe continued

SERVES 10 TO 12
....

HAZELNUT MERINGUE

½ cup (125 mL) hazelnuts

7 Tbsp (105 mL) sugar, divided

1 tsp (5 mL) cornstarch

1 tsp (5 mL) all-purpose flour

7 egg whites

¾ cup (180 mL) icing sugar

ORANGE BUTTERCREAM

¾ lb (340 g) unsalted butter

½ orange

½ cup (250 mL) water, divided

1½ cups (360 mL) sugar, divided

7 egg yolks

2 Tbsp (30 mL) orange liqueur

GANACHE ICING

10 oz (283 g) bittersweet chocolate

1 cup (250 mL) whipping cream

. . . Birthday Cake (cont.)

Put the egg yolks in the bowl of a stand mixer; set the bowl over a pan of simmering water, not touching the water, and whisk gently until warm to your finger. Move the bowl to the stand mixer, attach the whisk, and let it whisk on low speed while you make the syrup.

Scrub the inside of a small saucepan thoroughly; add ¼ cup (60 mL) water and 1 cup (250 mL) sugar, set it over medium heat, and bring to a boil without stirring (swirling the pan is fine). Turn the heat to low and cook for 5 minutes, or until the surface is completely covered with bubbles: the syrup is ready.

With the mixer on low speed, very slowly start to pour the hot syrup into the warm eggs, adding the rest in a slow steady stream. Increase the mixer speed to medium and leave the machine running for 10 to 15 minutes, until the outside of the bowl is just slightly warm to your hand.

Remove the whisk and attach the paddle. With the motor on medium, add 2 pieces of the softened butter. The eggs should be warm enough to soften but not melt the butter. If the eggs are too warm and the butter melts, lower the speed to slow and cool the eggs further before adding more butter on medium speed. Continue to add the butter a few pieces at a time; if the buttercream should start to separate (i.e., lose its smooth appearance), turn up the speed and beat until it comes back together. If it starts to look lumpy, the butter may not be at room temperature, or the eggs may be too cool: warm them a little over warm water.

When all the butter has been added and the buttercream is smooth and shiny, remove the rind from the orange slices and chop it finely until you have ¼ cup (60 mL). Add the orange liqueur and the chopped rind to the buttercream and gently mix to incorporate. Set aside; discard the orange flesh and any leftover peel.

Place 1 meringue circle on a sheet of parchment paper set on a flat surface (it makes it easy to rotate the cake for icing), and with a palette knife spread a little less than half the buttercream evenly over the top. Place a second circle on the first, press down gently, and spread most of the rest of the buttercream on top. Set the last circle on top, upside down and level. Don't spread it with buttercream, but use the leftover buttercream to fill any gaps on the sides and to make them as smooth as possible—the chocolate icing will hide any imperfections.

Cover loosely with plastic wrap and leave in a cool place for several hours or overnight.

GANACHE ICING Cover the cake with the icing at least 2 hours before serving.

Chop the chocolate into small chunks and set aside.

Rinse out a small saucepan with water but don't dry it. Set it over medium-low heat, pour in the cream, and bring it to a simmer. Remove the pan from the heat, add the chocolate chunks, and leave them to soften for 10 minutes. Stir gently with a whisk until the chocolate has melted and the mixture is smooth; pour into a bowl and set aside to cool. It may be covered and refrigerated for several days, then rewarmed over a pan of simmering water.

Ganache can be used as a poured icing when still warm; it gives a smooth, glossy and professional look. Cooled ganache is thicker and must be spread with a spatula, which dulls the finish, but makes icing the sides of the cake easier.

For a lighter, airier, Betty Crocker-style frosting, beat the ganache with a whisk until thick.

Summer Pudding

....

Summer pudding is one of the great treats of summer. In a world where every kind of food is available at any time of year, summer pudding stands alone. It has the shortest of windows, a brief few weeks in June and July when raspberries and red currants are both in season. For me, summer pudding conjures up memories of idyllic long-ago summers. I don't know whether they only existed in my imagination, but today when I taste the tart red currants, sweet raspberries, and the deep red bread, the memories are as real and intense as they ever were, and real or imagined does not matter.

Regular sliced white bread with no artisan pretentions is best; it absorbs the juice and becomes one with the fruit. If you don't have day-old bread, buy fresh bread and leave it out overnight to dry (by which time it will in fact be day old).

....

Find an old-fashioned pudding bowl (deep rather than wide) that can hold 7 or 8 cups (1.7 or 2 L).

Remove the crusts from the bread, and spread it on the counter to dry while you proceed with the recipe.

Remove the stems from the red currants. Put them and the sugar in a saucepan, and cook over medium heat until the juices run. Add the raspberries and continue cooking until the raspberries start to release their juice, too. Remove from the heat and set aside to cool—there will be quite a lot of juice, which will be absorbed by the bread.

Reserve 2 or 3 slices for the top and use the rest of the bread to line the bowl, cutting and pasting until the base and the sides are covered up to a height of about 4 inches (10 cm). Pour the fruit and juice into the bowl, arrange the reserved bread slices on the top, and cover with a sheet of wax paper or parchment paper.

Apply a weight by putting a saucepan, small plate, or saucepan lid inside the bowl; make sure it rests on the bread, not against the sides of the bowl. Apply 2 or 3 lb (900 g to 1.4 kg) pressure by placing a large can of beans or tomatoes on the lid or plate, or filling the saucepan with water. Refrigerate for at least a day (up to 2 days).

To serve, remove the weight, plate, and wax paper, and carefully run a knife inside the bowl to release the pudding. Set a serving plate upside down over the bowl and invert bowl and plate together. Give it a few seconds to release, then gently remove the bowl. The pudding should be firm enough to hold together, but even if it collapses a little, the taste will be the same.

Cut the summer pudding into wedges. It may be at its best served just as it is, without cream. Whipped cream on its own does not have the edge of tartness needed to bring out the sweetness of the red currants, but crème fraîche or whipped cream mixed with plain yogurt are both good accompaniments.

SERVES 6

....

1 loaf day-old white bread, cut into slices (approx. ½ inch [13 mm] each)

2 cups (480 mL) red currants, stems removed

1 cup (250 mL) granulated sugar

4 cups (1 L) raspberries

Tiramisu

SERVES 10
••••••••••••

5 large egg yolks (reserve the whites)

5 Tbsp (75 g) granulated sugar, divided

18 oz (500 g) Mascarpone

5 Tbsp (75 mL) dark rum

5 egg whites

2 Tbsp (30 g) granulated sugar

30 Italian ladyfinger biscuits (approx.)

1 to 1½ cups (250 to 360 mL) strong black coffee

¾ cup (180 mL) unsweetened cocoa powder

The first Tiramisu I ever saw was when we hired Daphna Rabinovitch as our pastry chef at the Yonge Street (at the time, the only) shop. She had just returned from Italy, where she had been shown how to make it, entirely in sign language, by an older Italian lady. It was not long before it had become a staple at the shop and of our catering menus. Nowadays Tiramisu is pretty much everywhere, and deservedly so. It looks best in a straight-sided glass bowl, but the taste is the same, regardless of the dish.

In a stand mixer (or by hand) whisk the egg yolks and 5 Tbsp (75 g) sugar together until pale yellow and quite thick. Stir in the mascarpone and the rum and set aside.

In a separate bowl, whisk the egg whites to firm peaks, adding 2 Tbsp (30 g) sugar halfway through. Stir a third of the whites into the mascarpone mixture to lighten it, then gently fold in the rest; set aside.

Place about a third of the ladyfingers in a shallow dish. Brush them with coffee, enough to colour and soften but not soak them, then arrange them in a single layer on the bottom of the serving dish. Spread a third of the mascarpone on top. Scoop about half of the cocoa powder into a fine sieve and sift it over the mascarpone until covered in chocolate. Repeat the process with 2 more layers of coffee-infused ladyfingers, mascarpone, and chocolate, finishing with chocolate.

Cover with plastic wrap and refrigerate for 4 hours or overnight.

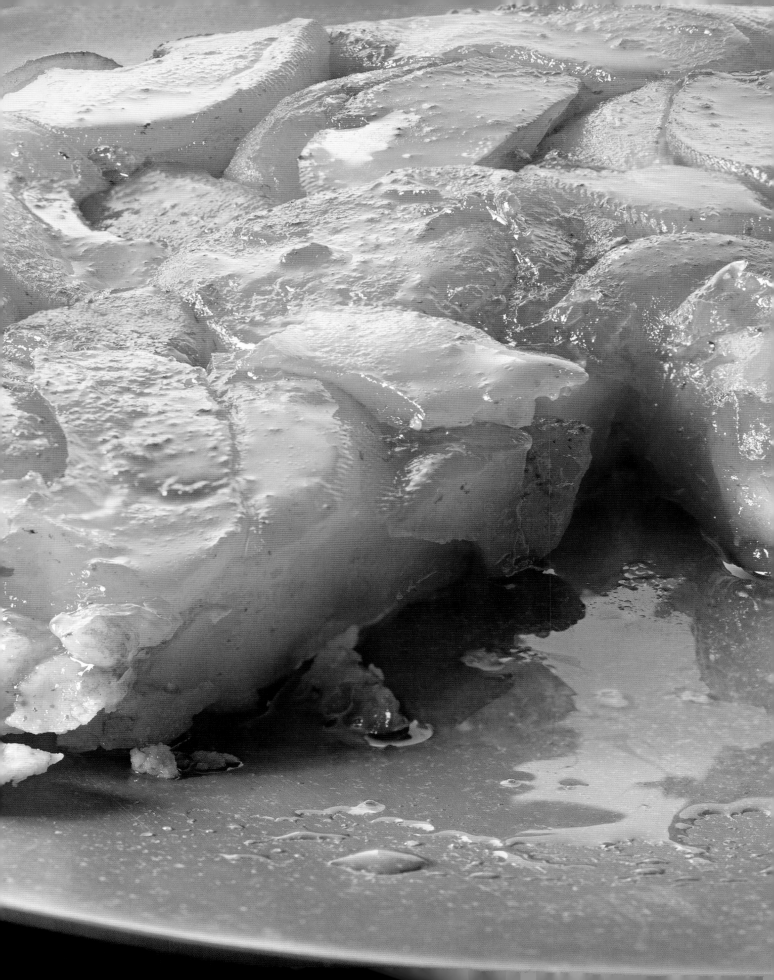

Tarte Tatin (Upside Down Apple Tart)

·······································

One of the best desserts in the world, made famous more than 130 years ago by les desmoiselles Tatin at their inn in the Loire Valley. No one knows if it was a happy recovery after an apple tart fell on the floor, or if they simply took a popular local dish and introduced it to a wider audience. Whatever the truth, it is an excellent tart: the caramelized butter and sugar permeate the apples, while the crust, baked on top of the apples and only turned the right way up (or upside down) just before serving, stays crisp and buttery.

Use apples that hold their shape when cooked, such as the traditional Granny Smith and Golden Delicious, or the modern hybrids such as Jazz, Gala, Braeburn, and Pink Lady. The tart can be made with pears, and also with quinces; both are excellent, and lovely mixed together.

There are two important points in making it—one is to caramelize the butter and sugar to the desired colour before adding any fruit to the pan, and the other is to make sure the fruit is fully cooked and the caramel sauce thick and syrupy before covering it with pastry.

·······································

Measure 5 oz (150 g) butter for the pastry and put it in the freezer for 30 minutes or more.

Peel, quarter, and core the apples; cut each quarter into 2 wedges and set aside.

Set the frying pan over medium heat, melt 4 oz (113 g) butter and add the 1 cup (250 mL) sugar. Shake the pan to combine them (don't stir), and have a kettle of hot water ready. The sugar will melt and then start to take on colour. When it reaches the desired colour (darker is better), hold the kettle in a gloved hand, avert your face, and pour a cup (250 mL) of water into the pan; it will bubble and spit, but the browning will be stopped dead in its tracks. (If the caramel is not dark enough after adding the water, leave the pan on the heat and allow the water to boil off. The caramelizing process will restart and you can cook to a darker colour.)

Add the apple wedges to the pan. Cook the apples until tender, turning and stirring from time to time; they can take a surprisingly long time to soften, and you may need to add more water. Continue cooking until the caramel is thick, syrupy, and much reduced, with just enough sauce to moisten the apples; stir frequently at the end to prevent burning on the bottom of the pan. Remove the pan from the heat and set aside to cool completely. The tricky part is done.

Whisk the flour, the ¼ cup (50 mL) sugar, and salt together in a large bowl. On the coarse side of a box grater, grate the frozen butter into the flour, and gently mix with your fingers.

Whisk the egg yolk with 2 Tbsp (30 mL) cold water and mix into the flour. Turn the dough onto your work surface and smear it over the surface using the heel of your hand as a pusher; it will take about 8 pushes altogether.

. . . recipe continued

SERVES 8 IN A 10- OR 11-INCH (25 OR 28 CM) ROUND FRYING PAN

·······················

5 oz (150 g) unsalted butter

10 apples (medium to large)

4 oz (113 g) butter

1 cup (250 mL) granulated sugar

1 cup (250 mL) water

1¼ cups (300 mL) all-purpose flour

¼ cup (60 mL) granulated sugar

½ tsp (2 mL) salt

1 egg yolk

2 to 4 Tbsp (30 to 60 mL) cold water

. . . Tarte Tatin (Upside Down Apple Tart) (cont.)

Scrape it up and knead briefly until it comes together, only adding more water if absolutely necessary to form a ball. Wrap in a plastic bag or plastic wrap and set aside (in the fridge if for more than 3 hours).

Preheat the oven to 375°F (190°C).

On a floured surface, roll the pastry to a circle the size of the pan; if it is cold and hard to roll, beat it a few times with a rolling pin to soften. Roll the pastry around the rolling pin and unroll over the cool apples; trim the edge with a small knife, and cut some vents to allow steam to escape.

Place the pan in the middle of the preheated oven and bake for 25 minutes, until the pastry is a light golden brown. The apples are already cooked and just need to be heated.

Remove the pan from the oven and cool for 5 or 10 minutes. Set a serving plate upside down over the tart, hold the plate and pan together with oven mitts and flip them over together, so that what was up is now down, and vice versa. Leave for half a minute for the apples to detach themselves, then lift the pan away, removing any clinging fruit and adding it to the tart.

Tarte Tatin is at its stellar best when warm, but it can be made ahead and kept in the pan in the fridge for 2 days. If reheating, put it in a 225°F (110°C) oven about 20 or 30 minutes before serving, or over a very low heat on the stove; warm it enough to melt the caramel and allow the apples to detach when inverted.

Serve with lightly whipped cream, crème fraîche, or plain Greek yogurt, or a mixture thereof; ice cream is good, too.

PEAR TARTE TATIN OR QUINCE TARTE TATIN (VARIATION) Exactly the same recipe as Tarte Tatin (page 215), but substituting pears for the apples. It is as good if not better than the better-known original, though perhaps the best of all is Quince Tarte Tatin. You can make Tarte Tatin with quince alone, but I like its tart, lemony flavour best combined with pears or apples, or even both. The recipe is the same as for Tarte Tatin, with one variation and a note of caution.

The variation is that the quinces (peeled and cored, with the hard parts around the stem and bud removed, then cut into 6 or 8 lengthwise segments as you would a pear) are cooked in the butter and sugar separately from the apples or pears. Quince take longer to cook, and dealing with the fruits separately allows each to get just the amount of cooking it needs.

When tender, remove the quinces from the syrup with a slotted spoon and set aside, put the apples or pears into the pan, and cook them in the remaining syrup (adding water as needed) until they, too, are tender. Finally, return the cooked quince to the pan and gently mix the fruit together before setting aside to cool.

Note of caution concerning the quince flesh, which is firmer and more brittle than that of most other fruit: it takes more force to make a cut, so make sure you have a sharp knife and take great care that your knife does not slip on the hard flesh and do you an injury.

Pear *and* Ginger Galette

....

This is a rustic tart, baked free-form on a cookie sheet, using a shorter and more melt-in-the-mouth pastry than might work in a conventional tart. The pears are softened in butter and sugar before baking.

....

Measure 5 oz (150 g) butter and put it in the freezer, in 1 piece, for 30 minutes or more.

Whisk together the flour, sugar, and salt in a large bowl. In a cup, whisk the egg yolk and cold water until well blended, and set aside.

On the coarse side of a box grater, grate the frozen butter into the flour. Mix together with your fingers, sprinkle the egg and water over it, and mix again: it should be barely moist and quite crumbly.

Tip the pastry onto a work surface and, with the heel of your hand, smear it across the surface. It will take about 8 pushes to spread all of it. Gather it into a ball, working it gently with your hands to bring it together; add a little more water if it needs it to form a ball. Wrap it in plastic and set aside at room temperature for up to 3 hours (refrigerate if longer).

Peel the pears and cut them in half lengthwise. With a melon baller, remove the core from each half, and trim away any hard parts around the stem and the bud with a small knife.

Melt the other 2 oz (60 g) butter (should equal about ¼ cup [60 mL] once melted) and ½ cup (125 mL) sugar in a large frying pan over low heat.

Cut each half-pear lengthwise into ¼-inch (6 mm) slices, then add them to the frying pan. Cook, stirring occasionally, until the juices run and the pears are almost tender, adding water as needed to stop the sugar browning. When softened, turn up the heat to medium, add the chopped ginger, and stir gently until the juices are thick and syrupy—you only need enough juice to moisten the pears. Remove from the heat and set aside to cool.

Preheat the oven to 375°F (190°C).

On a well-floured board, roll out the pastry about ³⁄₁₆ of an inch (5 mm) thick and 16 inches (40 cm) across—it does not matter if the circle is not round or its edges are rough. Line a baking sheet with parchment, roll the dough around your rolling pin and unroll in the centre of the paper.

Arrange the pears in the middle of the pastry, in a circle about 10 inches (25 cm) across, leaving a pastry border all around. Lift a point on the edge of the pastry up and over the pears toward the centre. Continue round the perimeter, folding the outside toward the centre, each fold covering part of the previous one. It will take 6 or 8 folds until all of the pastry has been folded in, leaving a circle of uncovered pears in the centre. You can give the pastry a nice gloss by glazing it with an egg yolk mixed with 1 Tbsp (15 mL) water.

. . . recipe continued

SERVES 6
....

7 oz (210 g) unsalted butter, divded

1½ cups (360 mL) all-purpose flour

⅓ cup (80 mL) granulated sugar

½ tsp (2 mL) salt

1 egg yolk + 1 extra for glazing the pastry (optional)

2 to 3 Tbsp (30 to 45 mL) cold water

3 lb (1.4 kg) pears

½ cup (125 mL) sugar

3 Tbsp (45 mL) ginger (preserved or crystallized), chopped in small chunks

. . . Pear and Ginger Galette (cont.)

Bake in the middle of the preheated oven for 25 to 30 minutes. When the pastry is nicely browned, remove from the oven and leave to cool for at least 30 minutes. Serve with lightly whipped cream, crème fraîche, or plain Greek yogurt (or any mixture of these).

STRAWBERRY RHUBARB GALETTE (VARIATION) This is a delicious alternative to the Pear and Ginger Galette, made almost the same way, except that the rhubarb needs to be cooked and drained and its syrup reduced before being mixed with the fresh strawberries. To prepare this recipe you'll need ¾ lb (340 g) rhubarb and 2⅓ cups (580 mL) cut-up strawberries instead of the pear and ginger.

Make the pastry as described in the recipe for Pear and Ginger Galette, and set aside in a plastic bag at room temperature for 1 hour or more.

Take the rhubarb and trim any damaged bits, but be sure to keep the pink end where the stalk was attached to the root—it has the best flavour. Rinse the rhubarb under cold water and put in a stainless steel saucepan. Add ⅓ cup (80 mL) sugar, cover with a lid, and set over the lowest heat you can—the lower the heat, the better the rhubarb will keep its shape, but the taste is the same either way. It will take 15 minutes to 2 hours until it is soft, depending on how low you can get the heat. Remove from the heat and set aside to cool.

When the rhubarb is cool, set it in a strainer over a bowl to catch the juice. Return the juice to the pan and, over medium heat, reduce it to 2 or 3 Tbsp (30 or 45 mL). Remove from the heat, stir in the cut-up strawberries, and set aside.

Mix all the fruit together when it has cooled to room temperature. If the mixture is sloppy, drain off some of the juice and reserve—you don't want it to soak through the pastry. You can add back the reserved juice after baking, or serve it separately.

Preheat the oven to 375°F (190°C).

Roll out the pastry, spread on the fruit filling and fold up the edges as in the recipe for Pear and Ginger Galette. Bake 25 to 35 minutes in the preheated oven; remove and allow to cool for at least 40 minutes. Serve with whipped cream, crème fraîche, or plain Greek yogurt (or any mixture thereof).

Spiced Pears *in* Red Wine

This is one of the most elegant desserts of all. Bosc pears, with their long stems and slender necks, flavoured with sweet spices and lemon zest and served with lightly whipped cream sliding down the wine-dark flesh, are as sophisticated as a dessert can be.

The pears can be served either whole or in half. There is no doubt that a whole pear is a more impressive presentation, and the half-pear an easier one. However, I would encourage you to leave them whole—faint heart never won fair maiden, and all that.

Put everything except the pears, water, and cream in a large stainless steel saucepan; bring to a simmer over medium heat, and turn down the heat to low.

With a vegetable peeler, peel the pears in long smooth strips, leaving the stem on if possible.

Remove the core from the pears with a small melon baller, working from the bud end (the opposite end to the stem). Scoop out the bud, then keep scooping, working upwards and into the pear, until the core is removed. Place the peeled and cored pear in the saucepan with the wine mixture, and repeat until all the pears are done.

Add enough water to float the pears, and turn up the heat to medium. Bring to a simmer, turn the heat as low as it will go, and cover the pan with the lid. The poaching time depends on the size and ripeness of the pears, at least an hour. From time to time, test for tenderness with a fork (a knife is too sharp), mindful that too many piercings do not make for a pretty pear (or person, for that matter).

When tender, remove the pan from the heat, leaving the pears in the poaching liquid to absorb colour and flavour as they cool.

When the pears are cool (sooner if time is short), lift them into a serving dish or bowl.

Strain the poaching liquid through a fine sieve into a large bowl to remove the spices and bits of pear. Rinse the pan, pour the wine back into the pan, and return to the stove. Turn the heat to high, bring the wine to a boil, and reduce it over high heat; from time to time, spoon back into the pan any liquid that drains from the pears.

Have ½ cup (125 mL) water on hand, ready to pour into the sauce if the sugar looks like it's burning—this will stop it immediately without harming the syrup.

When most of the liquid has evaporated and small bubbles start to cover the surface, the syrup is almost ready. Turn down the heat and test by lifting the syrup with a spoon and dripping it back into the pot—the syrup is ready when it falls in thick, sticky drops rather than a steady stream.

Set the pears on a serving dish (white looks good) and pour the syrup over them. From time to time, baste the pears with the syrup; with each spoonful the pears take on a little more colour, the surface gloss becomes a little deeper, and your soul becomes a little calmer. You will eventually have to tear yourself away and cook the rest of the dinner.

Just before serving, whisk whipping cream to soft peaks.

Set the pears on a plate and spoon over some sauce. Pass the cream separately.

SERVES 8
••••••••••

1 bottle (750 mL) red wine (full bodied)

1 cup (250 mL) granulated sugar

½ tsp (2 mL) ground nutmeg

1 stick cinnamon

Pinch allspice

6 cloves

Peel of 1 lemon

8 Bosc pears (not quite ripe)

½ cup (125 mL) water

¾ cup (180 mL) whipping cream

Pears *in* Caramel Ginger Sauce

This is a very elegant pear dessert, sophisticated enough for any occasion. The pears are halved (which makes them easier to prepare) and poached in white wine, the hollows in the pears are filled with a scoop of crème fraîche, and ginger is added to the sauce, which is then reduced and poured over the pears just before serving.

SERVES 8

½ bottle (360 mL) white wine

1 cup (250 mL) granulated sugar

½ tsp (2 mL) grated nutmeg

1 stick cinnamon

Pinch allspice

4 cloves

Peel of 1 lemon

4 large pears (any variety, close to ripe if possible)

¼ cup (60 mL) ginger (crystallized or preserved), finely chopped

1 cup (250 mL) crème fraîche

Put everything except the pears, ginger, and crème fraîche in a large stainless steel saucepan; bring to a boil over medium heat, and turn down the heat to low.

With a potato peeler, peel the pears in long smooth strips; cut them in half lengthwise, and use a melon baller to remove the core in a neat ball. With a small knife, cut away the bud and the hard strip that runs from the stem to the core. Put the peeled, halved, and cored pears in the wine mixture.

Add enough water to the pan to float the pears; turn up the heat to medium and bring to a simmer. Cover the pan, turn the heat as low as it will go, and poach the pears, testing for tenderness with a fork from time to time—they will take a surprisingly long time to cook.

When tender, turn off the heat and set aside to cool in the pan (or continue with the recipe if time is short.)

Remove the pears to a serving dish. Strain the poaching liquid through a sieve into a bowl to remove any bits of spice and pear. Rinse out the pan and return the strained sauce to the pan. Add the chopped ginger and turn up the heat to high.

When most of the liquid has evaporated and small bubbles start to cover the surface, the syrup is almost ready. Turn down the heat and test by lifting the syrup with a spoon and dripping it back into the pot; the syrup is ready when it falls in a sticky, steady stream, and has a pale pink or gold colour. Remove from the heat and allow to cool.

Dry the pear halves on paper towels, scoop a generous amount of crème fraîche into the hollow of each, and set them on a platter or individual plates. If the syrup has cooled and become too thick to pour, warm it gently over low heat. Spoon it over the pears, making sure each gets some of the ginger.

Dried Figs *in* Red Wine *with* Pepper, Fennel, *and* Orange

···

These figs accompanied by a creamy blue cheese are a lovely way to end a meal. Individually dried figs will have a better shape than the ones squashed together in the package.

···

Arrange the figs upright in a single layer in a large stainless steel pan. Add the red wine, peppercorns, fennel, and orange strips, and bring to a boil over medium heat. Reduce the heat to very low and cover the figs with parchment paper. Apply some weight to the figs with a pot lid that will just fit inside the pan; if there is no such lid available, press down the parchment paper by hand and cover the pot with its own lid.

Poach on very low heat (or bake in a 225°F [110°C] oven) for 1½ hours until the figs are very soft; remove the figs to a serving dish. Reduce the liquid until thick and syrupy, and pour it over the figs.

Serve at room temperature, sprinkled with the Grappa or Cognac.

MAKES 24 FIGS

··················

24 dried figs

3 cups (720 mL) red wine

1 Tbsp (15 mL) whole black peppercorns

½ tsp (2 mL) whole fennel seeds

4 strips orange peel

2 Tbsp (30 mL) Grappa or Cognac

BASICS

....

There is a point in cooking when you draw on your experience to create dishes of your own, no longer dependent on recipes from others. It can happen out of necessity or a sense of adventure, but whatever the catalyst, the shift in cooking from recipe-based to ingredient-based is a great step. It opens the door to buying whatever looks good at the market or in the store, and coming up with a way to use it. Leftovers no longer linger in the back of the fridge, but become new ingredients you can work with, as the French say in their lovely phrase, *"l'art d'accommoder les restes."*

Polenta

......

Polenta makes a very nice but often forgotten starchy alternative to potatoes, rice, and pasta, as a vehicle for a flavourful sauce. Great with short ribs and oxtails.

......

In a medium saucepan, bring 4 cups (960 mL) stock or water to a boil, then add the polenta and salt. Whisk until thoroughly incorporated, turn down the heat to medium low and cook, uncovered and stirring frequently, until the polenta is tender and has the consistency of grits (assuming you know what that is; watch *My Cousin Vinny* if in doubt). It takes about 20 minutes. Add more water if necessary.

MAKES ABOUT 5 CUPS (1.2 L)
......

4 cups (960 mL) chicken stock or water

1 cup (250 mL) polenta

½ tsp (2 mL) salt

Crostini

......

These crisp little rounds of baguette are a much more interesting vehicle for dips and pâtés than store-bought crackers. They are easy to make, and will keep for a few days in a tin or plastic container.

We all know not to cook with wine we would not drink, but for most of us it is a rule more honoured in the breach than in the observance. When it comes to cooking with bread, however, always start with a good baguette—something with a bit of heft, not a lightweight stick that looks like it has just been varnished.

......

Preheat the oven to 400°F (200°C).

With a pastry brush, spread half the olive oil over a large baking sheet. Arrange the bread slices on top in a single layer; brush the topsides with the rest of the oil.

Put the baking sheet in the middle of the preheated oven and bake for 5 minutes. Remove from the oven and check that the bread is starting to brown on the underside; it may need a minute or two longer. Turn all the slices over and bake for another 3 minutes; check again. The bread should be very lightly browned and still pliable, not completely crisp.

MAKES ABOUT 40 CROSTINI
......

¼ cup (60 mL) olive oil

1 baguette, cut across into ¼-inch (6 mm) slices (or on the diagonal for large crostini)

Nancy's Vinaigrette

MAKES ABOUT 2 CUPS (500 ML)

1 Tbsp (15 mL) Dijon mustard
(Grey Poupon)

2 Tbsp (30 mL) red wine vinegar

1 Tbsp (15 mL) lemon juice (or an
extra 1 Tbsp [15 ml] vinegar)

¼ tsp (1 mL) salt

1¼ cups (300 mL) olive oil

Nancy is my ex, and most things we have disagreed about in the past are water under the bridge—except for the question of who makes the best vinaigrette (also whether to trim one or both ends off a green bean, but I am not optimistic about a settlement on that). On the vinaigrette front, we are not far apart: her recipe has lemon juice where mine does not.

In a medium bowl, whisk together the mustard, red wine vinegar, lemon juice, and salt by hand, until blended. Gradually pour in the olive oil in a thin stream, whisking vigorously to create an emulsion (a smooth blend of oil and vinegar). Using a immersion hand blender toward the end produces a firmer emulsion, but use these powerful little machines with caution as they may spray the vinaigrette around the room.

The dressing will keep at room temperature for 2 weeks. (In the fridge the oil solidifies and the emulsion separates, and it is hard to bring it back together.)

Basil Balsamic Vinaigrette

MAKES ABOUT 1 CUP (250 ML)

1 Tbsp (15 mL) coarsely chopped
fresh basil

1½ tsp (7 mL) grainy mustard

½ tsp (2 mL) black pepper

½ tsp (2 mL) salt

2 cloves garlic, peeled

¼ cup (60 mL) balsamic vinegar

¾ cup (180 mL) olive oil

Sweeter than the classic vinaigrette, this is best made in a blender.

Put everything except the olive oil in the jar of the blender, and blend until smooth. With the motor running, pour in the olive oil in a steady stream. The dressing will be quite thick.

Walnut Oil Vinaigrette

Walnut oil makes a dressing that is light enough to allow the distinctive flavour of a lettuce fresh from the garden or market to shine; hazelnut oil works very well, too.

In a small bowl, whisk together the vinegar, salt, and pepper until the salt is almost dissolved. Gradually whisk in the olive oil followed by the walnut or hazelnut oil. It will not form a thick emulsion, but should be firm enough not to separate.

Store at room temperature for a few days.

MAKES ⅓ CUP (80 ML)
....

1 Tbsp (15 mL) wine vinegar

¼ tsp (1 mL) salt

Pinch fresh ground black pepper

2 Tbsp (30 mL) mild olive oil (not extra virgin)

2 Tbsp (30 mL) walnut oil or hazelnut oil

Mayonnaise

When I first became interested in food, I read a lot of cookbooks, and none with so much pleasure as those by Elizabeth David—to the point where Nicola, my wife at the time, took to calling me David Elizabeth. One of my recurring images was of Elizabeth sitting at her kitchen table, the sun streaming in through the window, making mayonnaise in an old-fashioned china bowl as if she had all the time in the world. Whether she ever did any such thing I have no idea, but the image still comes back; mayonnaise seems to taste better by hand, and for the 10 minutes it takes, the busyness of the world slips away and I can imagine myself sitting with Elizabeth in her kitchen.

There is no denying that Hellmann's works well for many things, but there are occasions when only homemade will do, including cold lobster and good salmon, eggs mayonnaise, an aioli platter, vitello tonnato, and cold, slightly pink roast pork.

MAKES ABOUT 2½ CUPS (600 ML)
....

3 egg yolks (or, using a food processor, combine 2 egg yolks and 1 whole egg)

1 Tbsp (15 mL) Dijon mustard

1 Tbsp (15 mL) lemon juice + extra as needed

Pinch salt + extra as needed

2 cups (480 mL) olive oil (or a mix of olive and another vegetable oil)

Put 3 egg yolks into a large bowl, or the bowl of a stand mixer (or put 2 yolks and 1 whole egg in the work bowl of the food processor.)

Add the mustard, lemon juice, and salt, and whisk together (or pulse 2 or 3 times). Strong whisking is important for a successful mayonnaise: the physical action binds the oil to the egg yolks and forms an emulsion. Add the oil very slowly in the beginning—a few drops at a time—to establish the emulsion, increasing to a slow stream once the mixture is smooth and homogeneous (or in a food processor, with the motor running, fill the feed tube with oil and let it flow through the hole in the bottom.)

If the mayonnaise becomes too thick (more likely to happen with a processor than by hand), dilute it with lemon juice or water as necessary.

Adjust for taste with salt and lemon juice.

Store in the fridge for up to 4 days.

Béarnaise Mayonnaise

¾ cup (180 mL) Mayonnaise
(page 229)

1 Tbsp (15 mL) Dijon mustard

1 clove garlic, very finely chopped

1 Tbsp (15 mL) very finely chopped
shallot

1 Tbsp (15 mL) lemon juice

3 Tbsp (45 mL) chopped fresh
tarragon

1 Tbsp (15 mL) tarragon vinegar

Pinch salt

A tarragon-flavoured mayonnaise that works wonders on roast beef sandwiches and cold beef tenderloin.

Put all the ingredients in a medium bowl and stir until well mixed. Cover with plastic wrap and set aside in the fridge for the flavour to develop.

Store for up to 4 days, refrigerated.

TARRAGON VINEGAR Tarragon vinegar is what makes the difference in this recipe. You can make your own by warming ¼ cup (60 mL) of white wine vinegar in a small saucepan over low heat and mixing in 2 Tbsp (30 mL) of fresh (preferably) or dried tarragon leaves. When it simmers, remove from the heat and set aside to cool; strain the liquid and use it in place of the tarragon vinegar.

Moroccan Preserved Lemons

12 lemons, washed (or as many as
the jar will hold)

½ cup (125 mL) salt

Lemon juice

The peel of lemons preserved in salt becomes soft and fragrant, and makes a very flavourful addition to chicken dishes and desserts.

You will need a wide-mouth glass container with a tight-fitting lid. Preserving enough lemons to fill the jar reduces the need for extra lemon juice and prevents the growth of mould.

Make a lengthwise cut in each lemon, as if cutting in half from top to bottom, but stopping about three-quarters of the way down, before the halves are separated. Make a second cut at right angles to the first (as if cutting in quarters), again, not cutting all the way to the bottom. Open the lemon like a flower and sprinkle the cut surfaces with salt.

Sprinkle 1 Tbsp (15 g) of salt on the bottom of the jar. Open up a lemon like the petals of a flower, and push the cut side into the salt pressing down firmly to release the juice. Sprinkle more salt on top, and continue with the rest of the lemons, opening them up and pressing down firmly on each one, sprinkling salt between the layers. When all the lemons are packed into the jar, add enough lemon juice to cover them.

Seal the jar tightly and store the lemons in a cool place (may be stored in the fridge) for 20 to 30 days. Turn the jar upside down every other day, to ensure all the lemons are covered with juice and to prevent mould growth.

Hollandaise Sauce

••

Hollandaise is a sauce with a reputation for being difficult, which can be well enough deserved if you use the classic method. Some of the store-bought alternatives are not bad, but homemade is so much better that it is worth the small amount of extra work required. This simple version frees you from anxiety about failure (but unfortunately only where hollandaise sauce is concerned—the rest of life remains a challenge).

••

Melt 7 oz (200 g) butter in a small saucepan over low heat; remove the pan from the heat and set aside to keep warm.

In a separate small stainless steel saucepan, whisk together the egg yolks and lemon juice. When thoroughly mixed, add 1 Tbsp (15 g) of the cold butter and set the pan over medium-low heat. Stir constantly, reaching all over the bottom of the pan with the whisk, and lifting the pan off the heat from time to time to slow down cooking and stop curds forming. Take your time.

The yolks will become warm and start to thicken. When the lines left by the whisk in the egg mixture linger briefly and do not immediately fill in (i.e., form a ribbon) remove the pan from the heat, add the rest of the cold butter, and whisk vigorously until it is incorporated. This stops the eggs cooking any further.

Now ladle about 1 tsp (5 mL) of the melted butter into the eggs and whisk it in. Add another small amount of the butter and whisk again. Continue, gradually increasing the amount of butter, as if making mayonnaise with melted butter instead of oil. Don't use the milky liquid under the melted butter—these are the milk solids and will dilute the sauce.

Set aside in a warm place until ready to serve. If the sauce cools, the butter may solidify and the sauce become too thick. If this should happen, set the pan very briefly over an extremely low heat (a bain marie works well) and whisk as the butter melts, just enough to regain the soft consistency.

Do not keep it warm for more than 2 hours due to the risk of harmful bacteria developing in the egg yolks.

Leftover hollandaise cannot be reused.

MAKES ALMOST 2 CUPS (480 ML)
••••••••••••••••••••••••••••••••

7 oz (200 g) unsalted butter

3 egg yolks

2 Tbsp (30 mL) lemon juice

2 Tbsp (30 mL) cold unsalted
butter, divided

Roasted Peppers

......

MAKES 6 PEPPERS

......

6 red, yellow, or orange
peppers

These are easy to make on a gas stovetop or barbecue, or a little more work over charcoal. In the absence of ether of those, store-bought roasted peppers from Spain are a good choice.

......

Turn the gas burners on the stovetop or barbecue to high and place the whole peppers directly on the flames or grill. Turn them with tongs every couple of minutes until charred and black all over; they will not blacken evenly, but it does not matter. Set them aside in a plastic bag, tightly closed so the moisture does not escape, for 15 minutes.

Take out 1 pepper at a time and rub the charred skin with your fingers—it flakes off easily, even where the skin is not burned. Wipe the pepper clean with a paper towel and set it aside while you skin the rest.

Clean any charred skin from your work surface. Cut a pepper in half lengthwise and trim off (and discard) the stem, membranes, and seeds. Scrape the back of a small knife across the inside surface to remove the last of the seeds; set aside and clean the rest.

Peppers can be served immediately, or kept in a closed container in the fridge for several days, longer if covered with olive oil.

Crème Fraîche

......

MAKES ALMOST 3 CUPS (750 ML)

......

2 cups (480 mL) whipping cream

¾ cup (180 mL) sour cream

Crème fraîche is sharper than whipping cream and has more fat than yogurt, combining an acidic edge with a rich mouthfeel in a very sophisticated manner. It is easy to make, but it's important to start at least 3 days before you plan to use it.

......

In a small bowl, mix the 2 creams together until completely combined. Cover the bowl with plastic wrap and leave it in a warm place for 2 or 3 days—at least 3 at room temperature. It will thicken as the dairy cultures in the sour cream work their magic.

Crème fraîche will keep for 2 weeks in the fridge.

Jalapeño Tartare Sauce

Good with crab cakes, fish, and seafood.

Combine all the ingredients in the work bowl of a food processor; process until the vegetables are finely chopped, but not puréed.

Sauce will keep in the fridge for 4 days.

MAKES 1½ CUPS (360 ML)

1 cup (250 mL) Mayonnaise (page 229) or Hellmanns

1 Tbsp (15 mL) chopped green onions

2 tsp (10 mL) chopped cornichons

2 tsp (10 mL) capers

1 Tbsp (15 mL) chopped fresh Jalapeño pepper

1 Tbsp (15 mL) lemon juice

2 tsp (10 mL) chopped parsley

Pesto Sauce

Homemade pesto is simply the best.

Combine all the ingredients in the work bowl of a food processor; process briefly, until still slightly chunky.

Pesto will keep for a week in the fridge, or much longer in the freezer—but fresh is best.

MAKES 2 CUPS (480 ML)

2 cloves garlic, crushed

½ cup (125 mL) pine nuts

¾ cup (180 mL) olive oil

½ cup (125 mL) grated Parmesan cheese

1 large bunch basil leaves, thick stems removed

½ tsp (2 mL) salt

Béchamel Sauce

2 cups (480 mL) milk

1 small onion, peeled

1 bay leaf

8 black peppercorns

3 Tbsp (45 mL) butter

3 Tbsp (45 mL) plain flour

½ cup (125 mL) whipping cream
(optional)

Salt

This classic white sauce can be made more liquid as a base for soup, medium thick as a filling for crêpes, or very thick for crab cakes. How thick it is depends on the amount of flour the recipe specifies for each 1 cup (250 mL) of milk—between 1 Tbsp (15 mL) per 1 cup (250 mL) for a thin sauce, or up to 3 Tbsp (45 mL) for a very thick one. The quantities below are for a medium sauce, right for cauliflower au gratin.

Rinse out a small saucepan with water but don't dry it. Pour in the milk, onion, bay leaf, and peppercorns, and bring to a simmer over medium heat, being careful not to let it boil over. Remove from the heat and set aside.

In a medium saucepan, melt the butter over medium-low heat. Add the flour and stir together for 2 minutes without browning.

Strain a third of the hot milk into the pan and whisk until smooth. Strain in more milk, whisk until smooth, and repeat with the last of the milk. For a richer sauce, stir in the whipping cream. Add salt to taste.

Remove the sauce from the heat and cover with plastic wrap if not being used straightaway.

Peanut Sauce

1 Tbsp (15 mL) finely chopped garlic

2 Tbsp (30 mL) vegetable oil

2 Tbsp (30 mL) Thai red curry paste

2 lemon grass stalks

4 cups (960 mL) coconut milk

1 cup (250 mL) unsalted peanut
butter

¼ cup (60 mL) lemon juice

1 Tbsp (15 mL) sugar

2 Tbsp (30 mL) fish sauce

An excellent spicy sauce for grilled meat or chicken, satays, and spring rolls, and a good addition to a stir fry.

In a medium pan, sauté the garlic in the oil until pale gold. Add the curry paste and stir over low heat until the paste starts to look dry; set aside

Remove and discard the dry, fibrous parts of the lemon grass; cut the rest into 1-inch (2½ cm) lengths, and add them to the curry. Pour in the coconut milk and bring the mixture to a boil over medium heat. Add the peanut butter, turn the heat down to low, and cook for 20 minutes, until the sauce thickens.

Take the pan off the heat and set aside to cool. Remove and discard the chunks of lemon grass, and stir in the lemon juice, sugar, and fish sauce.

Store in the fridge.

Spring Roll Sauce

···

This sweet chili sauce is an essential accompaniment to Chicken Fat Rice (page 114) and many other Southeast Asian dishes. It will keep in the fridge for 2 months.

···

Put the sugar and water in a medium saucepan and bring to a boil over high heat, stirring until the sugar has dissolved. Boil rapidly for 10 minutes, then remove from the heat and set aside to cool; some sugar may crystallize on the sides, which is fine.

In the work bowl of a food processor (or blender) combine the garlic, red pepper, and about ½ cup (125 mL) of the sugar syrup; process to a smooth purée.

Add the fish sauce, lemon juice, salt, hot sauce, and the rest of the sugar syrup; process again until well blended.

Store in a closed container in the fridge.

MAKES 4 CUPS (1 L)
·····················

2 cups (480 mL) granulated sugar

1 cup (250 mL) water

4 cloves garlic

½ red pepper (flesh, seeds, and membrane—not the stem)

3 Tbsp (45 mL) Thai or Vietnamese fish sauce

5 Tbsp (75 mL) lemon juice

1 tsp (5 mL) salt

1 Tbsp (15 mL) Vietnamese hot sauce

Chicken Stock

MAKES 6 CUPS (1.4 L)

2 lb (900 g) chicken (bones, skin, and scraps; fresh or cooked, whatever is available)

1 onion, peeled

2 carrots, scrubbed

2 stalks of celery

1 bay leaf

1 sprig of thyme

Chicken stock is an essential ingredient, and very useful to have in the freezer. You can make it from raw chicken bones, but also from the remains of a cooked chicken, including the skin and bones left on plates at the end of a meal (to the horror of some, but it will all be sterilized during cooking). The addition of vegetables improves the flavour of even the most ordinary chicken.

Fill a large saucepan with cold water and add all the chicken, both fresh and cooked. Set it over high heat and, as soon as it boils, strain and discard the liquid. Return all the chicken to the saucepan, cover with fresh water, set over medium heat, and bring to a boil. Reduce the heat to a simmer (active boiling makes the stock cloudy) and add the vegetables and herbs, whatever is available.

(The vegetables need less cooking than the chicken and, in an ideal world, they could be added later. There are many places in cooking where extra care pays off but, frankly, this is not one of them.)

Simmer the stock, partially covered, with the surface of the liquid barely moving, for 4 to 8 hours. Remove from the heat, cool briefly, and strain into a bowl.

Cool to room temperature, cover with a lid or plastic wrap, and refrigerate. Skim off and discard the fat that has solidified on top. Pour the stock into containers (warm it if the stock has gelled). It will keep in the freezer for months.

Demi-Glace

••

Demi-glace is veal or beef stock skimmed of fat and reduced to a thick, gelatinous liquid. It is a classy way to add depth, body, flavour, and texture to meat sauces and stews. It sounds daunting, but it is just one step beyond making stock, and worth the extra work.

••

Preheat the oven to 400°F (200°C).

Arrange the bones and vegetables in a large roasting pan, transfer to the oven, and roast, uncovered, for 45 minutes, turning from time to time, until the vegetables are well browned.

Remove the pan from the oven and transfer everything to a large stock pot. Deglaze the hot roasting pan with the wine and pour it into the stock pot.

Pour in cold water to cover the bones and vegetables, set the pot over medium-high heat, and bring to a boil. Turn the heat down to low and skim the scum off the surface with a slotted spoon. Add the bay leaves and a sprig of thyme, and simmer, with the liquid barely bubbling, for 8 hours.

Strain the stock into a clean bowl and transfer to the fridge when cool.

Skim the solidified fat from the surface and discard. Strain the stock back into a clean pot (warming it if necessary), bring to a boil over medium-high heat, and reduce it down to about 1 cup (250 mL). Set aside to cool.

Freeze demi-glace in an ice-cube tray, then pop the cubes out and store in a plastic freezer bag. Demi-glace is very concentrated, and 1 or 2 cubes are enough to transform a sauce.

MAKES 1 CUP (250 ML)

5 lb (2.2 kg) veal or beef bones (not previously cooked)

2 large onions, peeled and cut in half

2 large carrots, scraped and cut in half

2 stalks of celery, cut in half

1 cup (250 mL) white wine

2 bay leaves

1 sprig of thyme

Short Crust Pastry

A simple general-purpose pastry for everything from quiche to the topping for a chicken pot pie.

MAKES A 9- TO 11-INCH
(23 TO 28 CM) TART SHELL
OR PIE COVER

5 oz (150 g) unsalted butter

1½ cups (360 mL) all-purpose flour

½ tsp (2 mL) salt

1 egg yolk

2 Tbsp (30 mL) cold water

Measure the butter and put it in the freezer in 1 piece for 30 minutes or more.

Whisk together the flour and salt in a large bowl; mix the egg yolk and cold water together in a small bowl and set aside.

With the coarse side of a box grater, grate the frozen butter into the flour. Mix the dough with your fingers until it resembles fine crumbs; sprinkle the egg and water mixture over it, and mix again—it should be barely moist and quite crumbly.

Tip the pastry onto a work surface and, with the heel of your hand, smear it across the surface. It will take about 8 pushes to spread all of it. Gather it into a ball, working it gently with your hands to bring it together; add a little more water if necessary to form a ball. Wrap it in plastic and set aside at room temperature for up to 3 hours (refrigerate if longer).

Raspberry Purée

Great with anything chocolate or lemon.

MAKES ABOUT 1½ CUPS (360 mL)

2 cups fresh raspberries
(or 12 oz [340 g] unsweetened
frozen raspberries)

Icing sugar, to taste

Process the raspberries in the work bowl of a food processor until smooth. Add icing sugar to taste.

Custard *or* Crème Anglaise

....

In the Britain of my youth, custard was the standard accompaniment to dessert (pudding, as it is called), and I am sure it still is. In those days, "Bird's" and "custard" were synonymous, and only a rare few made it from scratch. This was not because it's difficult—quite the opposite, in fact—it just never occurred to them. Adding a little cornstarch to stabilize the custard provides a confidence-building safety net.

Much as I admire whipped cream, there are some desserts that without custard are as unbalanced as a two-legged stool—bread pudding and baked apples, to name two—and it is an essential part of trifle.

....

Rinse out a small saucepan with water but do not dry it. Pour in the milk, set it over low heat, add the vanilla pod (if using, add the vanilla extract later), and bring to a simmer, taking care it does not come to a full boil. Remove from the heat and set aside to infuse.

Whisk the egg yolks, sugar, and cornstarch in a small bowl (or a stand mixer fitted with the whisk) until pale yellow. Remove the vanilla pod, and slowly pour in the hot milk, whisking as you go.

Wash out the pan to remove any milk solids, return the custard to the pan, and set it over a low heat.

Stir steadily with a spoon or spatula as the custard heats and thickens. When the custard reaches the point where the film on the back of the spoon is thick enough that you can draw your finger across it and leave a clear line (a point not surprisingly called "coating the back of a spoon"), it is ready. Any more heating will curdle the eggs and make the sauce lumpy, so remove the pan quickly from the heat and stir for half a minute longer.

Strain the sauce through a sieve, and stir in the vanilla extract if you did not use the pod.

Cover the sauce with plastic wrap and set aside to cool. It will keep in the fridge for 3 days.

MAKES 1½ CUPS (360 ML)
....

1½ cups (360 mL) milk

1 vanilla pod (or ½ tsp [2 mL] vanilla extract)

4 egg yolks

⅓ cup (80 mL) granulated sugar

½ tsp (2 mL) cornstarch

MAKES ONE 9- TO 11-INCH
(23 TO 28 CM) TART SHELL
·····························

5 oz (150 g) unsalted butter

1½ cups (360 mL) all-purpose flour

⅓ cup (80 mL) granulated sugar

½ tsp (2 mL) salt

1 egg yolk

2 Tbsp (30 mL) cold water + extra
as needed

Sweet Short Crust Pastry

·································

This is melt-in-the-mouth pastry, ideal for an open-faced fruit tart or free-form sweet galette (page 217).

·································

Measure the butter and put in the freezer in 1 piece for 30 minutes or more.

Whisk together the flour, sugar, and salt in a large bowl. Whisk the egg yolk and cold water in a small bowl until well blended, then set aside.

With the coarse side of a box grater, grate the frozen butter into the flour. Mix the dough with your fingers until it resembles fine crumbs. Sprinkle the egg and water mixture over it, and mix again; it should be barely moist and quite crumbly.

Tip the pastry onto a work surface and, with the heel of your hand, smear it across the surface. It will take about 8 pushes to spread all of it. Gather it into a ball, working it gently with your hands to bring it together; add a little more water if necessary to form a ball. Wrap it in plastic and set aside at room temperature for up to 3 hours (refrigerate if longer).

To make a fully baked tart shell, roll out the pastry evenly to fit the bottom and sides of the tart pan; roll it around your rolling pin, and unroll it over the tart pan. Press the pastry onto the bottom and sides of the pan, and trim the edges. Refrigerate the pastry-lined pan for half an hour or more.

Preheat the oven to 375°F (190°C).

Place the chilled tart in the centre of the oven and bake for 20 to 25 minutes, or until very lightly browned all over. Remove from the oven and allow to cool, then gently remove the pastry shell from the pan.

Acknowledgments

To begin at the beginning: without my Mother and Father there would be no beginning, and without my Mother, no appreciation of food. I am grateful to her, and very sad that we did not have more time to enjoy it together.

Years later, at the Food Shops in Toronto, I worked with some very talented people who have, I am very happy to say, gone on to considerable success in their own careers. Karen Barnaby, Daphna Rabinovitch, and Darlene Mac-David will recognize particular recipes and the pervasive influence of their own styles and ideas on the way I cook. Krystyna Schmidt, who ran our catering business, was a stylist *par excellence,* and she taught me so much. Over the years, I have taken a great deal of credit that properly belonged to them (and I continue to do so with this book). They gave me the confidence to believe that I have something worth sharing.

Many years ago in Toronto, Nick Rundall (now recently retired from Whitecap Books) persuaded me to write the first *David Wood Food Book* (it was not a particularly hard sell). The sales were encouraging enough for him to talk us into a second book, and while it did not go over as well as the first (the idea of making their own desserts was definitely less appealing to the public), Nick remained undaunted. Twenty-five years later, over the course of dinner on Salt Spring with our very good mutual friends Mary and Peter Grove, he found himself agreeing once again that we should do a book. There is absolutely no doubt that without his support, it would never have seen the light of day.

After two years of struggling to find my voice in a food world so radically changed in the years since I left Toronto, I was getting nowhere and found myself on the verge of quitting. That I did not give up is entirely due to another dinner conversation, this time with Barbara and Bruce Housser and Shirley and John Dawe. Each of them casts a wide net that reaches far beyond Salt Spring, and they convinced me that there were people—not perhaps people they actually knew, but friends of friends—who were still keen to hear what I might have to say about food, and who might even be prepared to pay money for it. I gratefully allowed myself to be persuaded and, in the afterglow of their encouragement, the book started to come together. (I should perhaps mention that if these friends of friends are still out there, now would be a good time for them to step up to the plate.)

In the old days, cookbooks did not have photographs (which dates me, but that's the way it was). Nowadays most people who buy cookbooks spend as much if not more time looking at the pictures than they do on the actual cooking; having classy, mouth-watering photographs is now an essential element. The fact that this book can hold up its head among the current array of cookbooks is due entirely to my very good friend Gillean Proctor, who is also a very talented photographer. (It helps, too, if the recipes work, which they do.)

It has been a joy to collaborate with Gillean on this venture, and I owe him a deep debt of gratitude. Together we would like to acknowledge the many kindnesses of Linda Meinhardt and Colin Stacey, Georgia Taylor Proctor, and the lovely people at Stowell Lake Farm, just across the road from us on Salt Spring, for so generously offering such good-looking locations and props for the photographs.

I cannot speak too highly of the talent and professionalism of Andrew Bagatella, the book's designer, and of Penny Hozy, my editor. Together, they have created an elegant vessel out of the raw clay.

Patrick Geraghty, formerly at Whitecap, as well as Holly Doll and Sharon Fitzhenry, who remain, have supported my vision of the book through the years. In the beginning, I did not dare dream that it could turn out so well. It is thanks to all of the people I have mentioned, as well as many whom I am sure I have forgotten (which happens as we get older) that the book you hold in your hands is as well-formed as it has turned out to be.

Index